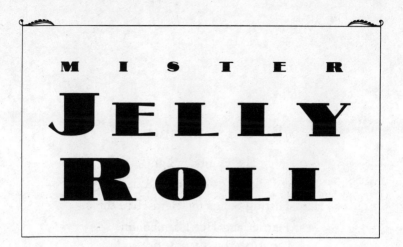

MISTER
JELLY
ROLL

MISTER JELLY ROLL

The Fortunes of Jelly Roll Morton,
New Orleans Creole and
"Inventor of Jazz"

ALAN LOMAX

Drawings by David Stone Martin

Pantheon Books   New York

TO BILL RUSSELL

AND

ALLAN JAFFE,

WHO HELPED TO KEEP JAZZ ALIVE

IN THE TOWN WHERE IT WAS BORN.

Preface copyright © 1993 by Alan Lomax

Copyright © 1950 by Alan Lomax

Copyright renewed 1978 by Alan Lomax

All rights reserved under International and Pan-American Copyright Conventions. Published in the United States by Pantheon Books, a division of Random House, Inc., New York, and simultaneously in Canada by Random House of Canada Limited, Toronto. Originally published in hardcover by Duell, Sloan and Pearce in 1949 and in paperback by Grove Press Books and Grosset in 1950.

Library of Congress Cataloging-in-Publication Data

Lomax, Alan, 1915–
Mister Jelly Roll: the fortunes of Jelly Roll Morton, New
Orleans creole and "inventor of jazz" / Alan Lomax.
p.   cm.
Originally published: New York: Duell, Sloan and Pearce, 1949.
Discography and bibliography: p.
ISBN 0-679-74064-3
1. Morton, Jelly Roll, d. 1941. 2. Jazz musicians—United States—Biography.
I. Title.
ML410.M82L6   1993
781.65'092—dc20
[B]   92-50469

Book design by Guenet Abraham

Manufactured in the United States of America

Pantheon Books Edition 1993

Contents

Preface

When Jelly Roll was a boy, his loving godmother sold his soul to the devil in return for a gift of boundless musical talent. For him, I believe, this bargain with Satan became quite real. In spite of his outcaste origins, he fulfilled all of his ambitions. He defeated all comers on the piano and at the pool table and, as the leading composer and conductor of early jazz, could afford to wear diamonds in his teeth and on his sock-supporters. When he lost all that he had gained, he attributed his misfortune to sinister unseen influences. And on his death-bed, so his mistress said, he was calling for holy oil to cheat the devil of his godmother's bargain.

His Faustian story parallels that of Robert Johnson, the great bluesman, in fact, of many believers in voodoo. Zora Hurston, the great black folklorist, tells of the crossroads encounters of would-be bluesmen with a satanic figure who clipped their fingernails or brushed his demonic hands across their guitar strings to make them masters of their instruments. Peetie Wheatstraw, who called himself the Devil's Son-in-Law, was said to have acquired his gifts in that way. A quirky old Irish fiddler told me about an unfortunate fiddler that "didn't have but the one tune," till one of the little people took pity on him and ran her hand along his bow, and he became the best fiddler in all the country. In olden times remarkably talented people were believed to be God-inspired, whether by Apollo or some other deity. But in these ancient and widespread beliefs there is usually no retribution, as there is in the Christian world, no sense of deadly sin as there was in Jelly's Catholic heart.

Wherever he is now, whether in heaven or hell, Mister Jelly Roll is probably well pleased that the recognition he sought—and which many critics feel he richly deserves—is coming his way. The august Smithsonian has reissued his great Red Hot Peppers orchestral series with worshipful scholarly notes. He figured prominently in *Pretty Baby*, the best film about Storyville. Twyla Tharp has devised a delightful and frothy suite of dances, called *The Four Jellies*, to his music. Bob Greene and others have edited fine editions of his piano scores and orchestrations. His music is now standard fare at jazz festivals the world over.

I know of at least two performers who tour America enacting *Mister Jelly Roll*, with words and music that recreate his memorable recital on the Library of Congress stage. Two musicals about him are concurrently running in New York. There will be more to come, doubtless—movies, television, better musicals (I hope), and, God help us, deconstruction—all the recognition that our ravenous culture denies to the geniuses it neglects and punishes when they are alive, and lavishes upon them when they are dead. It appears that Jelly Roll, the Dizzy Dean of jazz, may outlast both his critics and his contemporaries.

The Broadway musical of considerable flair, *Jelly's Last Jam*, treats the Faustian side of Jelly's life with great imagination. It also confronts his Creole color prejudice, which estranged him from some of his fellow musicians. However, quite unfairly, the script gives the impression that Jelly was unique in his feeling that blackness was a mark of social inferiority. This prejudice was not only normal to his Creole mulatto background, it has poisoned most Afro-American communities. Well-born mulattoes objected when their children wished to marry down the color line. This painful color-caste attitude, which divided New Orleans into hostile neighborhoods, was not only a source of conflict in Jelly's life but, as I discovered later, an issue in the lives of all the old-time jazzmen of the city. I applaud the writer of *Jam* for confronting this painful theme, but it is unjust for him to send Jelly off to hell as the singular carrier of this hateful prejudice.

Jam seems to go out of its way to misrepresent its anti-hero. It has him "jamming," a practice Jelly Roll loathed. "This is something I never allowed in my bands, because most guys when they improvise, they'll go wrong"—that is, they would depart from the classic canons of New Orleans music. Jelly himself is portrayed as a tap dancer or hoofer, a role that as a musician he looked down on. In spite of the warm and brilliant performance of Gregory Hines, it is taps on the floor rather than fingers on a keyboard that interpret the subtle ideas of this remarkable American pianist and composer. Moreover,

the square rhythms traditional in East Coast tapping obscure
the subtle Caribbean beat which throbs in Morton's music.

I was astounded to see that the Harlem team which created
this musical hardly touched upon the rich New Orleans folk
traditions that Jelly Roll celebrated in his music and in his
reminiscences. There is no hint of the jazz parades, the Indian
maskers with their collective improvisations of Afro-Caribbean
music and dance, which are the wonders of American folklore.
Instead, we are given second-rate blues and cootch songs,
mounted on routine New York choreography and pit-band
arrangements, which succeed in making this supposed testa-
ment to regional originality look and sound as much like a
routine Broadway musical as possible.

Jelly Roll was the first jazz composer, the equal or, some
feel, the superior of Ellington. His arrangements form part of
the basic vocabulary of jazz, but most of his music still has not
won public recognition. It could have brought a fresh sound to
Broadway, yet his innovative compositions are neglected by
the producers of *Jam*. New York and Harlem, as they so often
have done in the past, substituted their supposedly sophisticated formulas for this unique and charming regional music.
They might have had something better than *Porgy and Bess*.
Instead they have another slick Harlem musical hit. What a
shame, for Jelly's sake especially.

In the roar of dance halls, the rush of recording sessions,
handling a clutch of temperamental musicians, Jelly felt he
had never managed to have his compositions properly played.
He came back to this again and again. I remained a bit skep-
tical until, some time after his death, I was fortunate enough
to attend an all–Jelly Roll concert at Steinway Hall. That
afternoon Bob Gibson, leading an orchestra of great jazzmen,

who had rehearsed Jelly Roll's scores for several months, produced sheer magic. Here in Jelly's exquisite program music— *Milneburg Joys, The Pearls, Wolverine Blues, Doctor Jazz, Steamboat Stomp, Black Bottom Stomp*—an American Vivaldi at last emerged. He had created what Copland and Gershwin had fallen short of: an easy-going, sophisticated American orchestral idiom that was a match for Twain and Sandburg. Almost all of this charming regional music was omitted from or submerged in the show-biz hubbub of a musical whose title might better be *Harlem's Last Treacle*.

The author of *Jam* condemns Jelly Roll to hell for his boastfulness, for his obviously exaggerated claim to have invented jazz. Hasn't this gentleman heard of jiving and shucking, of rapping and sounding, which are the currency of street and barroom talk? Here anything goes to make your point. When Jelly told his audience that he had invented jazz, he was speaking up for his hometown in New York's Harlem, which so often has taken all the credit for black cultural innovations. Jelly had squelched Handy for asserting that jazz was born in Memphis. And here in Harlem, where the carriers of the great tradition were few, where big bands with horn sections were replacing the lacy counterpoint of New Orleans, he was sticking up for his hometown. He was grieved and shocked when he saw his musical acquaintances jumping on the bandwagon, which he and his hometown friends had started to roll, without learning to speak the language of jazz in classic New Orleans style.

As is true of everyone with a cause, his forcefulness annoyed some folks and has continued to provide fuel for his critics. But even when his star was fading, most of his listeners agreed that he could back what he said with what he knew and what

he could do. His listeners were aware that the main innovations in jazz had come from Middle America— ragtime from
Missouri, the blues from the Delta south of Memphis, jazz
from New Orleans and Chicago, boogie-woogie and swing
from Kansas City. In fact, New York contributed little and
late to jazz, although Van Vechten and other '20's critics created the impression that jazz was born in Harlem. The
roots of Harlem's entertainment tradition were rather in the
minstrel show, modernized for Broadway. I say this, not in
criticism of the elegant artists of Harlem—Fats Waller,
Rosamund Johnson, Cab Calloway, Duke Ellington, and all
the great men of bop—but only to cavil at the inhospitable
treatment that New York gave to the great music of New
Orleans and its cantankerous proponent, Jelly Roll Morton.
Harlem's indifference crushed Morton, and the author of this
Harlem musical also has it in for him.

On PBS he posthumously berated Jelly Roll for not ac-
knowledging his sources, as if this great original were somehow a plagiarist, a credit stealer, when in the heat of barroom
arguments he claimed credit for "inventing" jazz. This was
Jelly's way of saying, "Jazz is from my hometown. I was
rocking the cradle of jazz before you guys were born." All Jelly
couldn't say—the whole complex and orchidaceous story he
had in his mind—came pouring out in the recordings he made
at the Library of Congress. Far from stealing credit, here Jelly
introduced a huge cast of New Orleans musicians who would
otherwise have been forgotten, and then brilliantly played
their music and superbly sang their songs so that they will
always be remembered. In language as raunchy as the life in
this city of pleasure, he portrayed its streets, bars, neighborhoods, customs, and celebrations, depicting the whole rich

background out of which jazz grew. In two weeks he recited a masterful history of the origins of jazz, including all its best tunes and harmonies. Sources! It was Jelly who first took us to the wellsprings of America's most original music!

In the 1970's a television series brought me back to New Orleans to probe into the origins of jazz. Again the essential truth of Jelly Roll's story impressed me. He tells us "we had people there from every nation." Sure enough, the Preservation Hall old-timer's band, packing in the crowds in the French Quarter, was an intercultural melting pot, manned by Creoles with French, Spanish, and Anglo-American names, led by an ex-levee-camp worker from across the river, and managed by a tuba-playing German from Pennsylvania.

The jazz parades, which in Jelly's view had been the seedbed of the jazz band, are still very much alive. Even now they turn almost every weekend into a small Mardi Gras. The jazz funeral of a popular figure becomes a huge street ballet, lasting for several hours and involving a cast of hundreds or thousands of dancers, all doing their own thing. Some leap, some twist, some roll on the pavement, some dance on top of or slide about under cars, some jive on telephone poles, others caper on housetops. Often they surround the band, taking off from its beat and in turn shaping it. As one horn man told us, "We ain't got no soul—*they* [the dancing crowd] got the soul!"

By then I knew enough about world performance styles to realize that this concept and the parades themselves were very West African. For example, the orchestra—a brass-and-drum combo improvising collectively in hot rhythm, within a throng of dancers, each one taking in and feeding rhythmic cues to the musicians—is a uniquely African transformation of the European marching band. The movements of the "second line,"

with their foot-sliding steps, their co-acceleration in perfect
tynch, and their dramatic shifts in level, could be matched
with shots from Africa. African elements were equally apparent in the activities of the black Indian tribes of Mardi Gras—
their red-hot percussive rhythm bands, the dueling war-dances
at rehearsals, the cylindrical costumes so like the bulbous raffia
ancestor masks of West Africa.

"New Orleans," Jelly tells us, "has always been very
organization-minded . . . ." The unions and lodges, so important among the black Creoles, sponsored marching bands to
bring out the black vote after the Civil War. In the bad old
days of Reconstruction, when all black political activity was
savagely repressed, the joyful sound of these bands was the
only way that blacks could voice their democratic aspirations.
Today lodges, clubs, and burial societies still flourish in New
Orleans, providing a safety net of community help in black
neighborhoods. On all sorts of special occasions these organizations—the Invincibles, the Big Jumpers, the Zulus, and
scores more—take to the streets with their gorgeous uniforms
and their irresistible street ballets, displaying an almost tribal
unity and pride. As one of them told me at the end of a parade:

"We call our parades super-Sunday, that's the way we feel
about it. You see all those people there that participate in your
parade and you say to yourself, 'How in the world did we do
it?' Well, we doin it . . ." Another man chimes in:

"*Finances are tight, people can't get jobs it's hard. So everybody
need to come together. You want communication. You want happiness
between the brothers and the sisters . . .*" And another voice:

"*You have your clothes made, you have your streamers made, you
wants to have it all together when you hit the street, cos you gonna
have a congregation of people lookin at you. You want to look good*

and feel good and get out there and do some good . . ." And more
soberly:

*"The vast majority are poor people. Some of the kids want so bad
to be part of it that the parents will spend their last dime so a son or
a daughter can be involved. Some kids who may have got in a little
trouble, you know, they know that if they get into too much stuff they
can't belong, so that kind of keeps them straight. . . ."*

These are neighborhood people talking about what the parades mean to them and to their organizations—unity, pride,
and high morale. Clearly a vigorous black aesthetic is at work
here. Such are the insights that Jelly's penetrating memoirs led
us to.

While I was busy with other things, Rudi Blesh, the jazz
pundit, without bothering to tell me about it, edited and
issued most of my interview with Jelly Roll in a set of 12-inch
record albums. Jelly, with his growling bedroom voice and
mordant wit, became an international household god of jazz.
The ethnomusicologist and ardent jazz fan Alan Merriam was,
I believe, much influenced by this work. In his standard text
on ethnomusicology, he recommends the in-depth interview of
native musicians as the best way to understand exotic musical
systems.

The Jelly Roll recordings defined the roots of jazz and led to
the taping of every old-time jazz musician in the city and to
the formation of the jazz archive now housed at Tulane. A
more significant outcome was the establishment of recorded
history as a literary and historical genre of its own. I had
experimented with the idea of recorded folk history in my
fieldwork for the Library of Congress for some time before I
met Jelly Roll. My notion was that the great talkers of America could, if lovingly transcribed, contribute enormous riches

of prose style and varied points of view to literature. What
they had to offer was not literal history, as so many oral
historians have mistakenly thought, but the fruit of their life-
long experience, the evocation of their periods, and their imagination and style—the things that every good writer brings us.
I knew that Jelly Roll had given me, as Woody and Leadbelly
had done earlier, the living *legend* of his existence. I spent five
years adding the voices of other jazzmen to Jelly's account, and
in polishing all this earthy spoken prose so that the reader
could feel the presence of the speakers while turning the pages.

The present book, an almost best-seller in 1949, turned
many people on to the idea of "oral history." Among these was
Studs Terkel, who interviewed me on radio about the book
when it appeared, and who has since used this "oral history"
approach to create a fresh and democratic vision of American
life. *Mister Jelly Roll* was, I believe, the first altogether recorded book. Since it appeared in 1949 there have been others
that have kept to the mark—tapings of wise and witty talkers
lovingly translated into print—such as *He Pointed Them North*
by Teddy Blue and *All God's Dangers* by Theodore Rosengar-
ten. Unfortunately, libraries are also stuffed with the boring
"oral histories" of important figures and "typical" ordinary
folks, with no fresh perspective to share and no style at all. In
these cases a notebook serves posterity better than a tape machine.

Now it is almost time to let Jelly take over the mike.

Alan Lomax
New York, February 1993

Prelude

In foreign lands across the sea,
They knight a man for bravery,
Make him a duke or a count, you see,
Must be a member of the royalty.

Mister Jelly struck a jazzy thing
In the temple by the queen and king,
All at once he struck a harmonic chord.
King said, "Make Mister Jelly a lord!"

No one could have guessed that Jelly Roll Morton was down on his luck that soft May day in 1938. His conservative hundred-dollar suit was as sharp as a tipster's sheet. His watch fob and his rings were gold, and the notoriety diamond, set in gold in his front incisor, glittered like gaslight . . .

Mister Jelly Lord,
He's simply royal at the old keyboard . . .

The quiet of the chamber-music auditorium in the Library of Congress and the busts of the great composers sightless in their niches disturbed Jelly Roll not at all. He felt at home with great men and with history. He knew that his music had rolled around the world. If he never actually played at Whitehall, if it was only in fancy that the king said, "Make Mister Jelly a lord," he knew that his New Orleans jazz had warmed up the atmosphere all the way from Basin Street to Buckingham Palace . . .

You should see him strolling down the street,
The man's an angel with great big feet!
With his melodies,
Have made him lord of ivories . . .
Just a simple little chord.
Now at home as well as abroad,
They call him Mister Jelly Lord . . .

His diamond-studded grin lit up the sombre hall as he feathered his barrelhouse rhythms out of the concert grand. "You hear that riff," he said. "They call swing that today, but it's just a little thing I made up way back yonder. Yeah, I guess that riff's so old it's got whiskers on it. Whatever those guys play today, they're playing Jelly Roll."

Creole child of New Orleans in the last days of her glory, Jelly Roll grew up to become the first and most influential composer of jazz. He and his Red Hot Peppers put the heat in the hottest jazz of the '20's, but the Depression generation forgot Jelly Roll and his music. He had to pawn his diamond sock-supporters and 1938 found him playing for coffee and cakes in an obscure Washington nightspot. Years of poverty and neglect, however, had neither dimmed his brilliance at the keyboard nor diminished his self-esteem. He came to the Library of Congress to put himself forever on record, to carve his proper niche in the hall of history and, incidentally, to lay the groundwork for his fight to climb back into big time. This lonely Creole, without a dime in his pockets or a friend in the world, began by outlining his plans to sue the Music Corporation of America and the American Society of Composers, Authors, and Publishers.

There was something tremendously appealing about the old jazzman with his Southern-gentleman manners and his sporting-life lingo. I decided to find out how much of old New Orleans lived in his mind. So with the microphone near the piano of the Coolidge Chamber Music Auditorium I set out to make a few records of Jelly Roll, little knowing that I had encountered a Creole Benvenuto Cellini. Jelly Roll was ready to pour out a colorful and complexly woven account of the birth of jazz in his hometown, New Orleans—a story that had never been told or written before and that has since become the keystone in the history of jazz.

The amplifier was hot. The needle was tracing a quiet spiral on the spinning acetate. "Mister Morton," I said, "how about the beginning? Tell about where you were born and how you got started and why . . . and maybe keep playing piano while you talk . . ."

Jelly Roll nodded and his hands looked for soft, strange chords at a lazy tempo . . .

"Well as I can understand . . ."
        a gray and olive chord . . .
"My folks were in the city of New Orleans . . ."
        . . . a whisper of harmony like Spanish moss . . .
"Long before the Louisiana Purchase . . ."
        . . . a chord of distant bugles . . .
"And all my folks came directly
I mean from the shores of France
And they landed in this New World years ago . . ."

. . . a gravel voice melting at the edges, not talking, but
spinning out a life in something close to song . . . each sentence almost a stanza of a slow blues . . . each stanza flowing
out of the last like the eddies of a big sleepy Southern river
where the power hides below a quiet brown surface . . .

That hot May afternoon in the Library of Congress a new
way of writing history began—history with music cues, the
music evoking recollection and poignant feeling—history intoned out of the heart of one man, sparkling with dialogue and
purple with ego. Names of friends long dead and of honky-
tonks quiet for a half century, songs and tunes and precise
musical styles of early New Orleans musicians forgotten by
everyone but Morton—he recalled these things as if they were
of the day before, smoothly filling in uncomfortable gaps in his
own story with the achievements of his friends, building a
legend.

As the legend grew and flowered over the keyboard of that
Congressional grand piano, the back seats of the hall filled
with ghostly listeners—figures dressed in Mardi Gras costumes, fancy prostitutes in their plumes and diamonds, tough
sports from Rampart Street in pegtop trousers and boxback

coats, cable-armed black longshoremen from the riverfront, octoroons in their brilliant *tiyons* giggling at Morton's tales, old ladies framing severe parchment faces in black shawls, jazzmen of every complexion playing a solid background on their horns—for this was their legend that Jelly Roll was weaving at the piano, a legend of the painful and glorious flowering of hot jazz in which they had all played a part.

> *In New Orleans, in New Orleans,*
> *Louisiana town . . .*

Something came along there where the Mississippi Delta washes its muddy foot in the blue Gulf, something that bullies us, enchants us, pursues us out of the black throats of a thousand thousand music boxes. This something was jazz, which took shape in New Orleans around 1900 and within a generation was beating upon the hearts of most of the cities of the world.

A half century later the lineage of every fine jazz musician can still be traced back to the handful of half-caste Creoles who performed the original act of creation. As Jelly Roll is the "father" of hot piano, so black Buddy Bolden opened the way for other hot trumpet players, and Papa Tio taught "us all how to play clarinet." All these men knew each other. As boys they followed the parades together, or split into neighborhood gangs and fought bloody rock fights in the alleys. Later they wove together the complex fabric of hot jazz, an American creation at first scorned by the aesthetes and banned by the moralists. Meantime the fox-trot became our national dance. Jazz lent its color to most American music and to Tin Pan Alley, to the musical, to the symphonic tradition, to hillbilly, and most recently, to rock. The worldwide acceptance of rock fifty years later may be considered a further expansion of the jazz impulse.

Maybe nothing quite like the jazz explosion had ever happened before. Maybe no music, no fresh emanation of the spirit of man ever spread to so many people in so short a time. Jazz, in this sense, is one of the marvels of the century—a marvel that has spawned a monster—a monster entertainment industry, feeding upon jazz, growing gigantic and developing a score of interlocking colossal bodies whose million orifices pour out each week the stuff of our bartered dreams.

Jelly Roll's life story spans the whole of the "jazz age," from the street bands of New Orleans to the sweet bands of New York. With him we can leave behind the marketplaces of Hollywood and Tin Pan Alley and return to the moment of germination in New Orleans. In his sorrows and his fantasies we can find the very quality which distinguishes jazz from the many other forms of American music rooted in Africa—from the spirituals, from the work songs, from the blues and ragtime.

"We had every different kind of a person in New Orleans," Jelly said. "We had French, we had Spanish, we had West Indian, we had American, and we all mixed on an equal basis . . ." So tolerant New Orleans absorbed slowly over the centuries African, Iberian, Cuban, Parisian, Martiniquan, and American musical influences. All these flavors may be found in jazz, for it is a sort of musical gumbo. But the taster, the stirrer, the pot-watcher for this gumbo was the New Orleans colored Creole. There were 400,000 free colored Creoles in Louisiana at the time of the 1860 census. Some began as privileged servants, others as the favored offspring of mixed liaisons. Thus they acquired education and property, some even owning slaves. They taught their children fine French manners, built beautiful homes, and prospered in trade. In their heyday there were Creole poetry societies, newspapers, and opera companies. Louisiana Creoles served under Jackson at the Battle of New Orleans and their regiments helped to defeat the South in the Civil War. The capital was New Orleans, where for a hundred years they raised the most beautiful girls, who cooked up the tastiest dishes and were courted with the hottest music of any place in the Mississippi valley.

It is within the folklife of these Creoles that the emotional character of hot jazz is to be found, for their music was not only an Afro-American offshoot, not merely a complex of many elements, but a new music of and by New Orleans—a wordless Creole counterpoint of protest and of pride. Thus New Orleans, in its own local, subtropical way, was a sort of Athens for the popular music of the world.

Why did the streets of Athens during one century throng with the brightest collection of souls that the world has ever seen? This must always be a matter for speculation, for Athens is lost to us in time. But New Orleans and its time of creativity is close at hand. Some of the old men who watched the first awkward and charming steps of the infant jazz were still alive when this book was first published in 1950. In their recollections, in their story of the hot music of New Orleans, we come close to the magic and mystery of cultural flowering.

For Jelly Roll and his fellows had participated in one of the rare moments of ecstasy by means of which cultural transmutations take place. They spoke of this experience with the special feeling of men who have lived through an earthquake or witnessed a dance of the elephants. They were, indeed, the children of a golden age, and, because they were part folk, they recalled the emotions of those bright days in vivid feeling. This volume is, I hope, a testimony to their eloquence and their sensitivity.

With Jelly Roll the days of the interview flowed on into a month; scores of records stacked up onstage at the Library of Congress in a rich evocation of underground America. I felt it an impudence to check or correct Jelly's story. Jazz musicians are strong on downbeats but weak on dates. There are almost as many versions of every happening as there were men in the band. The big outlines of his story are solid and true to life; if there is niggling about facts, there is unanimity among the feelings of Jelly and the other boys in the bands.

In fairness to Morton, I have tried to give his narrative as much inner consistency as possible, something he would certainly have done if he had written this history himself. Otherwise Morton and the boys in the bands tell the story their own way. Sometimes they brag; sometimes they remember exactly what was said or how things looked; sometimes they remember it the way they wished it; but somehow out of the crossing of misty memories comes truth—comes a hint at great secrets—how culture can suddenly leap forward—how music flowers in unexpected places—how artists can be pimps and still set the world dancing with fiery notes.

Mister Jelly Roll now bends close to the keyboard, his face saddened by a half smile, his soft and powerful hands stroking out tropical harmonies, and begins . . .

In New Orleans, in New Orleans,
Louisiana town . . .

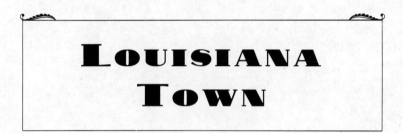

LOUISIANA TOWN

My Folks Was All Frenchmans

●●●**A**s I can understand, my folks were in the city of New Orleans long before the Louisiana Purchase, and all my folks came directly from the shores of France, that is across the world in the other world, and they landed in the New World years ago.

I remember so far back as my great-grandmother and great-grandfather. My great-grandfather's name was Émile Pechet—he was considered one of the largest jewelers in the South. My great-grandmother was Mimi Pechet—she traveled quite extensively and died when I was grown, at around one hundred years old. As soon as I can remember those folks, they was never able to speak a word in American or English.

My grandmother, her name was Laura. She married a French settler in New Orleans by the name of Henri Monette—a

wholesaler of fine liquors and cordials—that was my grandfather. And neither one of them spoke American or English.

My grandmother bore sons named Henri, Gus, Neville and
Nelusco—all French names; and she bore the daughters
Louise, Viola, and Margaret—that was the three daughters.
Louise, the oldest daughter, so fair she could always pass,
married F. P. La Menthe, also an early settler and considered
one of the outstanding contractors and demolishers in the
entire South. Louise happened to be my mother, Ferd (Jelly
Roll) Morton.

Of course, I guess you wonder how the name Morton came
in, by it being an English name. Well, I'll tell you. I changed
it for business reasons when I started traveling. I didn't want
to be called Frenchy. It was my godmother, Eulalie Echo,
helped to name me the christened name of Ferdinand, which
was named after the king of Spain—but the king of Spain
didn't do anything, it was the queen, Isabella.

When I was six months old, my godmother—a very dark
woman—would take me from my mother and, in absence of
mother, would pass me off for her child. It seems like she got
a special kick out of this because I was a very good-looking
baby.

One of these afternoons, in borrowing the baby now known
as Jelly Roll Morton, my godmother loaned me to one of her
acquaintances, some type of sporting-woman. This lady displayed me in saloons, setting me on the bar and so forth and
so on, making mirations. Then, through some kind of fracas or
riot, she was arrested. The officers decided not to put the baby
in jail with her and her associates, but she raised so much hell
that the young Ferdinand, named after the useless king of
Spain, was thrown right in jail at the age of six months.

The inmates were singing and making a lot of noise from time to time and it was there young Ferdinand got his first musical inspiration. The inmates would be singing and, as long as they would sing, it would keep the baby happy, and, the minute they would quit, I would go into a frantic rage. When they would start up again and sing, I would smile along with the singing. That was my first inspiration.

My first instrument was made up of two chair rounds and a tin pan. This combination sounded like a symphony to me, because in those days all I heard was classical selections. The next instrument tried was the harmonica at the time I was five years old. After trying to play harmonica for two years, I discovered I was the world's worst and changed to the jew's-harp, although this instrument sounded more like a bee humming than like music. When I had mastered this instrument, I set out to whip the world and conquer all instruments.

We always had some kind of musical instruments in the house, including guitar, drums, piano, trombone, and so forth and so on. We had lots of them and everybody always played for their pleasure—whatever ones desired to play. We always had ample time that was given us in periods to rehearse our lessons, anyone that was desirous of accepting lessons. At the age of six I gave up the jew's-harp and took my first lessons on the guitar with a Spanish gentleman in the neighborhood. My godmother paid for these lessons, as she always took an interest in anything her boy did.

At the age of seven I was considered among the best guitarists around, and sometimes I played in the string bands that were common at the time. These little three-piece combinations, consisting of bass, mandolin, and guitar, used to play serenades at late hours, from twelve to two, at the houses of

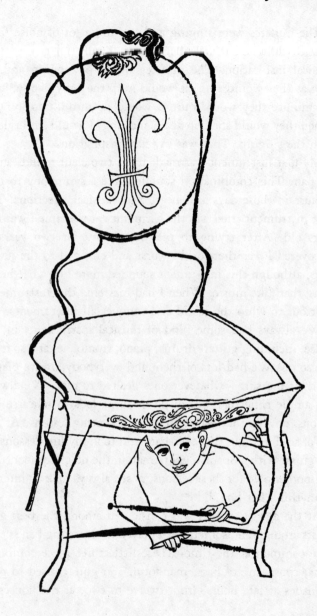

friends. Naturally, the folks would welcome us when they heard those old tunes like *Hot Time in the Old Town Tonight*, *Wearing My Heart for You*, *Old Oaken Bucket*, *Bird in a Gilded Cage*, *Mr. Johnson Turn Me Loose*, as well as different little blues and ragtime numbers we knew. There was plenty of liquor in these old-time New Orleans homes and they were liberal about entertaining us musicians. Soon the family would be up, all the friends would be informed and a festival would be on.

Of course, my folks never had the idea they wanted a musician in the family. They always had it in their minds that a musician was a tramp, trying to duck work, with the exception of the French Opera House players which they patronized. As a matter of fact, I, myself, was inspired to play piano by going to a recital at the French Opera House. There was a gentleman who rendered a selection on the piano, very marvelous music that made me want to play the piano very, very much. The only trouble was that this gentleman had long bushy hair, and, because the piano was known in our circle as an instrument for a lady, this confirmed me in my idea that if I played the piano I would be misunderstood.

I didn't want to be called a sissy. I wanted to marry and raise a family and be known as a man among men when I became of age. So I studied various other instruments, such as violin, drums and guitar, until one day at a party I saw a gentleman sit down at the piano and play a very good piece of ragtime. This particular gentleman had short hair and I decided then that the instrument was good for a gentleman same as it was for a lady. I must have been about ten years old at the time.

I had already become a very efficient guitarist. In fact, I was known to be the best, until I met Bud Scott, one of the famous

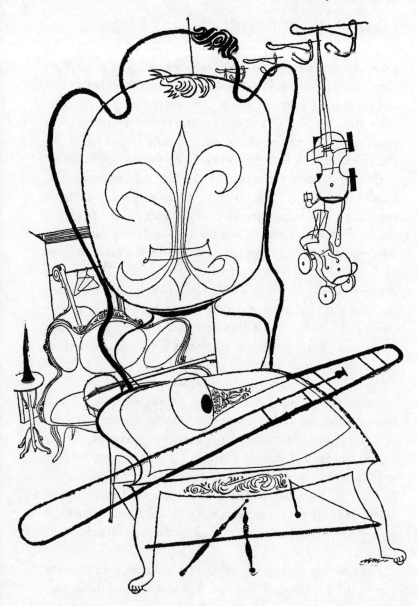

guitarists of this country, but, when I found out he was dividing with me my popularity, I decided to quit playing guitar and try the piano, which I did secretly. The only ones that knew was my family.

I tried under different teachers and I found that most of them was fakes those days. They couldn't read very much themselves. For example, a colored teacher I had, named Miss Moment—Miss Moment was no doubt the biggest ham of a teacher I've ever heard or seen since or before: she fooled me all the time. In those days the new tunes used to come out in the Sunday papers and it would be my desire to play those tunes correctly. When I would take these numbers and place them in front of Miss Moment, she would rattle them off like nobody's business and the third one she rattled off sounded about like the first one.

So I began to get wise and wouldn't take lessons any further. I demanded I would either go by myself and learn the best way I knew or be placed under an efficient teacher, which I was then placed under a teacher at St. Joseph's University, a Catholic college in the city of New Orleans. My denomination is Catholic which is how I came to learn under the Catholic tutelage, which was very efficient. Later I taken lessons from a well-known colored professor, who was considered very good, named Professor Nickerson. I tell you, things was driving along then.*

In my early youth I thought New Orleans was the whole world. I could speak only French at that time. I had been to

---

* The family wasn't sure whether young Ferd left school after the eighth or the fourth grade.

Shell Beach, Lake Pontchartrain, Spanish Fort, Milneburg,
Algiers, Gretna, all considered New Orleans suburbs, and I
was convinced this was the whole world: the names on the
map, such as New York, London, Paris, Berlin, Rome, Hong
Kong, etcetera, were just there to fill the map out—that was
my idea until my great-grandmother Mimi took a trip around
the world. She brought back toys for every one of the kids but
me and she told me in French, "Never mind, when I go again,
I'll bring you something real nice." She never did go again and
my heart was broken. It was then I decided that I wanted to
work for money, see the world on my own, get the things I
wanted for myself and not have to ask anyone for anything.

My first job was dishwasher after school, with permission
from my mother. Just to please me, she agreed. The salary was
seventy-five cents a week, three dollars payable monthly. At
the end of the month my boss said I ate enough for my pay and
would not pay me. That broke my heart, until my mother
gave me the money. She said she had collected it, but later I
could understand she, herself, had given it to me.

I was about eleven years old at the time and used to stay
with my godmother, Eulalie Echo, who spoiled me and gave
me a little freedom. When school closed, she permitted me to
go to pick berries at the strawberry farm. I thought I could eat
up the whole strawberry farm and ate enough to get sick and
so returned back home, about a forty-five-mile trip. Then I
was convinced that the world was a little larger than New
Orleans.

My godmother, Eulalie Echo, wasn't a handsome woman,
but she was very intelligent, had a pleasant personality and
plenty money. She used to monkey around with this spiritual
business. There were glasses of water around her house and

voices would come out of those glasses. Very prominent people would consult my godmother and she would give them stuff like uncooked turtle heart—*cowein**—she'd have them swallow that and, afterwards, they had good luck and no one could harm them. Here, late years, I have often thought many of my troubles came from my being around during those séances when my godmother fooled with that underground stuff.

New Orleans was a kind of haunted place anyhow, and in those days I was scared to death if I was caught away from home past curfew. I remember one night, when I came back home, I saw a big black man sitting on a fence blowing smoke at me through his nose. The minute I saw him, I started running. Nobody can convince me that there are no such things as spirits. Too many have been seen by my family.

My uncle met a girl on his way home one night and tried to flirt with her. He asked her if she didn't think it was rather late for her to be out. They talked for a minute and she asked him to see her home. When they got to the graveyard, the gate opened and she walked in and my uncle started running.

I was very, very much afraid of those things. In fact I was

---

* *Cowein* means turtle, a dish made of turtle meat, or by extension, a social get-together. New Orleans has always been the capital of voodoo (or *voudun*), the survival in black magic of the pantheistic religions of West Africa, still current in Haiti and Brazil. The famous priestess Marie Laveau flourished in the city in the nineteenth century. Zora Neale Hurston studied under Laveau's disciples in the 1930's, reporting only partially on her experiences in her book *Mules and Men* because she was afraid to break her vows of secrecy. In the '40's, Delta friends of mine were still going to New Orleans to get talismans, like Muddy Waters's mojo hand.

worried with spirits when I was a kid. Our family home, located on the corner of Frenchman and Robinson, seemed to be full of them. We heard dishes rattling at night, people walking around, the sewing-machine running, chains rattling, etcetera, and we used to keep the house filled up with holy water. I had it tied all around my bed. Even then it seemed like those spirits would touch my toes. I'd look up over the covers and see them and take one jump and be in my mother's bed. Those spirits at home was one of the most horrible things that ever happened to me.

Really Tremendous Sports

●●● **T**hose days I often used to like to stay with my god-mother. She kept boxes of jewels in the house and I always had some kind of diamond on. Through her I came to be considered the best dresser, and this caused me to get my invitation to be an honorary member of the Broadway Swells when I was still in short pants. The members figured I was a smart kid, so, in order to beat the other clubs, they decided to display a kid as an aide.

"What do you think about it, kid?" they said, "Do you think you could get a horse—that would cost you five dollars for the day? You'd have to have a streamer, too. But then you'd be an honorary member of the Broadway Swells."

I thought that was a swell idea and I personally accepted.

You see, New Orleans was very organization-minded. I

have never seen such beautiful clubs as they had there—the Broadway Swells, the High Arts, the Orleans Aides, the Bulls and Bears, the Tramps, the Iroquois, the Allegroes—that was just a few of them, and those clubs would parade at least once a week. They'd have a great big band. The grand marshal would ride in front with his aides behind him, all with expensive sashes and streamers.

The members that could afford it would have a barrel of beer and plenty of sandwiches and a lot of whiskey and gin waiting at their houses. And, wherever these supplies would be, the parade would stage a grand salute. The grand marshal would lead his boys up one side of the street and down the other while the band played on the front steps. Then the boys would go inside and get their drinks and have a hell of a time.

The day I rode with the Broadway Swells my horse wasn't exactly up to the minute. I thought I should have a small horse, since I wasn't nothing but a kid, and so the boys around that was jealous of me called my horse a goat and picked him up by his knees and hollered, "We can truck this horse on our back. . . . You shouldn't be riding the horse . . . he should be riding you." I got angry two or three times at the way my poor old pony was moving and I tried to beat him to death to show them that he could run fast. Until this day one of the things I feel most sorry for is the way I beat that poor horse.

Those parades were really tremendous things. The drums would start off, the trumpets and trombones rolling into something like *Stars and Stripes* or *The National Anthem* and everybody would strut off down the street, the bass-drum player twirling his beater in the air, the snare drummer throwing his sticks up and bouncing them off the ground, the kids jumping and hollering, the grand marshal and his aides in their expensive uniforms moving along dignified, women on top of women strutting along back of the aides, and out in front of everybody—the second line, armed with sticks and bottles and baseball bats and all forms of ammunition ready to fight the foe when they neared the dividing line.

It's a funny thing that the *second line* marched at the head of the parade, but that's the way it had to be in New Orleans. They were our protection. You see, whenever a parade would get to another district the enemy would be waiting at the dividing line.* If the parade crossed that line, it meant a fight, a terrible fight. The first day I marched a fellow was cut, must have been a hundred times. Blood was gushing out of him same as from one of the gushers in Yellowstone Park, but he never did stop fighting.

They had a tough little guy in the Broadway Swells named Black Benny. Benny hung around the charcoal schooners at the head of the New Basin, but on Sundays he'd get his broomstick and march as grand marshal of the second-line gang. He was a really tough egg and terrible to get along with, always in some argument.

---

* The line between two wards or neighborhoods—one of old-fashioned Creoles, the other of American newcomers, for example. Said Sayles, the banjo player: "If you lived on the riverfront and you go back of town, you liable to be run, whether you black or white. Or if you lived downtown, you go uptown, black or white, you liable to be run."

Some of the enemy would say, "Listen, don't cross this line."

"Why not?" Benny would say.

"If you cross it, it will be your ass."

"Whose ass?"

"Your ass."

"Well, lemme tell you something. I don't give a damn about you and your whole family."

"If I hit you, your old double grandfather will feel it."

And about that time the broomsticks and brickbats would start to fly, the razors would come into play and the seven shooters—which was a little bit of a .22 that shot seven times—would begin popping. I've seen one case when a fellow shot seven times and every bullet hit the other party and none of them even went into his skin. But, anyhow, everybody would move on out the way, because nobody wanted to take a chance with a pistol, because they'd known many of them to die that way. Myself, a razor was something I always moved from if I saw one in the fight. I knew what a razor was, my uncle being a barber. A razor is a very, very tough thing to come up against.

Well, if they'd have ten fights one Sunday, they didn't have many. Sometimes it would require a couple of ambulances to come around and pick up the people that was maybe cut or shot occasionally. This didn't happen all the time, but very seldom it didn't. The fact of it is, there was no parade at no time you couldn't find a knot on somebody's head where somebody had got hit with a stick or something. And always plenty to eat and drink, especially for the men in the band, and with bands like Happy Galloway's, Manuel Perez's and Buddy Bold-

And they'd sing on—

> *T'ouwais, bas q'ouwais,*
> *Ou tendais,*
> *T'ouwais, bas q'ouwais,*
> *Ou tendais.* *

And then they would stop for a minute, throw back their heads and holler—

> *Ala caille-yo ko*
> *Ala caille wais . . .*
> *Ouwais, bas q'ouwais,*
> *T'ouwais, bas q'ouwais,*
> *Ou tendais.*

They would dance and sing and go on just like regular Indians, because they had the idea they wanted to act just like the old Indians did in years gone by and so they lived true to the traditions of the Indian style. They went armed with fictitious spears and tommyhawks and so forth and their main object was to make their enemy bow. They would send their spy-boys two blocks on ahead—I happened to be a spy-boy myself once so I know how this went—and when a spy-boy would meet another spy from an enemy tribe he'd point his finger to the ground and say, "Bow-wow." And if they wouldn't bow, the spy-boy would use the Indian call, "Woo-

---

Tune 6, Appendix 1.

en's we had the best ragtime music in the world. There
many jobs for musicians in these parades that musicians
ever like to leave New Orleans. They used to say, "This
best town in the world. What's the use for me to go an
place?"*

Now everybody in the world has heard about th
Orleans Mardi Gras, but maybe not about the Indians
the biggest feats that happened in Mardi Gras. Ever
parades with floats and costumes that cost millions, wh
folks heard the sign of the Indians—

Ungai-ha!
Ungai-ha!

—that big parade wouldn't have anybody there: th
would flock to see the Indians. When I was a child, I
they really was Indians. They wore paint and blan
when they danced, one would get in the ring and
head back and downward, stooping over and be
knees, making a rhythm with his heels and singin
wais, bas q'ouwais—and the tribe would answer—(

---

* Johnny St. Cyr put it this way . . .
   "This is a town that would break up a show. What I m
shows came in here and the people fall so much in love wi
that they miss their train and didn't even try to catch up
Dixie Minstrels came here on their second trip, half the m
in New Orleans—just crazy about them Creole girls." I
pleasure-loving New Orleans had several hundred bands, a
work for them all at its feasts, balls, picnics, and celebra

woo-woo-woo-woo," that was calling the tribes—and, many a time, in these Indian things, there would be a killing and next day there would be somebody in the morgue.

In New Orleans we would often wonder where a dead person was located. At any time we heard somebody was dead we knew we had plenty good food that night. Those days I belonged to a quartet and we specialized in spirituals for the purpose of finding somebody that was dead, because the minute we'd walk in, we'd be right in the kitchen where the food was—plenty ham sandwiches and cheese sandwiches slabbered all over with mustard, and plenty whiskey and plenty of beer. Of course, the dead man would always be laid out in the front and he'd be by himself most of the time and couldn't hear nothing we would be saying at all. He was dead and there was no reason for him to be with us living people. And very often the lady of the house would be back there with us having a good time, too, because she would be glad he was gone.

Then we would stand up and begin—

> *Nearer, my God, to thee . . .*

very slow and with beautiful harmony, thinking about that ham—

> *Nearer to thee . . .*

plenty of whiskey in the flask and all kinds of crazy ideas in the harmony which made it impossible for anybody to jump in and sing. We'd be sad, too, terribly sad.

> *Steal away, steal away,*
> *Steal away home to Jesus . . .*

I tell you we had beautiful numbers to sing at those wakes.

Of course, as I told you, everybody in the city of New Orleans was always organization-minded, which I guess the world knows, and a dead man always belonged to several organizations—secret orders and so forth and so on. So when anybody died, there was always a big band turned out on the day he was supposed to be buried. Never buried at night, always in the day and right in the heart of the city. You could hear the band come up the street taking the gentleman for his last ride, playing different dead marches like *Flee as the Bird to the Mountain.*

In New Orleans very seldom they would bury them in the deep in the mud. They would always bury um in a vault. . . . So they would leave the graveyard . . . the band would get ready to strike up. They'd have a second line behind um, maybe a couple of blocks long with baseball bats, axe handles, knives, and all forms of ammunition to combat some of the foe when they came to the dividing lines. Then the band would get started and you could hear the drums, rolling a deep, slow rhythm. A few bars of that and then the snare drummer would make a hot roll on his drums and the boys in the band would just tear loose, while second line swung down the street, singing . . .

> *Didn't he ramble?*
> *He rambled.*
> *Rambled all around,*
> *In and out the town.*
> *Didn't he ramble?*
> *He rambled.*
> *He rambled till the butchers cut him down.*

That would be the last of the dead man. He's gone and
everybody came back home, singing. In New Orleans they
believed truly to stick right close to the Scripture. That means
rejoice at the death and cry at the birth. . . .*

Those boys I used to sing with were really tough babies.
They frequented the corners at Jackson and Locust and nobody
fooled with *them*. The policemen was known never to cross
Claiborne Avenue and these tough guys lived five blocks past
Claiborne at Galvez, way back of town!

It was a miracle how those boys lived. They were sweetback
men, I suppose you'd call them—always a bunch of women
running after them. I remember the Pickett boys—there was
Bus, there was Nert, there was Nonny, there was Bob. Nert
had a burned hand, which he used to wear a stocking over, and
he was seemingly simple to me. All these boys wanted to have
some kind of importance. They dressed very well and they
were tremendous sports. It was nothing like spending money
that even worried their mind. If they didn't have it, somebody
else would have it and spend it for them—they didn't care.
But they all strived to have at least one Sunday suit, because,
without that Sunday suit, you didn't have anything.

It wasn't the kind of Sunday suit you'd wear today. You was
considered way out of line if your coat and pants matched.

---

* Due in part to the influence of this book and the subsequent loving
care of jazz aficionados like Allan Jaffe, but largely to the strong cultural
attachment of the black neighborhoods of New Orleans, the jazz funeral
and the jazz parade are still very much alive in the city. Any weekend,
when the weather is good, there'll be a jazz parade in some part of town.

Many a time they would kid me, "Boy you must be from the country. Here you got trousers on the same as your suit."

These guys wouldn't wear anything but a blue coat and some kind of stripe in their trousers and those trousers had to be very, very tight. They'd fit um like a sausage. I'm telling you it was very seldom you could button the top button of a person's trousers those days in New Orleans. They'd leave the top button open and they wore very loud suspenders—of course they really didn't need suspenders, because the trousers was so tight and one suspender was always hanging down. If you wanted to talk to one of those guys, he would find the nearest post, stiffen his arm out and hold himself as far away as possible from that post he's leaning on. That was to keep those fifteen, eighteen-dollar trousers of his from losing their press.

You should have seen one of those sports move down the street, his shirt busted open so that you could discern his red flannel undershirt, walking along with a very mosey walk they had adopted from the river, called shooting the agate. When you shoot the agate, your hands is at your sides with your index fingers stuck out and you kind of struts with it. That was considered a big thing with some of the illiterate women—if you could shoot a good agate and had a nice highclass red undershirt with the collar turned up, I'm telling you were liable to get next to that broad. She liked that very much.

Those days, myself, I thought I would die unless I had a hat with the emblem Stetson in it and some Edwin Clapp shoes. But Nert and Nonny and many of them wouldn't wear ready-made shoes. They wore what they called the St. Louis Flats and the Chicago Flats, made with cork soles and without heels and with gambler designs on the toes. Later on, some of them made arrangements to have some kind of electric-light bulbs

in the toes of their shoes with a battery in their pockets, so
when they would get around some jane that was kind of simple
and thought they could make her, as they call making um,
why they'd press a button in their pocket and light up the
little-bitty bulb in the toe of their shoes and that jane was
claimed. It's really the fact.

Now these boys used to all have a sweet mama—I guess I
will have to tell it as it is—they was what I would call, maybe
a fifth-class whore. They got something when they could and
when they couldn't, they worked in white people's yards.
These were colored girls I'm talking about, but it applied to
the white girls, too, of the poorer class. They all practically
lived out in the same section together, because there was no
such thing as segregation at all in that section—in fact nowhere in New Orleans at that time.

Well, every night these sports I'm talking about would even
go as far as to meet their sweet mamas—sometimes they would
brave it and walk to St. Charles Avenue where their sweet
mamas were working; and sometimes it would be okay for
them to go in and their sweet mamas would bring a pan out
to the servant's room. Some of those pans were marvelous, I'm
telling you—in fact I, myself, have been in some of the homes,
seeking after a pan, and I know. Take a girl working for the
Godchaux or the Solaris—she would bring you gumbo, Bayou
Cook oysters, and maybe turkey with cranberry sauce—this
wouldn't have to be on Christmas, because New Orleans is the
place where no doubt the finest food in the world prevails.
When sweet mama cooks and carves that fowl, sweet papa is
sure to eat the choicest portions, no argument about that!

I was quite small, but I used to get in on those pans occa-

sionally. Always hanging out with older men, anyhow. And
sometimes I'd be with um when they all get together—a
whole lot of sweet mamas and their sweet papas—to have a
little bit of a ball off to their self. Josky Adams would play the
blues . . .

> See, see, rider, see what you have done,
> You made me love you, now your man done come.

Josky had a beautiful sister and I always had it in my mind I
wanted to marry her. Used to take her to these parties and had
a wonderful time. It seemed like a family there—Josky playing and singing . . .

> I want a gal that works in the white folks' yard,
> A pretty gal that works in the white folks' yard.
> Do you see that fly crawling up the wall,
> She's going up there to get her ashes hauled.
> I got a woman lives right back of the jail,
> She got a sign on her window—Pussy For Sale.

But the one blues I never can forget out of those early days
happened to be played by a woman that lived next door to my
godmother's in the Garden District. The name of this musician was Mamie Desdoumes. Two middle fingers of her right
hand had been cut off, so she played the blues with only three
fingers on her right hand. She only knew this one tune and she
played it all day long after she would first get up in the
morning.

I stood on the corner, my feet was dripping wet,
I asked every man I meet . . .
  Can't give me a dollar, give me a lousy dime,
  Just to feed that hungry man of mine . . .*

Although I had heard them previously I guess it was Mamie first really sold me on the blues.**

---

* Tune 1, Appendix 1.
** Bunk Johnson, old-time New Orleans trumpet player, remembered Mamie . . .

"I knew Mamie Desdoumes real well. Played many a concert with her singing those same blues. She was pretty good-looking—quite fair and with a *nice* head of hair. She was a hustlin' woman. A blues-singing poor gal. Used to play pretty passable piano around them dance halls on Perdido Street.

"When Hattie Rogers or Lulu White would put it out that Mamie was going to be singing at their place, the white men would turn out in bunches and them whores would clean up."

Danny Barker, the great jazz guitarist and raconteur, was leafing through a family photograph album. He pointed to the faded picture of a sweet-faced Creole girl. "That's Mamie Desdoumes, a cousin of mine," he said. "That's what she looked like before that pimp got hold of her. She was the family darling. Then she disappeared. He had taken her out of town. Then later he put her to work for him in one of those houses in Storyville. They often held those girls against their will. Well, Mamie tried to escape one night. She jumped out of a second-storey window and broke her hip, so that she was always deformed after that. Then she couldn't get away. Later she became famous for the blues. That was something that happened in this great city of ours." I looked at the sweet young face in that old photograph and I wept.

Money in the Tenderloin

●●● **Y**ou see, my young friends had brought me into the tenderloin district at a very young age, even before we were in long pants. In fact, we used to steal long pants from our fathers and brothers and uncles and slip on in. When the policemens caught us, they would slip us on in jail. One of them, I remember, was named Fast Mail Burwell. He was known to be Fast Mail because he had two legs and feet that couldn't be beat, and he would take the straps on the ends of his club and cut our legs to ribbons. We kids were very much frightened of him and, at times, would climb those high-board fences to escape. In those days we had curfew in New Orleans and, when the curfew bell rung at nine, all the kids was supposed to be at home. Of course, it was our ambition to show that we were tough and could stay out after curfew.

When I was about fourteen, my mother died and left my favorite uncle as guardian. He was in the barber business and he gave me a job at the fabulous salary of twenty-five cents a week and promised a suit for New Year's. My assignments were chambermaid, apprentice and note messenger to his different girls, plus excuses to his wife. He was punctual with my salary, and with the few pennies I made on shines I was able to help my sisters for whom I had a fatherly feeling, since I was the oldest.

When New Year's came I waited for my new suit. Uncle's wife was very good at sewing and I believe it was agreed between both uncle and wife to cut down one of uncle's suits. This was done and the suit was presented to me, very much to my disapproval. Uncle was a very fat man, weighing about two hundred and ten pounds. So the suit was tried and did not fit me anywhere. All the kids had holiday clothes but me. I was so peeved at my uncle and his wife that I tried to kill their cat, Bricktop.

The older generations were passing away and friends were vanishing. The estate was being mortgaged and grandfather was losing his liquor business. My favorite horse, Tom, died during a very drastic September electric storm, and things were generally going bad.

I had heard of some boys getting jobs in the cooperage, lining barrels, making not less than two dollars a week, more than I had ever made working. (Lining is the small strip nailed around the head of a sugar barrel to make it secure—two strips to each head—five cents to each strip.) School closed. I went to the Brooklyn Cooperage Company, was hired and, positively green to the job, made three dollars the first week. My heart was jumping with joy. I could see success by my own hands. I finally got to be one of the best in the shop and was promoted to higher departments to learn the trade of cooper.

By this time I was considered one of the best junior pianists in the whole city. Everywhere I went I was accepted as a king. I was always dressed well by my folks, but I, myself, wanted to dress myself. Of course, my father wanted me to be a hard-working boy in the bricklaying trade, like he was. He was a contractor, bricklayer, making large buildings and so forth and so on. He offered to pay me two dollars a day as a foreman, but I decided, after I learned to play music, I could break more money playing piano in the tenderloin district.

This is the story of how I got my first job in music . . . I had leave to stay out at night on Saturday and Sunday till 11 P.M., so when some boys enticed me to go to the tenderloin district I finally accepted the invitation. I liked the freedom of standing at a saloon bar, passing along the streets crowded with men of all nationalities and descriptions. There were women standing in their cribs with their chippies on—a crib is a room about seven feet wide and a chippie is a dress that women wore, knee length and very easy to disrobe.

One Saturday night whilst on one of the wild jaunts, we heard that one of the houses was stuck for a pianist. My friends encouraged me to go for the job, but my fear was so great that the only way I would go was if my friends would go with me. I felt sure it was a plot to kidnap me, since I had had a narrow escape when I was younger on Melpomene and Willow streets. So they finally agreed to take the other upstarts along and put them into a rear room where I could see them but their guests could not.

I was so frightened when I first touched the piano, the girls decided to let me go immediately. One of my friends spoke up, "Go ahead and show these people you can play." That encouraged me greatly and I pulled myself together and started playing with the confidence of being in my own circle. "That boy is marvelous"—this was the remarks of the inmates. Money was plentiful and they tipped me about $20, which I did not want to accept because I was not taught that way.

They wanted to give me the job of regular professor, but I could not see the idea. I was making about $15 legitimately, and furthermore I knew that if my folks were ever to find out I had even passed through the tenderloin, they would deal with me drastically. I asked what salary they would pay.

"One dollar a night is the regular salary," was the landlady's answer. I flatly refused.

Then my friends showed me how I had made $20 in tips in maybe an hour's playing. "You see, the $1 is a guarantee in case there happens to be some kind of a bad night, so you will be sure of some salary," the landlady explained. "But I will guarantee you $5 a night, if you don't make it in tips."

My friends coaxed me. I thought of all the incidents that might happen, maybe in the thousands. I decided I could tell my folks I had changed to the night watch in the cooperage and I would notify my boss I had taken ill. This plan would possibly make things safe all the way around. Anyhow, I thought, whatever happens in a family, all you have to do is take some money home and everything is all right. I then accepted the job, but would not stay that night. I reported the next night promptly at the given time, nine o'clock.

The streets were crowded with men. Police were always in

sight, never less than two together, which guaranteed the safety of all concerned. Lights of all colors were glittering and glaring. Music was pouring into the streets from every house. Women were standing in the doorways, singing or chanting some kind of blues—some very happy, some very sad, some with the desire to end it all by poison, some planning a big outing, a dance, or some other kind of enjoyment. Some were real ladies in spite of their downfall and some were habitual drunkards and some were dope fiends as follows, opium, heroin, cocaine, laudanum, morphine, etcetera. I was personally sent to Chinatown many times with a sealed note and a small amount of money and would bring back several cards of hop. There was no slipping and dodging. All you had to do was walk in to be served.

The girls liked their young professor and they worked the customers for big tips for me. I began to make more money than I had ever heard of in my life. I bought a new suit and a hat with the emblem Stetson in it and a pair of St. Louis Flats that turned up, I'm telling you the truth, nearly to my ankles. I was wearing these clothes on my way home to work one Sunday morning when I met my great-grandmother coming from early mass.

She looked at me and, I'm telling you, this Mimi Pechet could look a hole right through a door. "Have a good job now, Ferd? Making plenty money?"

Being very, very young and foolish, I told her what I was making. My grandmother gave me that Frenchman look and said to me in French, "Your mother is gone and can't help her little girls now. She left Amède and Mimi to their old grandmother to raise as good girls. A musician is nothing but a bum and a scalawag. I don't want you round your sisters. I reckon you better move."

My grandmother said all this and then she walked up the path to the white columns of the front porch, went inside, and shut the door.

INTERLUDE ONE

The Family

The boy stood at the gate, hearing the cold snap of the lock inside the door and staring at the pleasant house of his childhood. The early morning sunlight gleamed on the white clapboard walls and there, among the little gray railroad cottages of Frenchman Street, his old home looked very fine. In his mind it became a mansion with fluted columns and a noble broad gallery, a mansion that hid the real storey-and-a-half house with its narrow porch and its small square columns.

For young Ferdinand Morton the door had closed upon the secure, secret, and confined Creole family life. The beauty and glory of this life (indeed, for an American Negro, it was a comparatively rich one) were forever lost to him. Already an orphan, he became a wanderer, searching for a golden world that existed only in the memories and prejudices of respectable old Creole ladies like his grandmother.

He turned and walked away down the sunny street, the poison of Mimi's words entering and taking hold of his heart. She had judged him a danger to his sisters, a threat to the family reputation, and unworthy of the name of a Pechet, a Monette or a La Menthe. Her rejection wakened an unquenchable ambition and drive in the boy.

"One of the best junior pianists in the city of New Orleans"— would now be the king of ivories, glorifying a new name. Shut out of the warm heart of Creole New Orleans, he would bring the whole world close to the fire of New Orleans music. In the end he would have a respectable Creole girl, whom he would guard as jealously as Mimi watched his sisters.

This moment of fantasy prepared the way for later, almost paranoid feelings of self-love and persecution. Defeated by his family respectability, Morton would never again admit that he had been bested in anything. He met the whole world, including those who loved him best, with a diamond-encrusted and defiant smile. Back of this smile were hidden the shame

and sorrow of his childhood; these were secrets too painful for
him to recall, but along the narrow streets of New Orleans
they were still whispered—they were still to be discovered
in bits and fragments during an afternoon of casual Creole
gossip. . . .

The streets of the Seventh and Eighth wards—the "best"
part of what Jelly calls "Downtown" (actually, the district lies
to the west and north of the French Quarter and the Old
Cemetery above Claiborne Avenue)—have not wholly changed
since Jelly Roll rode with the Broadway Swells. Tonti, Rocheblave, Ursulines, Durbigny, St. Antoine—they have remained
dusty and quiet with small groceries or neighborhood bars on
many corners. These little establishments are flanked by rows
of one-storey houses, each joined to its neighbor and abutting
directly on the sidewalk. Most of these little houses are un-
painted and have grown gray with years of weathering. The
two front windows are almost always shuttered and the front
door is likewise hooded with shutters. At first one feels lonely
there, shut in by this blind and shuttered gray wall. Then
delicate strokes of fancy and love begin to stand out, silver
against gray.

The wooden stoops bear worn hollows for familiar feet. The
lintels above the doorways are strung with faded gray pearls.
Up along the cornices of the single gables the eye follows the
pleasant and rather silly music of scrolls and flowers and acan-
thus leaves sawn into the wood. Below, at the level of the
sidewalk, the shallow cellars breathe street air through delicate
medallions of wrought iron. Each house is slightly different in
such details and, as one notices these tracings of old-time
craftsmen, the blocks of humble and narrow houses take on a

*Guide to Jelly Roll's
New Orleans around
1900*

1) Where Jelly was born, corner Frenchman and Robinson.
2) Where Lala lived, corner 4th and Howard.
3) The Frenchman's.
4) Cemetery — Marie Laveau's tomb.
5) Gypsy Schaeffer's.
6) Pete Lala's.
7) Eloise Blackenstein's.
8) The Tuxedo.
9) Billy Phillips's.
10) Congo Square—The Globe Hall.
11) Tom Anderson, King of the District.
12) Parish Prison.
13) Music publishers here in business district.
14) Chinatown, opium available.
15) The French Market.
16) Dago Tony's — sponsor of Buddy, Bunk, and Louis.
17) Spanol's tonk.
18) Masonic Hall.
19) The Red Onion.
20) Hattie Rogers' place.
21) A few blocks to corner where Robt. Charles sold papers.
22) Jackson Hall corner Melpomene and Dryades.

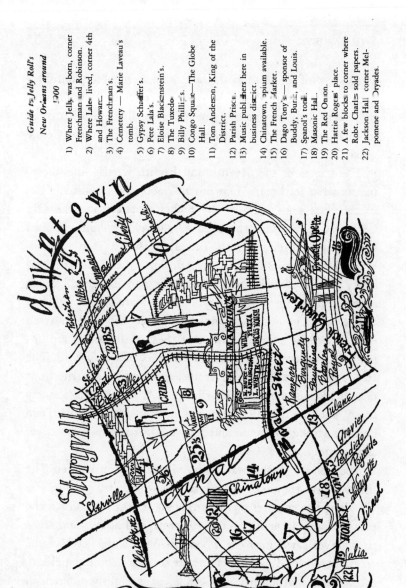

distinguished look—decorous rows of weatherbeaten and impoverished old ladies of good family, wearing stained lace
fichus and bending with age toward the dusty street.

The house on St. Antoine Street, where Jelly Roll's sister
lived, leaned gently against its neighbors, but indoors, behind
the shutters, where the air was cool and the light was dim, the
parlor still had a certain elegance. Amède Colas was neither
faded nor decadent. Her smile was warmer than Jelly Roll's
and in repose her glance was not withdrawn and cool like his,
but tender and animated. What secrets belonged to this lady,
she enjoyed.

She busied about the high-ceilinged room, turning up the
lights to show off the family portraits. "That's my daughter
who lives in California, Mister Lomax. She could pass any time
she want to but she think too well of herself," Amède said
with no irony intended. "My girl look like Mama and Mimi
yonder." Among the three handsome octoroons in the tinted
enlargements on the wall it was quite easy to.pick out Mimi—
the strong-minded fine old French lady with a determined
mouth and a big twist of hair high up. "What eyes she had,"
Amède laughed. "She never had to *tell* us to do anything. Just
open her eyes at us and we'd *move*. See, when my Mama died
we went to live with grandmother Mimi. My real mother I
don't even remember . . . You could say the same thing about
Jelly . . . I hardly knew him. When he left New Orleans, we
were just kids and we didn't hear no more from him until
1917 when he wrote and sent us money."

Jelly hadn't spoken about sending money. "He was a wonderful brother," Amède explained. "Do you know he sent me
something almost every week for years? It was a holiday in this
little family when his letters arrived—sometimes with twenty-

five and thirty-five dollars—whatever he could send, if it was
only five. Jelly never told us if he had any hard times, but we
would know from the amount of money. Just a week before he
died he sent ten dollars, and never even told us he was sick. He
didn't *have* to do that, but he knew I had a husband . . . see,
M. Colas has been sick along, not able to work so much. . . ."

From the bedroom that opened on the front parlor came an
apologetic coughing and in shambled M. Colas, wearing his
paint-spattered carpenter's overalls. He looked for all the world
like a white crane out of a bayou—tall and stooped, the hollows of his cheeks and temples showing dark against silvery
skin, and up towards the ceiling a swatch of silvery hair—a
silver crane with a Cajun accent.

"That Ferd. He was a gentleman. You know? Sho he was."
Tuberculosis had so deepened and softened his voice that M.
Colas habitually wagged his big, saw-marked forefinger for
emphasis. "When he heard about *me,* he sent me clothes—
shirts, suits, socks, everything. One time he sent five overcoats, brand new. Ten pairs of shoes, the very best. Ferd would
wear his things a couple of times and buy new and send me the
old. I didn't have to buy anything for years. He was a *man.* He
understood I had it hard because of my chest. . . ."

Colas stared into my face with a frank, country look, then
dropped his eyes to the cigarette he was rolling in his big
hands. Amède seemed a little pained by him, a little embarrassed, and yet every gesture of her warm brown face showed
her pride in having caught this tall, soft-voiced Cajun from the
western parishes. Sometime later on, when she was out of the
room, old Colas chuckled over the days when he had been
something of a rounder. "You know what she told the woman

who come to her with gossip about *me*? She tol' that woman, 'Well, it's a mighty po' rat ain't got but one hole!' "

We were still laughing when Amède returned. "I called up Uncle Henry and invited him over," she said. "He's my mama's oldest brother and he can tell you everything about our family. Uncle Henry is awful old, but he gets around, he really gets around." She threw back her head and laughed a liquid, joy-swollen laugh that swept Colas and myself—a couple of inhibited crackers—along with it.

Presently Uncle Henry popped into the door, like Uncle Rat of the ballad, twitching a Velasquez moustache. Spare, trim, quick, with a hawk-like Roman nose and parchment skin, he was the little Mediterranean gentleman who spread Roman law, wine-drinking, and gallantry to the ends of the earth. Uncle Henry was the kind of a feisty old bachelor who would never take his hat off except in church, yet so dignified that the diamond on his finger somehow matched his faded blue work clothes. Here was the proper family chronicler for Mister Jelly Roll.

"I have just attained my seventy-fifth birthday," said Henry, with comic solemnity, eyes as sharp upon me as if I had been state's prosecutor. "But don't think those boys can get rowdy in *my* barroom. I handle um. And some of those guys as tall as the trees they grow in Mississippi . . . feel my strength." He proffered his arm and his stringy old man's muscle.

"The Pechet family—look at me, I'm a Pechet, but old Mimi there, she was *born* Felicie Baudoin. She married in with us—Pierre Pechet, a cigar manufacturer and a real Creole. What I mean by *real* Creole, he was French and Spanish and spoke both languages. Like me. I change languages as I change clothes—French, Spanish, Italian, English, and back again. . . .

"Old Pierre, my grandfather, wasn't never rich, but he was well educated and a *man,* too. Knocked out two sets of twins among his ten children. Five lived to be men and women and five died. . . ."

"I thought hees name was Émile,"* Amède remarked.

"No, no, Émile was old Pierre's son—his only son, and a cigarmaker, too," Henry said, rolling a cigarette in his claw-like fingers and then passing the makings on to M. Colas. "Émile was the boy and the rest was daughters. That cause old lady Mimi to have to work out. You remember she used to cook for the Solaris out on Palmer's Avenue?"

"Me remember?" Amède began to giggle. "Times I used to stay out at Solaris! Mimi, she used to tell us, if you want to stay out here with these fine folks and all their money you got to act decent. Mimi was strict, strict! And those Solaris thought a lot of her, used to take her along when they went traveling to The Hague, Paris, Germany, and all them places."

(The bitterest hatreds are those of servants for their masters, and the most pitiable pretensions and the fantasies belong to children of servants. Jelly's "rich" grandmother traveled around the world as a ladies' maid.)

Old Henry struck the right note. "Ours was a highly-thought-of family, because Mimi was strict and all her daughters the same. My mama, Laura, was just like Mimi and *she*

---

* Henry's statement shows that both Jelly Roll and his sister had confused Émile and Pierre.

married well. Good blood on both sides of the family. My daddy, Julien Monette*—he was a tailor by trade—got elected state senator in 1868. Yes, Papa was a big politician —a big racketeer like all these politicians, I reckon—but in his days, he was *known*. Then he left New Orleans and died of yellow fever in Panama, working on the canal job."

"Well, that's all news to me," said Amède. "It all happened before I went to live in the Monette home."

"You keep talking about the Monette home! It wasn't ours," Uncle Henry said. "We *rent* it so long, everybody *think* it belong to us. . . . Don't look at me, Amède. This young man want the facts and I ain't gonna lie."

Amède looked embarrassed. "My people never told us children nothin'," she said. "I barely know anything about my own father and mother."

"Well, honey, I'll tell you one thing," said old Henry. "Your mama was a very pretty woman—not as pretty as I am because I favor the Pechets—but she was handsome, had hair hanging down to her waist, always very gay dispositioned. And I thought she was smart till I found out who she was gonna marry."

"You mean Ed La Menthe?" said Colas.

"That's who, F. P. La Menthe—Jelly Roll Morton's father—a nice-lookin' light brown-skin Creole, but wild." Old Henry wagged his head. "Very wild."

"Ed had himself a good livin', too," Colas sighed. "Carpenter, demolished buildings, and owned a couple of properties, but he was a fourflusher."

---

* Not Henri, as Jelly remembered the name.

"Sho he was. Do you remember how him and Paul went to Haiti in the big war? Government interpreters. Interpreted so much government money they landed in the pen," old Henry chuckled.

"Is that why Mama left him?" Amède asked.

"No, no, honey," said old Henry. "She left him long before. Louise taken it from Ed till it came up to here." Henry made a vivid gesture across his throat. "And then she threw it off. Ferd was just a kid then. . . ."

There was a pause while old Henry squinted back at the past through the curling cigarette smoke, remembering big-timing Ed La Menthe. How close-mouthed Jelly had been about his father!

"You couldn't dislike that Ed," said Henry, half to himself. "Ed enjoyed himself, he always did. Went to the French Opera House all the time and loved music, loved music. . . ." He slapped his narrow thigh. "Why, that's it, that's *it*. It just came back to me!"

"Hey, old man, what you talking about?" from Colas.

"That's where the *music* came into this boy. Listen—Ed La Menthe was a trambone player! Played a slidin' trambone! I didn't think of that. Why, I danced to his music many and many an old time." Old Henry laughed with excitement. "That's where Jelly got his music. Ed could cooperate pretty well in a band. Slidin' trambone, too, at that . . . !"

Here was a real discovery. Jelly Roll had occasionally mentioned playing trombone, but the influence of his father ran deeper. Obsessively, in almost every line of his compositions, Jelly Roll wrote base figures in tailgate style and so-

norous, bursting melodies; trombone phrasing is the trade-
mark of Jelly Roll's compositions . . .

So the man who hardly mentioned his father in conversation
never stopped talking about him in his music. Certainly he
must have heard the worst of Ed La Menthe. Certainly he was
ashamed of him and felt terribly rejected by him. Jelly even
claimed to have been "a foundling raised in an orphan's home";
yet, in a sense, his whole career—the gambling, the sporty
clothes, the fondness for notoriety, and especially the music in
every line of which one can find the voice of the "slidin'
trambone"—was a search for his lost father and a triumph over
him.

Here in the shadows of this Creole parlor, the ghosts that
haunted Jelly Roll Morton were coming into the light. Amède

said, "Maybe some of us is 'outside' children, because I don't know for sure that Mama was really married to Jelly's daddy or to mine. I'm not even certain how old I am or Jelly, either. I *believe* Mimi said I was born in 1897 and I always heard Jelly was eleven years older, but I don't *know*."

This explained why Jelly Roll could juggle his age as it suited him—writing 1888 on his insurance policy, giving 1885 on the Library of Congress records, a date that puts him in Storyville earlier than most other jazzmen and gave him plenty of historical elbow room, and telling his wife the year was 1886. It was this last date that checked with Amède's recollection.

"I don't know for sure," she sighed. "We tried to find out, but the old parish church had burnt with all the birth records."

Old Henry chuckled, "Don't worry. You wouldn't find nothing about Ed La Menthe in no parish record."

"Where did the name Morton come in?"

"That was *my* daddy, Willie Morton," said Amède, answering my unspoken thought. "I can't tell anything about *him*. I don't even know whether he was living or not after mother died. All I know is I didn't see no daddy and I didn't see no mama."

"He was dead, honey," said Henry softly. "This Willie Morton, he wasn't no Creole—he was a sort of light brown-skin man, did portering jobs around hotels and clubs and things—a nice type of fellow." Jelly Roll preferred not to remember his porter father at all, but chose to say he invented the name Morton for business reasons.

"Just how Willie Morton died, I can't tell you," said uncle Henry. "Off traveling somewhere. I think he drowned. Anyhow, Louise didn't live long after that. She was always healthy, but the pneumonia took her. Yes, it did. . . ."

"After that," Amède said, "Ferd stayed most of the time with his godmother, Eulalie Echo. Used to *love* to stay Uptown with her. Lalee, he called her."

"Did you know her, M. Monette?" I asked Henry.

"I reckon so," he grinned. "I knew her so well, the first child I had birthed, she birthed it for me! She was a girl friend of mine for three years while she lived next door to the Monette house. Then she went back to Paul Echo and they moved in the Garden District.* I believe later on she married this Ed Hunter, drove a coal cart. . . ."

In the South you have to know people mighty well before they will talk about voodoo and old Henry hooted at the idea that Lalee had been a practitioner. Yet it seemed to me that perhaps old Henry was suspiciously overemphatic in his protests that voodoo was just humbug.

"No, Lalee was nothing of the kind," he said, while old man Colas smiled quietly to himself, "But she *was* crazy about that boy, much as if he was her own son. She sent him to professors and she pushed and advised him in every way to perfect himself on the piano. The family wanted to make a bricklayer of him, but Ferd was too smooth and clever a fellow. He preferred to sit in the parlor out of the sun and play piano. And he got to be the very best. At least that's what I *hear*. I never heard him actually play in life."

"It's real sad to me," said Amède, "that I never heard Ferd

---

* To the corner of Fourth and Howard, only a trumpet toot from Perdido Street, Louis Armstrong's hangout.

in person but one time in my life. He came by the house and
I asked him to go across the street to a neighbor's and play for
me. That day I remember Ferd was wearing a loud silk candy-
striped shirt and loud suspenders. . . ."

"Kind you have to put under the mattress to keep um from
running off," M. Colas chuckled.

"Yes," Amède agreed, "he *was* dressed kind of rowdy.
Grandma got to fussin at him and he told her he wasn't goin
to stay around to be fussed at, and then he left New Orleans
and never did come back. When we'd get letters he'd always
tell us to pray and make novenas. We had to look up the places
he was traveling in the geography."

"Well, he was like that from a boy," said Henry. "Never
stopped running. Always on the go. After he began that piano, we never had any of his time at all."

"I always used to tell Amède I wished Jelly could have come
back home. There's no place like New Orleans, after all," said
M. Colas.

"Well, I reckon you *have* to hustle to get as far as Ferd did,"
said old Henry with a dry chuckle, seeming very pleased with
himself that he had never tried to get away.

"Hustling was just what Grandmother called it," said
Amède. "She told Ferd that anybody who went on the stage,
doing things in public, was just *common*. And she raised us not
to boast about Ferd's playing. Of course, *now* I'm real proud of
my brother. . . ."

An afternoon of casual gossip in a little gray house of the
Eighth Ward, an hour or so of chuckling with Morton's ami-
able relations, and then the painful burden of his secrets, the
sorrow of his orphaned and illegitimate youth, gradually began to show behind the diamond-crusted grin. Jelly Roll, in

all candor, could have begun by saying, "I never have been sure of the exact year of my birth and I can't be certain that I'm legitimate. My mother came from a line of respectable Creole house-servants and cigarmakers. My father was a fourflusher, who left me with nothing. . . ." Instead, Morton buried the hurt of his thrice-orphaned heart in a legend about a fine and noble family. . . . Nonetheless, the evening of the day his grandmother shut him out of his family, the boy wept.

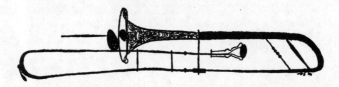

STORYVILLE

*In 1896 a New Orleans alderman, Sidney Story, promul-
gated a city ordinance which restricted prostitution to a
thirty-eight-block red-light district adjoining Canal Street.
Much to the mortification of the alderman, some joker nick-
named the area* Storyville. *And the name stuck. Storyville
it remained until, in 1917, the navy finally closed the
tenderloin for good. In Jelly Roll's time the district's legal
boundaries were: North Robertson, St. Louis, Basin, and
Iberville (Customhouse) streets. See map on page 36.*

Where the Birth of Jazz
Originated From

●●● The first night after my great-grandmother told me to go, I attended the Grand Theatre and saw a play in which they sang a very sweet song, entitled *Give Me Back My Dead Daughter's Child*. I thought about how my mother had died and left me a motherless child out in this wide world to mourn, and I began to cry. Fact of the business, I was just fifteen and so dumb I didn't even know how to rent a room. So I walked the streets till morning and then caught a train for Biloxi, where my godmother had her country place in the summer. I knew she would take me in, no matter what happened.

While there in Biloxi I began hanging out with older boys and thinking of myself as quite a man, which I was still just a kid. These guys told me that you could be a real man if you could take a half pint of whiskey, throw it to your mouth, and drink the whole thing down without stopping. Well, I tried that and it knocked me completely out. I lay under the bed at my godmother's house for three whole days before they found me. That finished whiskey and me for that time.

Well, I played in various little places in Biloxi, but I never made the money I had in New Orleans. I worked at The Flat Top until one night the owner was hit in the head with a pool ball, which has made him crazy till this day. Then I moved on to a job in Meridian, Mississippi. Mississippi was always my bad-luck state. I came down with typhoid fever and returned to Biloxi on a stretcher. My godmother fed me for three weeks on a diet of whiskey and milk, which almost ended me with liquor entirely. (I never took another drink, except occasionally . . . Lord, this whiskey is just lovely!)

My next job was playing for a white sporting-house woman named Mattie Bailey. Nobody but white came there, and, as it was a dangerous place, I always carried a .38 Special. Mattie Bailey would keep me behind to close up the place for her, and, because I was always the last man out, talk began to get around that something was going on between the two of us. By her being a white woman, they didn't approve of my being intimate with her, as they thought. One day she told me they were talking about lynching me and right then I decided it was time for me to roll on back to my good old hometown, New Orleans.

So in the year of 1902 when I was about seventeen years old I happened to invade one of the sections where the birth of jazz originated from. Some friends took me to The Frenchman's on the corner of Villery and Bienville, which was at that time the most famous nightspot after everything was closed. It was only a back room, but it was where all the greatest pianists frequented after they got off from work in the sporting-houses. About four A.M., unless plenty of money was involved on their jobs, they would go to The Frenchman's and there would be everything in the line of hilarity there.

All the girls that could get out of their houses was there. The millionaires would come to listen to their favorite pianists. There weren't any discrimination of any kind. They all sat at different tables or anywhere they felt like sitting. They all mingled together just as they wished to and everyone was just like one big happy family. People came from all over the country and most times you couldn't get in. So this place would go on at a tremendous rate of speed—plenty money, drinks of all kinds—from four o'clock in the morning until maybe twelve, one, two, or three o'clock in the daytime. Then, when the great pianists used to leave, the crowds would leave.

New Orleans was the stomping grounds for all the greatest pianists in the country. We had Spanish, we had colored, we had white, we had Frenchmens, we had Americans, we had them from all parts of the world because there were more jobs for pianists than any other ten places in the world. The sporting-houses needed professors, and we had so many different styles that whenever you came to New Orleans, it wouldn't make any difference that you just came from Paris or any part of England, Europe, or any place—whatever your tunes were over there, we played them in New Orleans.

I might mention some of our pianists . . . Sammy Davis, one of the greatest manipulators of the keyboard I guess I have ever seen in the history of the world. . . . Alfred Wilson and

Albert Cahill, they were both great pianists and both of them were colored. Poor Alfred Wilson, the girls taken to him and showed him a point where he didn't have to work. He finally came to be a dope fiend and smoked so much dope till he died. Albert Cahill didn't smoke dope, but he ruined his eyes staying up all night, gambling. Albert was known as the greatest show player that ever was in existence as I can remember. Then there was Kid Ross, a white boy and one of the outstanding hot players of the country.*

All these men were hard to beat, but when Tony Jackson walked in, any one of them would get up from the piano stool. If he didn't, somebody was liable to say, "Get up from that piano. You hurting its feelings. Let Tony play." Tony was real dark and not a bit good-looking, but he had a beautiful disposition. He was the outstanding favorite of New Orleans, and I have never known any pianists to come from any section of the world that could leave New Orleans victorious.

Tony was considered among all who knew him the greatest single-handed entertainer in the world.** His memory seemed like something nobody's ever heard of in the music world. He

---

* Jelly, after thirty years, not only recalled the names of these bygone musicians but remembered their music, and as he named them one after another, he paused to play a selection in their various styles—a feat of creative ethnomusicology that has made the Library of Congress sessions into a treasury of the roots of jazz. This sonorous re-creation of the past was certainly not the work of a vulgar egotist, as some have portrayed him, but rather of a luminous and passionate musical intelligence.
** Johnny St. Cyr said . . . "Really the best pianist we had was Tony Jackson, but, with the exception of Tony Jackson, Jelly Roll was the man."

was known as the man of a thousand songs. There was no tune that come up from any opera or any show of any kind or anything that was wrote on paper that Tony couldn't play. He had such a beautiful voice and a marvelous range. His voice on an opera tune was exactly as an opera singer. His range on a blues would be just exactly like a blues singer. Tony had a blues that was a favorite with him . . .

> *Yes, Michigan water taste like sherry,*
> *I mean sherry, crazy about my sherry,*
> *Michigan water tastes like sherry wine,*
> *But Mississippi water tastes like turpentine.*
> *"Mama, mama, look at sis,*
> *She's out on the levee doing the double twis'."*
> *"Come in here, you dirty little sow,*
> *You tryin' to be a bad girl and you don't know how . . ."*

Tony happened to be one of those gentlemens that a lot of people call them lady or sissy—I suppose he was either a ferry or a steamboat, one or the other, probably you would say a ferry because that's what you pay a nickel for—and that was the cause of him going to Chicago about 1906. He liked the freedom there.

Tony was instrumental in my going to Chicago the first time, very much to my regret because there was more money at home. Anyhow he was the outstanding favorite in Chicago until I finally stayed for a battle of music that came up and I won the contest over Tony. That threw me first in line, but, even though I was the winner, I never thought the prize was given to the right party; I thought Tony should have the

emblem.* We were very, very good friends and whenever he spotted me coming in the door, he would sing a song he knew I liked—*Pretty Baby,* one of Tony's great tunes that he wrote in nineteen thirteen or fourteen and was a million-dollar hit in less than a year . . .

> *You can talk about your jelly roll,*
> *But none of them compare with pretty baby,*
> *With pretty baby of mine.*

Tony was the favorite of all who knew him, but the poor fellow drank himself to death. Well, I'm getting way ahead of my story.

When I first got back to New Orleans from Biloxi, I had a run of bad luck. I felt sick and bad. Something seemed to be wrong with my hands. When jobs came up in the district, they didn't come my way. One afternoon I was sitting around 25's and wondering if my grandmother hadn't been right after all, when old man Sona walked up to me.

"Son, you are sick."

"That's right, Papa Sona, somebody must have put something on me." I was just kidding when I said that, of course.

"Don't you worry, son, Papa Sona gonna cure you."

I didn't know how *he* could tell I was sick. I had seen him one time before when I was a kid. That day I walked in on a ceremony in a neighbor's house. Papa Sona was dancing

---

* Jelly Roll told Roy Carew that he won by making Tony nervous, leaning close and whispering, "Tony, you can't sing now. You can't sing now."

barefoot on a blanket, mumbling some type of spell. Afterwards they had a feast of jambalaya rice with some kind of peculiar odor to it and they gave us kids poppy seed to put in our mouths. The seed was supposed to make you highly successful—you could swing people your way.

These operators like Papa Sona did some kind of workmanship with frog legs and boa-constrictor tongues to make somebody fall in love with you, but you don't know how this is done. That's all I knew about Sona, that he operated in this underground stuff I didn't half believe in. He told me, "Come along, son. I'm going to give you three baths and you will be well by the last bath."

He took me to his house. He stripped me and put me in a tub with some kind of grass in it. Then he rubbed me with this grass and mumbled and shook so much it made me very, very nervous, I'm telling you. For three Fridays he gave me this bath and then he told me, "Son, I'm gonna get you a job now so you can pay me. Take me to the house where you want to work only don't say anything when we get there. Just touch me. In three days you will have that job."

I took Papa Sona past Hilma Burt's house, which was one of the highest class mansions in the district, and did as he had requested. Three days later at two o'clock in the afternoon I was sitting around 25's and a maid from Miss Burt's house walked in and said their regular piano player was sick. "Would I like to make a few dollars?"

Of course, I accepted and you never saw such a well man as I was that night when I sat down at the grand piano in Hilma Burt's mansion. Right away Miss Burt liked my style of music and she told me, "If you think you can come steady, I will be glad to have you."

In a week I had plenty money, but I never thought of paying Papa Sona for what he did, because I never really believed he had helped me. I should have realized that he used some very powerful ingredients. I should have been more appreciative, for I have lived to regret this ungrateful action.*

Hilma Burt's was on the corner of Customhouse and Basin Street, next door to Tom Anderson's Saloon—Tom Anderson was the king of the district and ran the Louisiana legislature, and Hilma Burt was supposed to be his old lady. Hers was no doubt one of the best-paying places in the city and I thought I had a very bad night when I made under a hundred dollars. Very often a man would come into the house and hand you a twenty- or forty- or a fifty-dollar note, just like a match. Beer sold for a dollar a bottle. Wine from five to ten, depending on the kind you bought. Wine flowed much more than water—the kind of wine I'm speaking about I don't mean sauterne or nothing like that, I mean champagne, such as Cliquot and Mumm's Extra Dry. And right there was where I got my new name—Wining Boy.**

---

* Here, in all likelihood, Jelly Roll is referring to the voodoo-induced troubles he had in New York City. See "It Like to Broke My Heart," page 268 below.

** *Wining* (pronounced with a long ī) is the term Jelly preferred to *winding*, for reasons that Johnny St. Cyr makes quite clear. In fact Johnny was more than a shade embarrassed when asked what the nickname meant, since *winding* also means rotating the hips in dancing or in sexual intercourse. He said, ". . . Winding Boy is a bit on the vulgar side. Let's see—how could I put it—means a fellow that makes good jazz with the women. See, Jelly lived a pretty fast life. In fact, most of those fellows round the district did. They were all halfway pimps any-

When the place was closing down, it was my habit to pour these partly finished bottles of wine together and make up a new bottle from the mixture. That fine drink gave me a name and from that I made a tune that was very, very popular in those days . . .

> I'm a wining boy, don't deny my name,
> I'm a wining boy, don't deny my name,
> I'm a wining boy, don't deny my name,
> Pick it up and shake it like Stavin Chain,
> I'm a wining boy, don't deny my doggone name . . .
>
> Every month, the changing of the moon,
> Every month, the changing of the moon,
> I say, every month, changing of the moon,
> The blood comes rushing from the bitch's womb,
> I'm a wining boy, don't deny my name . . .*

---

way . . . Jelly's Winding Boy tune was mighty popular in the early days."

* Other stanzas of this blues (see Tune 2, Appendix 1) would burn the pages they were printed on. They confirm St. Cyr's story. Also, Stavin Chain, to whom Morton compared himself, lived off women. Chain was the hero of a long, rambling ballad known all through the Southwest; his prowess was sexual.

Uptown—Downtown

●●● The tenderloin district in New Orleans was considered the second to France, meaning the second greatest in the world, with extensions for blocks and blocks on the north side of Canal Street. *Downtown* was supposed to be the highclass part, although, fact of the business, the highest caliber district ran from the highest to the lowest in price and caliber alike. We also had an *Uptown* side in the district, which was considered very big, but the price was pretty much even all the way around.

They turned out many different artists *Uptown,* but never first-class artists because the money wasn't there.

Every place in New Orleans had a gambling-house, and I don't know of any time that the racetracks were ever closed—a hundred days of races at City Park, then they would be at the

Fair Grounds for another hundred days—and so they would go
on continuously for three hundred and sixty-five days a year.

I'm telling you this tenderloin district was like something
that nobody has ever seen before or since. The doors were taken
off the saloons there from one year to the next. Hundreds of
men were passing through the streets day and night. The
chippies in their little-girl dresses were standing in the crib
doors singing the blues. Then you could observe the fancy
Dans, dressed fit to kill, wearing their big diamonds—sports
like Willie the Pleaser, Bob Rowe (the kingpin of the district), Clark Wade (who took over after Rowe went to California), Chinee Morris (the best-looking guy in the district),
Okey Poke (the bartender), Ed Mochez (who left a hundred
and ten suits when he died) and so many more I can't think of
them. These guys were all big gamblers, and had all the best
women and a lot of them smoked hop or used coke. In fact
those days you could buy all the dope you wanted in the
drugstore. Just ask for it and you got it.

They had everything in the district from the highest class to
the lowest—creep joints where they'd put the feelers on a guy's
clothes, cribs that rented for about five dollars a day and had
just about room enough for a bed, small-time houses where the
price was from fifty cents to a dollar and they put on naked
dances, circuses, and jive. Then, of course, we had the mansions where everything was of the very highest class. These
houses were filled up with the most expensive furniture and
paintings. Three of them had mirror parlors where you
couldn't find the door for the mirrors, the one at Lula White's
costing $30,000. Mirrors stood at the foot and head of all the
beds. It was in these mansions that the best of the piano
players worked.

Kid Ross was the steady player at Lula White's. Tony Jackson played at Gypsy Schaeffer's, one of the most notoriety women I've ever seen in a highclass way. She was the notoriety kind that everybody liked. She didn't hesitate about spending her money and her main drink was champagne and, if you couldn't buy it, she'd buy it for you in abundance. Walk into Gypsy Schaeffer's and, right away, the bell would ring upstairs and all the girls would walk into the parlor, dressed in their fine evening gowns, and ask the customer if he would care to drink wine. They would call for the "professor" and, while champagne was being served all around, Tony would play a couple numbers.

If a Naked Dance was desired, Tony would dig up one of his fast speed tunes and one of the girls would dance on a little narrow stage, completely nude. Yes, they danced absolutely stripped, but in New Orleans the Naked Dance was a real art. For your information, I will give you Tony Jackson's *Naked Dance** the way he played it years ago . . .

Not all the piano players in the district were of the same type and class as Tony Jackson. At that time, back in 1901 and 1902, we had a lot of great blues players that didn't know nothing but the blues . . .

I could sit right here and think a thousand miles away,
Yes, I could sit right here and think a thousand miles away,
I got the blues so bad I cannot remember the day . . .

---

* Tune 3, Appendix 1, takes one back to those dark and impassioned hours at the westerns when a ragtime piano provided the soundtrack for the noble loves of William S. Hart.

This blues was a favorite of a musician we called Game Kid and it made Game Kid the favorite of the Garden District. He was a man that really wouldn't work. He was as ragged as a pet pig, wore a big smile on his face, and was a nice-looking brown-skin fellow until you got to his lips—he had nice, fat, greasy lips. Game Kid played the piano all day long after he got up, moving around from one girl's house to another—what we called the "good-time houses"—not for any financial purpose at all, but just to have a good time. That was when you could get a half-gallon can of beer for ten cents and a half pint of whiskey for twenty-five. So a real big sport in the party (not the piano player, of course, it didn't cost *him* nothing) would rush about ten straight cans of beer and get about a quart of whiskey. The whole doggone thing wouldn't cost him over two dollars and made him a big sport for a whole evening at a good-time house. And there was the Game Kid playing the blues and just swilling all the lush in the world. He was a bowler, I'm telling you, the best there was in the section when it came to playing blues. Of course, we had another man that was a very good blues player, too—old Buddy Carter—a man that could really play those blues and those thing we call stomps today.

Game Kid and Buddy Carter played around honky-tonks like Kaiser's and the Red Onion and Spano's. I'll tell you the fact, I don't think some of those places were swept up in months. Gambling went on night and day among a lot of rough people who made it dangerous for anyone that would go in there that didn't know what it was all about. Sometimes they'd have good-looking women of all kinds. Some was very, very ugly. Some had lips looked like bumpers on a box car.

I'm telling you they had all kinds of men—some wearing rags that looked like ribbons, some with big guns in their

bosoms, and many times you would see St. Charles millionaires right in those honky-tonks. Called themselves slumming,
I guess, but they was there just the same, nudging elbows
with all the big bums—the longshoremen and the illiterate
screwmens from down on the river.

You see, there wasn't no certain neighborhood for nobody
to live in in New Orleans, only for the St. Charles Avenue
millionaires' district, and that's why anybody could go any
place they wanted to. So in those days in honky-tonks the
St. Charles millionaires would bump up against the fellows
that was on the levee, some of whom didn't bathe more than
once in six months and, I'll go so far as to say, were even
lousy. They would reach up in their collars, when they saw
anyone that was dressed up, get one of these educated louses
and throw it on that person when his back was turned. Then
maybe a St. Charles Avenue millionaire would be in the
same situation they were—lousy—and didn't know how they
got to be that way. It was a funny situation. And away in
the dark there would always be an old broke-down piano and
somebody playing the blues and singing something like
this . . .

I'm a levee man,
I'm a levee man,
I'm a levee man,
I'm a levee man.

Captain, captain,
Let me make this trip,
I need some money
To fill my grip.

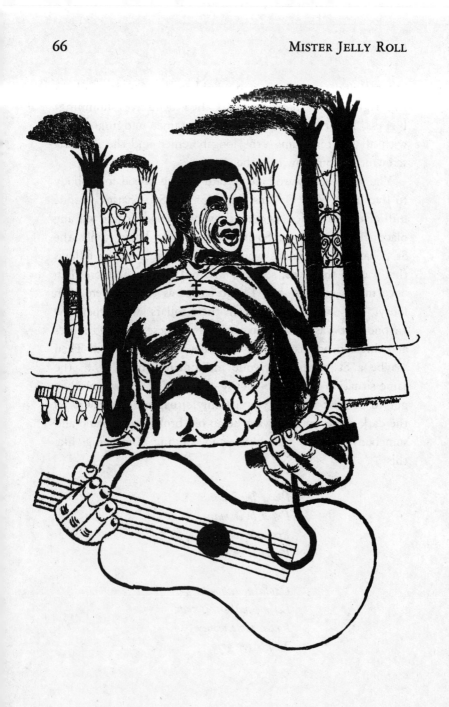

Yes I need the money
And I need it bad,
Wants a lot of things
That I never had.

These honky-tonks ran wide open twenty-four hours a day and it was nothing for a man to be drug out of one of them dead. Their attendance was some of the lowest caliber women in the world and their intake was the revenue from the little, pitiful gambling games they operated, waiting for a sucker to come in. When a sucker came, don't worry, he would really be taken. The odds were so much against him, he never had a chance, especially if he played Cotch, the three-card Spanish poker where you deal from the bottom of the deck. The way the dealer would shove the cards in the bottom of the deck he would have that sucker leegayed in no time.

If they didn't clean this sucker by legitimate cheating, one of the tough guys would take his money anyhow—men like Chicken Dick, who had shoulders and arms on him much more stronger-looking than Joe Louis—and Toodlum and Toodoo Parker, guys you couldn't afford to bother with—and Sheep Eye (I was raised with him), he was real loud-mouthed and, if he couldn't bluff you, he might murder you. Sheep Eye was a raider around these little Cotch games and when he would walk in, everybody would quit—

"Cash in my checks here, I've got to go."

And Sheep Eye would holler, "You gonna play! Sheep Eye's here and I'm the baddest sonofabitch that ever moved. Set down there and play. If you don't, I'm taking this pot."

Of course, it made no difference whether Sheep Eye won or lost. He'd take all the money anyway. Curse you, kick you, and slap you cross the head with a pistol. He was the toughest guy in the world until Aaron Harris showed up, but, when Aaron entered, Sheep Eye would become the nicest little boy anywhere—just lovely.

Aaron was the toughest of them all—a known and dangerous killer that had very little to say. The policemen wanted Aaron, but they couldn't afford to say much to him unless they intended to kill him. They were afraid to try that, because it seemed he never missed any time he got ready to kill anyone. Man or woman, it made no difference to Aaron. He had eleven killings to his credit, including his sister and his brother-in-law. I believe Aaron Harris was, no doubt, the most heartless man I've ever heard of or ever seen. Later on, as I'll tell you, I got to know him personally.

It was known that Madame Papaloos always backed him when he got in trouble—not with funds or anything like that—money wasn't really in it. Madame Papaloos was a hoo-doo woman. She was supposed, from certain evidences, to tumble up Aaron's house to discourage the judge from prosecuting—take all the sheets off the bed, turn the mattresses over, hang sheets in front of the mirrors, turn the chairs over, which was said and known to confuse the judge. Then she would get lamb and beef and veal tongues from the markets and stick pins and needles all through them in order to tie the tongues of the prosecuting attorney and the witnesses and the juries so they couldn't talk against whoever the victim's supposed to be—not the victim, but the one that's arrested. That way, Aaron Harris, the ready killer, was always successful in getting out of his troubles . . .

Aaron Harris was a bad, bad man,
Baddest man ever was in this land.

Killed his sweet little sister and his brother-in-law,
About a cup of coffee, he killed his sister and his brother-in-law.

He got out of jail every time he would make his kill,
He had a hoodoo woman, all he had to do was pay the bill.

Now listen to the story of the man who was maybe even more dangerous than Aaron. This was a seemingly harmless little fellow, but he tore up the entire city of New Orleans for a week.

Robert Charles sold newspapers on the corner of Dryad and Melpomene, back there around 1900. He never made any noise bigger than "Get your *Picayune,* get your paypire!" until the day he had an argument with his wife and she called the police. According to authentic information that I gathered, Robert Charles was arrested and the policeman wouldn't let him go back after his hat. He was a very orderly seeming guy, but this arose him to fury. He broke away, taken a Winchester rifle, killed the policeman, and from that the riot started in which all sorts of innocent people were killed.

Seemingly Robert Charles must have been a marksman. It was later learned that he had a couple of barrels of bullets in his house that he had made himself. Well, if you shoot one officer like Robert Charles had, it's no more than right that another one should take his place, but the way that newsboy was killing them off it looked like the department might run out of officers. Every time he raised his rifle and got a policeman in the sights, there'd be another one dead. It was never learned how many police were killed. Some said thirty-two. Some said eighteen. And they also told how a policeman was killed who was gazing at the last rites of a brother officer. Robert Charles shot him right between the eyes and didn't harm the priest.

The first day after the killing, which I believe was on a Sunday, the newspapers were full of it. Then the riot broke out. Men were beat up on streetcars—both white and colored. Any place a white man seen a colored man or a colored man seen a white man there was a fight. The streetcars had to stop. Transportation absolutely quit. Finally, B. A. Baldwin, considered one of the biggest ammunition dealers in the world, issued a statement that if they didn't quit killing the colored people, he would arm them all to fight back for their own rights. Through this there came a halt to the Robert Charles riot.

After the riot, nobody knows for sure what became of Robert Charles. He lived in twin houses and it was stated that they burned the house next to his and smoked him out. But there has never been anything authentic that Robert Charles was captured. Later on some friend wanted to betray him and was killed. Then years after we heard that Robert Charles had been taken very sick and had confessed who he was on his deathbed, but that isn't positive. Anyhow, like many other bad men, he had a song originated on him. This song was squshed very easily by the department, and not only by the department but by anyone else who heard it, due to the fact that it was a trouble breeder. So that song never did get very far. I once knew the Robert Charles song, but I found out it was best for me to forget it and that I did in order to go along with the world on the peaceful side.

It was right there in the Garden District, where the Robert Charles riot took place, that I heard all the great blues piano players. Yes, it was some terrible environments that I went through in those days, inhabited by some very tough babies. Of course, wherever there is money, there is a lot of tough people, no getting around that, but a lot of swell people too.

Speaking of swell people, I might mention Buddy Bolden, the most powerful trumpet player I've ever heard or that was known and the absolute favorite of all the hang-arounders in the Garden District.* Buddy played at most of the rough places like the Masonic Hall on Perdido and Rampart, at the Globe Hall in the Downtown section on St. Peter and St. Claude, and occasionally in Jackson Hall, a much nicer place on the corner of Jackson and Franklin. I had an opportunity to be in Jackson Hall one afternoon, when Mr. Bolden was playing a matinee. A little incident happened which will show you the type environments that produced hot music.

There was a man standing at the bar, a little bit of a short fellow. Seemingly he was sick with rheumatism. A great big husky guy steps on this little guy's foot (I was just in between them) and they got into an argument and the little guy didn't

---

* "Born about the time of the Emancipation, Buddy typifies the Negro's expression of the political and social motifs in the creation [of jazz]. A barber with his own shop, as well as editor and publisher of a scandal sheet, *The Cricket*, Buddy Bolden found time to play the cornet as few men and to form, in the early 1890's, a band which was to typify nearly all that jazz has meant even to today. . . . Before the Spanish American War, he was a public figure of immense popularity, well known to white New Orleans . . . he and his band were in demand everywhere. . . ." Rudi Blesh, *Shining Trumpets: A History of Jazz* (New York: Knopf, 1945), p. 180. See also Donald M. Marquis, *In Search of Buddy Bolden: First Man of Jazz* (Baton Rouge: Louisiana State University Press, 1978).

want to stand for it and pulled out a great big gun, almost as long as he was old, and shot, and if I hadn't pulled my stomach back, I wouldn't be here to tell you the history of jazz. This big guy laid there on the floor, dead, and, my goodness, Buddy Bolden—he was up on the balcony with the band—started blazing away with his trumpet, trying to keep the crowd together. Many of us realized it was a killing and we started breaking out windows and through doors and just run over the policemen they had there.

After I got on the outside, I felt that I was safe and I decided I would look on and see what would happen. When the patrol pulled up, they took the dead man and laid him in the bottom of the patrol wagon and then here comes the little cripple man that shot him, and, finally, Buddy Bolden. I've often wondered why they would put Mister Bolden in the patrol when he was up there blowing high notes to keep everyone quiet.

Of course, things like this killing weren't taken too seriously in New Orleans in those periods. It was a law in New Orleans that anyone could carry a gun that wanted to, almost; the fine was only ten dollars or thirty days in the market, your job being to clean up the market in the morning. Most of prisoners ran away, so the thirty days didn't mean anything.

We all felt funny when we saw Buddy Bolden riding the calaboose, because he was our favorite in the Garden District.*

---

* Bunk Johnson, who played with Bolden, confirmed this in a 1942 interview, adding . . . "Of course the whites said, 'We don't want no King Bolden. Robechaux's the band.' John Robechaux had a note-reading band that play the hotels and all the big places. *They* called Bolden's Band a 'routineer' bunch, a bunch of 'fakers.' But, amongst the

Buddy was a light brown-skin boy from Uptown. He drink all the whiskey he could find, never wore a collar and a tie, had his shirt busted open so all the girls to see that red flannel undershirt, always having a ball—Buddy Bolden was the most powerful trumpet in history. I remember we'd be hanging around some corner, wouldn't know that there was going to be a dance out at Lincoln Park. Then we'd hear old Buddy's trumpet coming on and we'd all start. Any time it was a quiet night at Lincoln Park because maybe the affair hadn't been so well publicized, Buddy Bolden would publicize it! He'd turn his big trumpet around toward the city and blow his blues, calling his children home, as he used to say.

The whole town would know Buddy Bolden was at the Park, ten or twelve miles from the center of town. He was the blowingest man ever lived since Gabriel. They claim he went crazy because he really blew his brains out through the trumpet. Anyhow he died in the crazy house.*

The tune everybody knew him by was one of the earliest variations on the real barrelhouse blues. Some of the old honky-tonk people named it after him and sang a little theme to it that went like this . . .

Negroes, Buddy Bolden could close a Robechaux dance up by 10:30 at night. Old King Bolden played the music the *Negro* public liked. He could step out right today, play his own style, and be called 'hot.' Old Buddy ruled in them days just like Louis Armstrong rules today."
* Another old-time jazzman said of Bolden, "That fellow studied too hard—always trying to think up something to bring out. He could hear you play something and keep it in his head—then go home and think up parts. . . ." Blesh, *Shining Trumpets*.

> *I thought I heard Buddy Bolden say,*
> *"Dirty, nasty stinky butt, take it away,*
> *Dirty, nasty stinky butt, take it away*
> *And let Mister Bolden play . . ."**

This tune was wrote about 1902, but, later on, was, I guess I'll have to say it, stolen by some author and published under the title of the *St. Louis Tickle*. Plenty old musicians, though, know it belonged to Buddy Bolden, the great ragtime trumpet man.

---

* Tune 4, Appendix 1.

Sweet, Soft, Plenty Rhythm

●●●I might name some of the other great hot men oper-
ating around New Orleans at this period and a little later.
There was Emmanuel Perez, played strictly ragtime, who was
maybe the best trumpet in New Orleans till Freddie Keppard
came along. John Robechaux probably had the best band in
New Orleans at the time, a strictly all-reading, legitimate
bunch. Before him, there was Happy Galloway. Both men had
the same type seven-piece orchestra—cornet, clarinet, trombone, drums, mandolin, guitar, and bass. A guy named Payton* had a band that played a very lowdown type of quadrille

---

* See Louis Nelson's story, Interlude 2, p. 110.

for the lowclass dance halls. Also a lot of bad bands that we used to call "spasm" bands, played any jobs they could get in the streets. They did a lot of ad-libbing in ragtime style with different solos in succession, not in a regular routine, but just as one guy would get tired and let another musician have the lead.

None of these men made much money—maybe a dollar a night or a couple of bucks for a funeral, but still they didn't like to leave New Orleans. They used to say, "This is the best town in the world. What's the use for me to go any other place?" So the town was full of the best musicians you ever heard. Even the rags-bottles-and-bones men would advertise their trade by playing the blues on the wooden mouthpieces of Christmas horns—yes sir, play more lowdown, dirty blues on those Kress horns than the rest of the country ever thought of.

All these people played ragtime in a hot style, but man, you can play hot all you want to, and you still won't be playing jazz. Hot means something spicy. Ragtime is a certain type of syncopation and only certain tunes can be played in that idea. But jazz is a style that can be applied to any type of tune. I started using the word in 1902 to show people the difference between jazz and ragtime.

Jazz music came from New Orleans and New Orleans was inhabited with maybe every race on the face of the globe and, of course, plenty of French people. Many of the earliest tunes in New Orleans was from French origin. I'm telling you when they started playing this little thing they would really whoop it up—everybody got hot and threw their hats away . . .

C'été n' aut' can-can, payez donc,
C'été n' aut' can-can, payez donc . . . *

Then we had Spanish people there. I heard a lot of Spanish tunes and I tried to play them in correct tempo, but I personally didn't believe they were really perfected in the tempos. Now take *La Paloma,* which I transformed in New Orleans style. You leave the left hand just the same. The difference comes in the right hand—in the syncopation, which gives it an entirely different color that really changes the color from red to blue.

Now in one of my earliest tunes, *New Orleans Blues,* you can notice the Spanish tinge. In fact, if you can't manage to put tinges of Spanish in your tunes, you will never be able to get the right seasoning, I call it, for jazz. This *New Orleans Blues* comes from around 1902. I wrote it with the help of Frank Richards, a great piano player in the ragtime style. All the bands in the city played it at that time.

Most of these ragtime guys, especially those that couldn't play very well, would have the inspiration they were doing okay if they kept increasing the tempo during a piece.** I decided that was a mistake and I must have been right, be-

---

* Various ways to translate this: *Can-can*—cucumber—the dance of that name—gossip. *Payez*—pay—shut up. Tune 7, Appendix 2. "There seems to be a vulgar meaning which I never understood," said Jelly Roll.
** Which is a West African way of doing things. Here Jelly imposes the European metronome idea of tempo upon the more fluid African idea of beat, just as he imposed rigid and intricate European harmony upon a simpler folk pattern.

cause everybody grabbed my style. I thought that accurate tempo would be the right tempo for any tune. Regardless to any tempo you might set, especially if it was meant for a dance tune, you ought to end up in that same tempo. So I found that the slow tunes, especially the medium slow tunes, did more for the development of jazz than any other type, due to the fact that you could always hit a note twice in such a tune, when ordinarily you could only hit it once, which gave the music a very good flavor.

About harmony, my theory is never to discard the melody. Always have a melody going some kind of way against a background of perfect harmony with plenty of riffs—meaning figures. A riff is something that gives an orchestra a great background and is the main idea in playing jazz. No jazz piano player can really play good jazz unless they try to give an imitation of a band, that is, by providing a basis of riffs. I've seen riffs blundered up so many times it has give me heart failure, because most of these modern guys don't regard the harmony or the rules of the system of music at all. They just play anything, their main idea being to keep the bass going. They think by keeping the bass going and getting a set rhythm, they are doing the right thing, which is wrong. Of all the pianists today, I know of only one that has a tendency to be on the right track and that's Bob Zurke of the Bob Crosby Band. Far as the rest of them, all I can see is ragtime pianists in a very fine form.

Now the riff is what we call a foundation, like something that you walk on. It's standard. But without breaks and without clean breaks and without beautiful ideas in breaks, you don't even need to think about doing anything else, you haven't got a jazz band and you can't play jazz. Even if a tune

haven't got a break in it, it's always necessary to arrange some kind of a spot to make a break.

A break, itself, is like a musical surprise which didn't come in until I originated the idea of jazz, as I told you. We New Orleans musicians were always looking for novelty effects to attract the public, and many of the most important things in jazz originated in some guy's crazy idea that we tried out for a laugh or just to surprise the folks.

Most people don't understand the novelty side of jazz. Vibrato—which is all right for one instrument but the worst thing that ever happened when a whole bunch of instruments use it—was nothing at the beginning but an imitation of a jackass hollering. There were many other imitations of animal sounds we used—such as the wah-wahs on trumpets and trombones. Mutes came in with King Oliver, who first just stuck bottles into his trumpet so he could play softer, but then began to use all sorts of mutes to give his instrument a different flavor. And I, myself, by accident, discovered the swats on drums. Out in Los Angeles I had a drummer that hit his snares so loud that one night I gave him a couple of fly swatters for a gag. This drummer fell in with the joke and used them, but they worked so smooth he kept right on using them. So we have "the swats" today—a nice soft way to keep your rhythm going.

A lot of people have a wrong conception of jazz. Somehow it got into the dictionary that jazz was considered a lot of blatant noises and discordant tones, something that would be even harmful to the ears. The fact of it is that every musician in America had the wrong understanding of jazz music. I know many times that I'd be playing against different orchestras and I would notice some of the patrons get near an orchestra and put their hands over their ears. (Of course, I wouldn't permit mine to play that way.) Anyhow, I heard a funny fellow say once: "If that fellow blows any louder, he'll knock my ear drums down." Even Germany and Italy don't want this discordant type of jazz, because of the noise.*

Jazz music is to be played sweet, soft, plenty rhythm. When you have your plenty rhythm with your plenty swing, it becomes beautiful. To start with, you can't make crescendos and diminuendos when one is playing triple forte. You got to be

---

* What would our hero think if he heard the hard-rock bands and fusion orchestras of Europe and other continents?

able to come down in order to go up. If a glass of water is full
you can't fill it any more; but if you have a half a glass, you
have the opportunity to put more water in it. Jazz music is
based on the same principles, because jazz is based on strictly
music. You have the finest ideas from the greatest operas,
symphonies, and overtures in jazz music. There is nothing
finer than jazz music because it comes from everything of the
finest-class music. Take the *Sextet* from *Lucia* and the *Miserery*
from *Ill Travadore,* that they used to play in the French Opera
House, tunes that have always lived in my mind as the great
favorites of the opera singers; I transformed a lot of those
numbers into jazz time,* using different little variations and
ideas to masquerade the tunes.

The *Tiger Rag,* for an instance, I happened to transform
from an old quadrille, which was originally in many different
tempos. First there was an introduction, "Everybody get your
partners!" and the people would be rushing around the hall
getting their partners. After a five-minute lapse of time, the
next strain would be the waltz strain . . . then another strain
that comes right beside the waltz strain in mazooka time . . .

We had two other strains in two-four time. Then I transformed these strains into the *Tiger Rag* which I also named,
from the way I made the "tiger" roar with my elbow. A person
said once, "That sounds like a tiger hollering." I said to myself, "That's the name." All this happened back in the early
days before the Dixieland Band was ever heard of.

---

* Tune 5, Appendix 1.

INTERLUDE TWO

The Boys in the Bands

Down in New Orleans they remember "Jelly Roll used to play piano all day and practice all night. . . . We used to ask him when do he sleep?—he fool at the piano so much."

Down in New Orleans one morning, down in one of those
Storyville dance halls, young Morton was fooling around with
an old-time quadrille—maybe it happened just this way—he
was just playing around with this old tune, sort of half asleep
after a hard night, and suddenly he rolled his left forearm
across two octaves of keys—a black and white tone cluster.
Somebody in there listening hollered, "Hey, Winding Boy,"
says, "Hey, that sound like a tiger hollering."

"Yeah?" says young Morton, deserted son of that fast-living,
trombone-playing contractor, Ed La Menthe, "Yeah, I believe
it does. Sounds just exactly like a tiger roaring. *HOLD THAT
TIGER!*"

The left arm tromboned that roar out of the honky-tonk
upright and then the right hand got away like a jackrabbit
with the left beagling right behind to a full-band finale. And
all his life Jelly Roll held a tiger by the tail.

In barrelhouse lingo "tiger" meant the lowest hand a man
could draw in a poker game—seven high, deuce low, and
without a pair, straight, or flush. It takes nerve to hold on to
a tiger and bluff it to win, but Jelly Roll had the nerve to take
the pot with bluff alone. He had learned some tricks from
Sheep Eye, the gambler, as well as from Tony Jackson. All he
had was the music of the Storyville bordellos—it was his tiger
and he bet his life on it.

For Jelly Roll, jazz was not just music. It was Creole New
Orleans; it was home and family; it was security and acceptance; it was the path to wealth and glory; it was power. He
spoke of it possessively ("I personally originated jazz in New
Orleans in 1902"). He wished he had somehow copyrighted

jazz and he groaned because he could not sue the white band leaders who were making their fortunes with "my ideas."

The facts justify Morton to some extent. Certainly he did not originate jazz. He was, however, the first true composer of jazz, the first who devised and notated jazz arrangements. His richly illustrated account of the music of New Orleans streets, bordellos, and honky-tonks shows that he saw jazz as a music that the whole New Orleans community had given rise to. It is impossible to know whether or not he "composed" *Tiger Rag*, but he certainly understood, explained, and illustrated its elements with total clarity.

Moreover, he became a leader and organizer of great orchestras and the producer of truly inspired recording sessions, long before Fletcher Henderson and Duke Ellington, who certainly took from him, as did the whole world of jazz. He also belonged to the great tradition of self-promoting showmen that began with Barnum and continues with Madonna. Unlike Louis or Sidney, he was an organizer and self-promoter. Not all his colleagues liked that side of him, but they all admired his music and his professionalism. What Jelly Roll did was to absorb the complex currents of the music of his hometown and, very early, to set about organizing and ripening them into a system of music. His compositions were inventions in the New Orleans style, reflections of what a whole musical community had to say: His "band piano style" brought together on the keyboard the polyphonic weave of voices in Storyville dance bands; his powerful left hand, with its constantly shifting riffs, reflected the polyrhythmic style of those bands; so, although it suited Jelly Roll to feel that he walked

alone, actually a generation of inspired New Orleans musicians
always marched by his side. He created formal arrangements of
the collective improvisations that formed the explosive sub-
stance of New Orleans music. This music was judged by the
radical composers of Europe to be the most intuitive sound of
its time.

To understand Jelly Roll and jazz, then, one must know his
comrades in music—his generation. His story—that jazz was
the creation of a cathouse pianist—has the virtue of simplicity,
but otherwise it presents enigmas. Babies are not born in
brothels. Jelly's tiger, whose roar was heard round the world,
is not just come-on music. The flames that illumine jazz are
not the cold red lights of the tenderloin. . . . But the more
one examined Jelly's own story, the deeper the mysteries became. He had lost his roots somewhere in those elegant
sporting-houses. Where could those roots, those fertile begin-
nings be found . . . ? What I did, to back up Jelly's brilliant
folk history of jazz, was to take my recording machine to the
great old-timers still alive in the Crescent City and set down
what they had to say. There follow excerpts of these interviews, made now a very long time ago, in the late '40's . . .

On a May afternoon down in New Orleans on a sunny corner
of St. Antoine Street. . . . An old man stood there, bald,
toothless, going on eighty, but every inch of his six feet
erect—a red-hot bass player, seventy-nine years old, a proud
Creole.

"Albert Glenny, painter by trade. Pleased to make your
acquaintance, Mister Lomax."

He looked at me shyly, squinting out of his hooded eyes. I
held the work-hardened, bass-toughened old hand, and asked

about Jelly Roll. "Well, I heard of him, but I never seen him that I remember," said Glenny. "That boy come along in late years."

Glenny, the oldest living hot jazzman, went woolgathering about early Creole musicians. I had difficulty in traveling along with his Creole-thickened English, but there was one proudly descriptive phrase that kept ringing through—*"painter by trade . . . plasterer by trade . . . cigarmaker by trade."* Apparently the Creole musician was also a craftsman. Glenny's conversation was a trade directory—a trade directory of the great names in New Orleans hot jazz:

PAPA BECHET, who played flute for fun, was a shoemaker.

LEONARD BECHET, who played trombone in Silver Bell Band, was a maker of fine inlays.

SIDNEY BECHET, the best of New Orleans musicians, always followed music.

PAPA DELISLE NELSON was an amateur accordionist and a butcher.

LOUIS DELISLE (BIG EYE) NELSON, maybe the first "hot" clarinet, worked as a butcher's apprentice.

PAPA DOMINGUEZ, a fine classical bass, was a cigarmaker.

PAUL DOMINGUEZ, first a violinist, then a ragtime fiddler, was always a professional musician.

BAB FRANK, who led the "first hot band" with his piccolo, ran restaurants.

ALBERT GLENNY, bass player, was a painter by trade.

FREDDIE KEPPARD, the greatest New Orleans trumpet, was a professional musician.

F. P. LA MENTHE fooled with slidin' trambone, but made money as a contractor.

FERDINAND MORTON (La Menthe) disdained manual labor.

MANUEL PEREZ, the favorite Creole trumpeter, also knew how to make cigars.

ALPHONSE PICOU, composer of *High Society,* tinsmith by trade.

PIRON, composer of *Sister Kate,* was by trade a barber and his shop was a musicians' center.

JOHNNY ST. CYR, the best hot guitarist, plasterer by trade.

PAPA TIO, classical clarinet, cigarmaker by trade.

LORENZO TIO, son, taught clarinet, cigarmaker by trade . . .

These light-skinned Creole craftsmen lived Downtown in the Seventh Ward, Morton's own neighborhood. In the nineteenth century music was a sideline for the older generation, becoming a profession for the sons and grandsons in the twentieth. Mister Jelly Roll, then, was typical of a period, but, though his contemporaries confirmed the main outlines of his story, few seemed to have had much personal contact with Morton, himself. At first this absence of congruity was puzzling; then, as these ancients of jazz spun out their own stories, not only did Jelly's life fall into perspective, not only were Jelly's main points confirmed, but, little by little, the central mystery of jazz came to light . . .

There was Alphonse Floristan Picou, the oldest living Creole clarinetist. On the telephone his accent was gumbo-flavored. His house, old Louisiana style, stood on brick pillars against the flood. My companion whispered with awe, "It is only one of his *seventeen* properties. Thees Picou, he has properties all over New Orleans."

Although it was nearly three o'clock of a Sunday afternoon,

Picou was still yawning. "Last night we had a little *cowein* with wine and whiskey. I believe I drunk a quart. Pretty good for an old man, eh!"

Picou was sixty-nine and didn't show it. A vigorous stocky body was topped by a strong square-jawed face. The skin was the color of fresh, slightly pinkish parchment, the eyes dim and light blue, the teeth seedlike. Serene and merry, he displayed the naive and dignified self-absorption that often marks an original man. He talked on totally undisturbed by the interruptions of his wife, whose acquisitive face spoke of those seventeen properties.

"I was born in 1879 in New Orleans," began Picou. "We spoke Creole at home. Being we were so poor, I had to go to work when I was fourteen. I went to learn the tinsmith trade and I put my father under insurance and took care of the family.

"In my family it was the brother before me that started playing clarinet, but, when *he* would blow, the clarinet would screech and my father would say, 'There's that boy, calling the ducks . . .'

"So, my father did not know I had taken lessons from a flute player at the French Opera House. I did not explain him nothing, but one time I just sat down and played *Cavalleria Rusticana*. My father hollered to my older brother, 'Listen to that. *He* ain't calling no ducks!' " Old man Picou chuckled so that his pale blue eyes almost disappeared in the wrinkles.

"One day Bouboul Augustat, the trombone player, heard me practicing at the house and ask me if I want to come to one of his rehearsals. I say, 'You got any music?'

" 'You don't need no music,' say Bouboul.

" 'That's impossible. What I'm gonna play? Just sit there and hold my instrument?' I ask.

" 'Don't worry. You'll know.' That's what Bouboul tell *me*.

"So I went. They were playing some good jazz that I didn't know nothing about . . .

Femme en dans lit,	*Woman in bed,*
'N homme en bas lit,	*Man under bed,*
Moi pas l'aimez ça,	*I don't like that,*
Moi pas l'aimez ça	*I don't like that,*
Ai, ai, ai,	*Ai, ai, ai,*
*Moi pas l'aimez ça.**	*I don't like that.*

"Well, I had a good brains at that time and I caught on quick. When Bouboul heard me filling in, he say, 'See, you know how to play without music.' So I played with Bouboul's string band then. We had guitar, bass, trumpet, clarinet, and a songster.

"Most of the time we played for birthday parties. . . . About ten at night we would come in a man's yard and play a number in the dark for surprise. Then they turn the lights on and grab this guy and kiss him and wish him happy birthday. Then they take all the furniture down and begin to dance, everybody kiss the girls and the girls kiss the men.** It was the old quadrilles from eight to four and a set would last two hours.

"In those days the girls were *crazy* about musicians. They

---

* Tune 8, Appendix 1.
** A visitor to New Orleans was surprised at the amount of second-hand jewelry in the antique shops. "There must have been lots of money in this town," he said. "Yes," said a wise young lady, "and lots of love."

all fight to carry your case home. Then they ask you to their house to take 'a little rest.' You see, you feel *so* tired you couldn't carry your own instrument home." Picou said this in a plaintive tone and then laughed as if perhaps some young girl had carried his clarinet home only the night before. There came a rustling and sniffling from the ladies in the dining room. . . .

"I joined The Imperial, the finest band in town at that time. Manuel Perez, a cigarmaker by trade, was our leader—a tough cornet, a man that never fail. I worked at my trade all week, but all day Saturday I would play in a wagon to advertise the dance that night. Play all night. Next morning we have to be at the depot at seven to catch the train for the lake. Play for the picnic at the lake all day. Come back and play a dance all Sunday night. Monday we advertise for the Monday night ball and play *that* Monday night. Sometimes my clarinet seemed to weigh a thousand pounds. . . ."

We heard feet on the stair and the door pushed open timidly. The little man who shambled in and edged across the room bore the same resemblance to sturdy old Alphonse as a withered orange peel does to an orange. He was a bag of stooped, toothless, withered, and debauched old bones, dressed in rags and greasy shoes and hat. This was Alphonse's "little brother" Ulysses, composer of Creole songs, junkman by trade, and anxious to sing.

As the recorder began to spin, Ulysses was seized by a spasm of coughing. He began again, fortified by a bottle. Again the horrible alcoholic cough choked his voice off to silence. At last, Ulysses managed the following Creole ditty in his hoarse fragment of a voice, while Alphonse sat back in the shadows, weaving clear, sweet clarinet passages behind him:

LA MISÈRE

Y'apé parlé pou' a̲l̲p̲r̲e̲s̲s̲i̲o̲n̲
Vo' pas conné ça c'est yé
Quand la misère prends chaudières-yé
Toutes chaudières cap côté.
  La misère, la misère,
  C'est qui-chose quitté-il?

Posé pas ta pot,
N'avé pas café,
Pou demain matin, mon cher ami,
Quand n'va levé.
  Prend le vieux café
  Sêché-li dans soleil,
  S'il-n'y-a pas du sucre, mon cher
    ami,
  Servi du sel.

Quand m'tapé longé, apé reposé
M' tendé frappé de M. Jouvert, li
  frappé la porte-la.
Moin dit "M. Jouvert, m'pas fait
  travaille,
M'pas gaignin l'argent vien
  prochaine semaine.
  Li metté ti notice-la, dans la
    chiffonier,
  Comme m'gardé ti-notice-la, li dit
    moin déménagé.

E—, c'est la misère,
La misère pou toutes allé,
Comme un chien, comme un chat,
Toutes gaigin la misère.

THE DEPRESSION

They speak of depression,
But they don't know what it is—
When trouble takes hold of the pots,
All the pots are turned upside down.
  Yes, the depression, the depression,
  Is there anyway to get rid of it?

Don't put on the pot,
We don't have any coffee
For tomorrow morning, my dear,
When we get up.
  Then take the grounds,
  Dry them in the sun—
  If there's no sugar, my friend,
  Serve salt instead.

Well, I was lying down, trying to
  take my rest,
And I heard M. Jouvert [the
  landlord] come knocking on my
  door.
I said, "Mr. Jouvert, I don't have a
  job,
I'm broke, come back next week."
  He put a little notice on the
    chiffonier, when I read that
    little notice,
  It said I had to move out of the
    house—

O it's the depression, depression . . .
Yes, the depression, the depression's
  everywhere,
Even the dogs and the cats, too,
Everybody's got troubles.

During the playback of his ironic Creole ballad, Ulysses'
wicked old eyes popped with delight. He slapped his withered

and flapping thighs and cheered himself passionately. The neighborhood apparently concurred, for the house debouched Creole ladies of all ages, who shrieked with laughter at every Calypsonian turn of the song.

When Alphonse played his own famous tune, *High Society*, rippling through the difficult solo passage, the audience drifted away: jazz for these ladies was not quite a part of the rich and secret life of the Creole district, whereas the songs, they were *Creole, même*. However, Alphonse didn't mind. He knew he was good and he listened to his playback with a serene smile, thinking of the old days.

"Those were happy days, man, happy days." Alphonse Picou shot a smile at me that was as warm as old New Orleans. "Buy a keg of beer for one dollar and a bag full of food for another and have a *cowein*. These boys don't have fun nowadays. Talking 'bout wild and woolly! There were two thousand registered girls and must have been ten thousand unregistered. And all crazy about clarinet blowers!"

Neither this rocklike old tinsmith nor his brother felt the torment that later crept into jazz. Picou played a joyous pure-toned Creole clarinet with never a dirty tone or a blued note. Only the syncopation reminded one that this was early jazz. As Picou saw it, jazz consisted of "additions to the bars—doubling up on notes—playing eight or sixteen for one." This urbane New Orleans ragtime, salty with West Indian rhythms, was the inspiration for Morton's best melodies, tunes that recall the days when he tagged the serenade bands along Rocheblave and Tonti streets, goggling at Picou and his Creole cousins.

These artisans, homeowners, and shopkeepers knew that they were better off than the mass of Southern blacks. Lodge members and union members, their parades voiced the strength and solidarity of their workingclass organizations. Their bands poured out a joyful and triumphant kind of music, music much safer to sing through instruments than to put into words, down in Dixie; music that spoke of a proud and militant history.

Under tolerant Spanish and French rule in Louisiana, mulatto children were sent to school, taught trades, and given professional jobs. Freedmen of color helped to win the Battle of New Orleans under Andy Jackson. Before 1861, these colored Creoles accumulated fifteen million dollars' worth of property, much of it in slaves; they organized literary societies and musicales and published their own newspapers, while the craftsmen amongst them built the lovely churches and homes of New Orleans and cast the lacy ironwork for its balconies and doorways.

The Civil War reminded the Creoles that they were Negroes and second-class citizens. A Creole lady welcomed Union General Butler to New Orleans with these words: ". . . No matter where I fight I only wish to spend what I have and fight as long as I can so that my boy may stand in the street equal to a white boy."

This was not just talk. Creole troops decided the battle of Port Hudson for the Union, to cite only one example of several. And in the first years of Reconstruction, New Orleans led the fight for the ballot, free schools, equal rights for women and other democratic reforms in the South. A Creole newspaper, the *New Orleans Tribune,* called upon all true democrats, regardless of color, to participate in the Louisiana Constitutional Convention of 1868:

> This will be the first constitutional body ever con-
> vened in the United States without discrimination
> of race or color. It will be the first mixed assembly
> clothed with a public character. As such, this con-
> vention has to take a position in immediate contra-
> diction to the white man's government. They will
> show that a new order of things will succeed the
> former order and that the long-neglected race will
> effectually share in the government of the
> state. . . .

Jelly Roll's grandfather, Henri Monette, sat in that convention with the grandfathers of other jazzmen, and together they
passed the most liberal constitution ever adopted in the history
of the U.S.A. establishing universal suffrage, equal rights for
all before the law, free and equal rights for women. Very soon
after this constitution was ratified, racists murdered several
black legislators, and in the notorious New Orleans race riots,
a mob of policemen shot down blacks who had assembled to
cheer the passage of the new constitution. Reaction deepened
in the South, and soon the black government of Louisiana was
violently swept out of office. Disillusioned, old man Monette
shipped out for Panama and never returned. But the Creoles
who stayed behind held on where they could. They struggled
to educate their children, or at least to give them a trade, and
they organized, as far as they dared, benevolent societies,
unions, secret lodges, and social clubs. Behind these closed
doors they could be themselves, could act out the legitimate
political aspirations repressed by Reconstruction. Above all,
they cultivated the art of music, always a permitted avenue of

achievement to a black from Jim Crow America, the one avenue where he could safely achieve success and prove himself "superior" to the white man. The black governor Pinchot had suggested that every organization should have its own orchestra to lead its members to the polls. This custom endured right through the bad old days of Reconstruction, and so, on days of celebration, the black clubs and lodges moved into streets with loud, defiant music.

Cheap instruments, left behind by the Confederate Army bands, filled the pawnshops. Creole freedmen could afford to buy instruments and pay for music lessons as few other Southern Negroes could. Almost any Creole old-timer can recall his childhood musical instruction—given in the strictest style of the French Academy. "I studied music for two years and *then* I chose my instrument," he will tell you pridefully. Even if this old gentleman had limited technical knowledge of music, he felt for it the passionate enthusiasm of a Brooklynite for baseball and could bore you to death with the esoterica of forgotten bands and their stars.

New Orleans and adjoining parishes became a world of brass bands and string orchestras. "The stomping grounds of all the best musicians in the world . . ." said Jelly Roll, ". . . very organization-minded." All the fraternities and lodges wanted bands for their balls and parades, and so, for an overblown half century, New Orleans Negroes experimented with European instruments. A strong tradition took form, and was passed on to eager apprentices, continually enriched by cosmopolitan musical currents from everywhere, yet maintaining its local character. French opera and popular song and Neapolitan music, African drumming (still to be heard at voodoo dances on Congo Square where Jelly was born), Haitian rhythm and

DOWNTOWN

Cuban melody, native Creole satiric ditties, American spirituals and blues, the ragtime and the popular music of the
day—all these sounded side by side in the streets of New
Orleans and blended in the rich gumbo of New Orleans music.
The people made a fine human gallimaufry, too. Whites and
Negroes lived as neighbors in the Creole quarter, and, as one
lady remembers it, "It was just over the fence whenever we had
dinner. We always swapped platters of our best cooking with
the French and Italians next door."

"Just over the fence"—with recipes for gumbo and for
jazz—so Creole music ripened, subsidized by a relatively
prosperous and tolerant Negro community. Time seemed to
flow like a dreamy rhumba in Picou's and Mimi's Downtown
world, but all over the South the old order, which had given
status to the Creole Negro, disappeared. Poor whites were
demanding and getting jobs that had formerly been Negro
prerogatives. By the 1890's the Creoles of New Orleans were
being pushed out of their old trades and down on the social
scale. Soon they were to be practically eliminated from the
skilled trades. Music had once been a hobby or at most the
source of a few extra dollars; now those few dollars became
the income for a family and music became a serious professional matter. On his way down the class scale the light-
skinned Creole met the black-skinned American musician
fighting his way out of the black ghetto. This meeting took
place in Storyville, which opened in 1897 and offered regular, well-paid jobs to any musician who wasn't too proud to
earn a dollar in a barrelhouse. The black Americans were in
there pitching for those jobs and getting them. Among the
great Americans from Uptown who gave the Downtown Creoles trouble were—

LOUIS ARMSTRONG, a trumpetman, who also worked on coal carts and was a smart hustler.

BUDDY BOLDEN, maybe the first hot trumpeter, a barber too.

MUTT CAREY, one of the great trumpeters, worked by the day sometimes.

BUNK JOHNSON, who took over from Bolden, also drove trucks.

JOE OLIVER, the King of Chicago trumpets, who worked as a butler at times.

JIM ROBINSON, a great trombone who followed longshoring.

BUD SCOTT, the guitarist who bested Jelly . . . just a musician.

By and large these black Americans were common laborers or service workers. They were not trained musicians, but won their Storyville jobs by sheer talent. Creoles who wanted to work in Storyville had to play in bands with them. So for the first time since Reconstruction, Creoles were compelled to accept blacks as equals. This was bitter medicine. As the mulatto group had been forced down, its caste prejudice had mounted. *"The mulattoes were actually more prejudiced than the white people at that time,"* dark-skinned Johnny St. Cyr somberly remarked, and his comment was confirmed every time a Creole opened his mouth.* Invariably, in describing

---

* Jelly Roll's race prejudice was not, therefore, a singular defect, but a commonly accepted Creole attitude, considered normal by Creoles and non-Creoles alike.

someone, a Creole would begin, "He's kind of light
brown .   " or, "He's real black, got bad (kinky) hair . . ."
or, "He's a real nice-lookin' light fellow. . . ." A man's pig-
mentation was his most significant human attribute in New
Orleans.

Light-skinned Downtown shared the bandstand with "real
black and nappy-headed" Uptown. Playing jazz on the job
every night required them both to cooperate, in spite of the
fear and disdain that they felt for each other. What emerged in
all my interviews with old-time New Orleans jazzmen was
how this drama of competition and collaboration, played
against the nightmarish backdrop of Storyville, had wrung
their hearts—

There was Paul Dominguez, fiddling son of a fiddling father. "Bon santé," he said, raising his glass to mine.

"Même chose," said I. And we suited our actions to our
words.

We were in 25's, at the "hot" corner of old-time Storyville,
where Iberville crosses Franklin and where, in Jelly Roll's
time, blacks and mulattoes first put the heat in hot jazz. The
highclass bordellos of Basin Street had been just around the
corner—Tom Anderson's and The Pig Ankle across the street,
Pete Lala's and The Frenchman's just a couple of squares away.
The 25's had never closed and the whiskey was still flowing
fast. Instead of a little band in the corner, a jukebox boomed.

Paul and I had spent the day together, visiting old man
Picou, peering at the black crayon scrawling on the unmarked
tomb of Marie Laveau, queen of voodoo in the Delta. Paul had
told me, in his own way, the history of his people. Now he
traced a slow design on the table top with his birdlike fiddler's

finger, smiling a little, looking at me speculatively and shyly. Remember, this conversation took place in the 1940's, when Jim Crow rules were in full force.

"What you say if they refused to serve you?" he said at last.

"What do you mean?"

"Well, after all, thees ees a colored place and they not suppose to entertain white guests. If I was to go in the Absinthe House, they wouldn't serve *me,* good as my hair is," Paul pulled at his stiff and unkinked white locks, "And good-looking as I *am.*" He smiled gently. But for his brownish-gray skin, Paul might have served as model for a bust of a proconsul.

"What *would* I tell them, Paul?" I smiled back.

"That you were colored, naturally. Then they would *have* to serve you. *You* can drink anywhere, that's *your* advantage over *me.*" His tone was friendly. "See, these people down here are very prejudiced. And your color makes all the difference. Now that guy just coming in. He's real dark, ain't he? I know him good. He's a fine man, but, much as I don't want to say anything about him, his color's against him." (The man was a dark, handsome and intelligent-looking Afro-American.)

"He's black and he's got bad hair," Paul went on. "If he should go down to vote, for an instance, he hasn't so much opportunity. . . . But when *they* see *me,* they know what type of fellow I am—a Creole. Not that I'm better than anybody, but they know I'm different. People on my light type have a better opportunity everywhere—stores, court, voting, all that stuff. But the Johnny yonder, they won't consider him. And if he's intelligent, so much the worse. . . ."

"Just what is a Creole, Paul, the way you see it?"

"I'll explain to the best of my ability," Paul replied, with utmost seriousness. "A Creole is a mixture of Spanish and white and must talk French. Now they are folks will *say* they Creole, but they ain't. You take in the Seventh and Eighth wards, we are Creoles, mostly, from way back, but you go on across Elysian Fields into the Ninth Ward and the people over there *call* themselves Creoles, but they're black and they got bad hair. They're from the country.

"Of course, they speak the language—speak French, but what does that prove? If you learn Italian, it don't make no Italian out of you. You catch my point? They're different from us. They don't have no education; maybe only been to school two or three years and just barely know their ABC's. And you don't see *none* of them fair like my niece. She's a real lady— so fair you wouldn't know—isn't that right?"

I thought of the girl, her creamy face heavy with scorn for her somewhat darker little uncle. She had barely turned from the television set in the plushy living room where Paul had dragged me to prove his policy-making brother's prosperity.

"And she's got a good education, too," added Paul, very humbly. "You see, we Downtown people, we try to be intelligent. Everybody learn a trade, like my daddy was a cigar-maker and so was I. All us people try to get an easy job that our education qualifies us for. We try to bar jail. . . . Uptown, cross Canal yonder, they are *used* to jail," he chuckled with real malice.

"There's a vast difference here in this town. Uptown folk all ruffians, cut up in the face and live on the river. All they know is—get out on the levee and truck cotton—be longshoremen, screwmen. And me, I ain't never been on the river a *day in my life.*"

Paul's heart was in this. Canal Street had been the dividing

UPTOWN

line between two worlds in Negro New Orleans. As long as
you stayed on the Downtown side, you were "not just another
Negro," but if you crossed Canal you "carried brickbats and all
forms of ammunition." The line was felt to divide:

DOWNTOWN . . . . and . . . . UPTOWN
  Mulatto . . . . and . . . . . Black
  Upper caste . . . . and . . . . . Lower caste
  Trades and professions . . . . and . . . . . Day laborers
  Accepted (somewhat) . . . . . and . . . . . Jim-Crowed
  Educated . . . . and . . . . . Illiterate
  Sophisticated . . . . and . . . . . From the country

The Storyville musicians broke this pattern. Hot music
forced mulatto Downtown to share musical knowledge with
"blacks," to compete with "blacks" as equals, to acknowledge
"blacks'" gifts and maybe even to love "blacks" as brother
artists. Yet the blues warns . . .

I don't want no black woman puttin' sugar in my tea,
'Cause "black is evil" and I'm skeered she might poison me . . .

"Have another beer, Paul."
"Thanks. That's all I can drink since I lost my wife. In fact
whiskey-drinking cause her to leave me. Then I come to realize
I had lost everything in life. My nerves is shot to hell now."
He brooded over his empty glass.
"You know what happen to us musicians—I mean us real
musicians from the Seventh Ward where we were all educated
in music and *knew* our instruments—when we came in here,
we had to change. Why, my daddy, he was recognized king

bass player in this town, but he wouldn't play *ratty*. He wouldn't play unless you put his part up in front of him, and then he could make a monkey out of the average player of today. Well, he couldn't make it here in the district. He couldn't make a *living!*"

Paul was still astonished and bitter over this.

"See, us Downtown people," Paul hurried on, "we didn't think so much of this rough Uptown jazz until we couldn't make a living otherwise.

"Say, for instance, I was working with the Olympia Band, working one or two nights a week for two dollars and a half a night. The 25's here in Storyville pay you a dollar and a quarter and tips, but you working seven nights. Naturally, wouldn't I quit the Olympia and go to this tonk? Wouldn't I?"

"Anybody would," I assured him.

"Well," Paul went on, "that's how they made a fiddler out of a violinist—me, I'm talking about. A fiddler is *not* a violinist, but a violinist can be a fiddler. If I wanted to make a living, I had to be rowdy like the other group. I had to jazz it or rag it or any other damn thing."

Playing hot jazz in Storyville meant for Paul not merely losing status, but jeopardizing the professional musical skill that his cigarmaker father had skimped to pay for. He had to check his Creole cultivation outside when he stepped up on the stand in 25's.

> *Downtown joined forces with Uptown*
> *Written Music was compromised by Head Music*
> *Pure Tone sounded beside Dirty Tone*
> *Urbanity encountered Sorrow*
> *Nice Songs were colored by the Lowdown Blues*

"Bolden cause all that," Paul said bitterly. "He cause these younger Creoles, men like Bechet and Keppard, to have a different style altogether from the old heads like Tio and Perez. I don't know how they do it." Paul's anger was mixed with admiration. "But goddam, they'll do it. Can't tell you what's there on the paper, but just play the hell out of it. . . ."

Paul and I stood in the rain and looked at the housing project that now stands where Gypsy Schaeffer's and The Frenchman's once rolled all night till morning. It was beginning to grow dark.

"Take me home, Alan," Paul said. "I don't like to be out on these streets after dark. I guess my nerves is shot. . . ." Old Paul Dominguez had run away from his black brothers and from the strong and sorrowful sound that blew out of their horns. He had turned his back on jazz. But what of the old-timers who had stayed on in Storyville and grown with the music? Bolden was thirty-five years dead. Perez was dead. Tio was dead. Keppard had drunk himself to death. Glenny was old and "getting mindless." Carey, Oliver, Baquet, Tony Jackson—the list of the dead was longer than that of the living.

"You might talk to Louis deLisle Nelson," someone said. "Old Big Eye about the first one play hot clarinet. You find him at the Arteezan Hall, but I hear he's mighty sick . . ."

It made you feel like running all the way. The Arteezan Hall—the Arteezan Hall? Was it a secret order or an outlandish Creole name?

"You standing right in front of it, mister." The young fellow jerked his thumb toward a weathered gray building. There above the sagging door was the dim insignia—a muscled arm holding a hammer, below this a square rule, and underneath, the words *ARTISANS HALL*.

The hall where the artisans—carpenters, plasterers, iron-workers, tinsmiths—had met to deliberate and then to dance was quiet and deserted. The floor sagged and the gavel marks on the rostrum had gathered dust. Presently, a slight brown woman peeped out of the inner door.

"Mr. Nelson is mighty sick," she said, "but I reckon you can come up if you don't stay long."

She led the way up the bare, poor stairs to the bare, poor room, where, flanked by medicine bottles, the old man lay upon his hard pillows. The door closed behind the woman. Big Eye Louis and I stared at each other.

"What you want—history?" he muttered. "Well, I know it."

"Were you acquainted with Jelly Roll Morton?"

"Why, I started him," he snapped. "I started him. Round about nineteen eight or nine.

"When Jelly Roll came around the district he knew note music—that's the way he started—started by messing around with piano scores. Course, he wasn't no real reader," Louis wanted to say nothing pleasant about this rival. "Jelly was just a *speller*. But he wasn't dumb like some of these fellows. He could pick up fast by ear."

It made one grin to think of the roar that would have come from Mister Jelly Lord if he had overheard this malicious remark.

"Years later," Louis went on sourly, "he come to be a real good piano player. I'll give him this: he was a *busy* soul, a hustler. Stay a couple of weeks one place and he was ready to go. Not like us fellows. We made ourselves satisfied and let well enough alone."

Perhaps Louis had worked with Jelly for two weeks

somewhere and felt snubbed when Jelly moved on to a better
job.

"Maybe he *had* worked in one of those sporting-houses,"
added Louis, vigorously, "but before I took him over he hadn't
never been on a bandstand. . . ." Right from the start, then,
Jelly had "played possum" on new jobs.

Louis deLisle Nelson knew little about Jelly Roll and cared
less. He went on to talk about himself. His father was from
one of the upcountry parishes, marching to New Orleans with
the Yankees, and adopting the name Nelson from his first
employer. Louis had worked in the family butcher shop until
he was fifteen, but early had "started fooling with my daddy's
corjun. . . ."

"I come to be thirteen years old and I should have already
made my Confirmation," Louis said, "but I had more music in
my head than catechism. Music caused me to miss my Confirmation at eleven and then at twelve. At last, the priest tell
my mama, say, 'That boy's gettin too big. He's got to be
Confirmed!' So I went to studyin my catechism and at fifteen
I made it.

"My sister sent me to Professor Nickerson* to study violin,
but after four or five months, I got disgusted: I was paying a
dollar a lesson and he just had me *holding* the violin—hadn't let
me pull the bow across the strings one time! I told my sister,
say, 'Shuh, no use to pay out that money. I ain't learning a
thing.' But that's the way it was in my time among us Creoles.
You had to take lessons before you could touch your instrument.

"*Downtown* here, the Creole people are slow. Maybe they

---

* The same teacher Jelly Roll mentioned.

depend a little too *much* on their pride. Don't mix with every-body. Don't trust everybody. They always in for society. But we had better-quality musicians down here. Mostly note read-ers. In the best bands, they was *Downtown* here with us. The American section it was Robechaux's and *he* use mostly *Down-town* men. . . .

"*Uptown,* in the American part, other side of Canal Street, the people had different way. They worked in white folks' houses or down along the river. They were more sociable and more like entertainers. They played more rougher, more *head* music, more blues. . . . The blues? Ain't no first blues. The blues always been. Blues is what cause the fellows to start jazzing."*

Louis' ironic speech, his dark skin, his short tight-napped hair, showed a strong African heritage. Probably the Creoles of the Seventh Ward never completely accepted him. Poor, dark and déclassé, Louis understood the blues and felt at home with the Uptown musicians he met in Storyville.

"The sporting district come to have all the best musicians because the pay was every night. Just take the corner of Iber-ville and Franklin—four saloons on the four corners—the 25's, 28, The Pig Ankle, and Shoto's. Those places had eight bands amongst them. Four on day and four on night. And they changed bands like you change underclothes.

"It was lively round there. In 25's they had a ham hanging from the chandelier about six feet up. Any woman could kick

---

* The blues were clearly an importation from upriver in the Delta. In New Orleans they were Creolized, becoming sweeter and more mellow, into bluesy songs like *Winding Boy, Michigan Water, Buddy Bolden's Blues* and *Mamie's Blues.*

that ham, she could take it home. I've seen many a one crack their butts crying, but they didn't mind and we sure didn't mind seeing their legs. Very often they got the ham, because they used to have a high-kicking bunch around this old town." Old Louis almost smiled.

"Me, I went in the district when I was fifteen and I tell you how it come about. I was carrying my violin and when the cops stopped me I told them I was taking the fiddle to my daddy. So I pass right on. Charley Payton's* band was playing at 25's. I stop and listen.

"Jesus, that man could make some pretty music. He wasn't no humbug musician. He come from Alabama, made and played all the string instruments. He'd holler 'follow me' and his bunch would rip out one of those old quadrilles which induce so much lively jazz. And he could play the *Anniversary Song* so the tears would run right out of your eyes.

"Well, I stood there and listen at Payton on that corjun. He say, 'Come in, son,' but I was afraid and I told him, 'I ain't comin in, but I can play the corjun you got.' He say, 'Come on in and try her.' That way he entice me in. I couldn't make it on that corjun the first time, but I kept comin back till I got so I could fool with it. One of them old musicians, passed me off as his son, used to tell the cops, 'That's my boy.'

"Pretty soon I had me a job with Payton—he was the man brought Bolden in there, too. I learned clarinet from Papa Tio's son, Lorenzo, and I played on in the district till they closed it down in 1916, played with every band *you* ever heard of and some you haven't.

---

* Jelly mentioned Payton as one of the pioneer "bad bands."

" 'Course, my people didn't know what I was doing till I was making too much money for them to stop me. They needed me to bring home that money. My papa hadn't been doing so well in his butcher trade. He was just holding on, and we were right poor. I felt like helping him out, because Papa had always been good to me. He hadn't never told me to leave my music and look for a trade. So they never ask me where the money came from and I never told them much.

"Some of our Creole boys didn't have my opportunity; their families wouldn't stand for them in the district. Take Manuel Perez—one of the toughest cornets we ever had, a sight reader and a horse for work—well, his people was very, very up to the minute, running back and forth to the church. A little bit of this is a sin and a little bit of that is a sin—they'd have died if they'd heard of him being in the district.

"See, all kind of people come through those joints—long-shoremens, roustabouts, cowboys, Yankees, and every kind of woman in the world. I seen plenty of knife-and-pistol play. Killings was a common affair, and in 1900 I seen a mass killing —that Robert Charles riot. I remember that night too well. It cause me to dig down deeper in my music more so yet. . . .

"Robert Charles got away, but they had his friend in the parish prison. When the jailer refuse to give him up to the mob, the mob said they was going down round 25's and kill all the Negroes.

"So a woman came in 25's and told us, 'If I was you, I'd knock off tonight!' Lord, I've wished many times I had gone home to warn my people, like I wanted to, but Payton, he was an unbeliever. He told me, 'Aah, we never had nothing like that in New Orleans yet and it won't happen tonight.' Then he stomped off the next tune and we kept playing.

"When they came—I reckon it was an hour later—we didn't know how they got there. We heard shooting. Me, I was sitting at the inside end of the bandstand, playing bass. All them boys flung themselves on me in gitting away from the door and out toward the back. The bass was bust to kindling and I sailed clear across the back of the room, so many of them hit me so hard all at once.

"We made it out the window of the gambling house into the alley in back but, man, that alley was already loaded with folks. Me and Bolden and Gipson was together. We thought Josie Arlington might let us through her house into Basin Street. When she saw who we was, she slammed the door, locked it, and start to screaming. So we cut on through the lot next door, made it over the fence and on down Basin. Not one of us had a shirt on him by then and Bolden had left his watch hanging on the wall near the bandstand. We might have been assassinated, but we was lucky enough to get to a friend's house. We locked ourselves in and barred the doors.

"How many they killed that night never has been told, but it was many a one. They claim the police was trying to stop the mob, but fact was the police were worse than the others. These rebels, my boy, are different . . . ! The national guard, nothing but a bunch of kids. When the mob came this way, *they* run the other. This thing went on about two days, until old man Baldwin—own the hardware store—told them he was going to arm the colored and *that* word stop them cold.

"Next day I found out my daddy was missing. Somebody said I'd better go on down to the hospital—it was full of folks all crippled and shot up. One of the sisters there told me a man had been brought in at two A.M. in very bad condition and had died about sun-up. Nobody knew him. When they showed him to *me,* I knew him. It was my daddy. They had snatched him off his meat-wagon down at the French market and killed him.

"Was I angry about it? Well, sure, sure I was. But what could I do?" Old Nelson made a sweeping gesture with his hands, palms up. "It just wash away. It all just wash away." He sighed, "Couple of days after my daddy was killed, I was back there at 25's playing harder than ever."

Louis paused and then half to himself, "They *claims* I'm the first hot clarinet."

"The first hot clarinet" went on to confirm Jelly's analysis of jazz; in fact Louis stated his theory of syncopation, harmony, and tempo in almost the same words that Jelly had used. Yet there was a profound difference in emphasis that corresponded exactly to their contrasting feeling about the Robert Charles riot—Jelly thought like a mulatto, Louis like a black.

"Jazz," said old Louis, "jazz is all head music." He raised himself up on his elbows to get a better purchase on his remarks. "Some player don't know a note as big as this house, he have an idea—he don't know—it kinda sound a little good to him and somebody takes a fancy to that idea and writes it down. That's how riffs come about. You must handle your tone. Happen sometime you can put some *whining* in the blowing of your instrument. There are a whole lot of different sounds you can shove in—such as *crying*—everywhere you get the chance. But you gotta do that with a certain measurement and not opposed to the harmony. Don't play like you're at no funeral."

Keep a lively tempo but "shove in crying wherever you get the chance." Then your listeners can dance and feel the tears behind. This is the master formula of jazz—mulatto knowingness ripened by black sorrow. Perhaps Nelson began this "whining" through instruments. At any rate the singing through the reeds and brasses—the instrumental imitation of the marvelous techniques of Afro-American folksong—this is a principal innovation of New Orleans jazzmen, responsible for a new array of orchestral sounds that has traveled everywhere with jazz, opening broad new musical horizons.

"That ain't all there is to it," said Louis. "No, that ain't all." He seemed to have run out of words. He plucked nervously at the covers, pulling them up to the neck of his heavy winter underwear. At last he said, not looking at me, "You've got to play with the heart. Picou, he come before me, he's a good enough musician, but they"—referring to the note-musicians who had taught him and to all the Downtown folks—"*They* don't play with the *heart.* . . ."

He looked sick and old. Alone and sick. Yet the heart of this man had warmed ten thousand thousand nights for all the world. "Do you know Sidney?" he suddenly asked, with a smile that had become really warm, with the feeling shared by anyone who ever heard Sidney Bechet blow sunshine out of his horn. "Sidney," said Louis, as if this explained everything. "He wouldn't learn notes, but he was my best scholar. The son-of-a-gun was gifted. Man, he ran away with that thing, playing from his heart. . . ."

Mulatto to black, black to mulatto—mulatto Tio to Nelson, Nelson (a black by inspiration) to mulatto Bechet: this was the chain reaction that at last exploded into jazz. A new generation of jazzmen suddenly appeared, blessed with the gifts of both Uptown and Downtown, and playing it all "with heart." The golden boy of this golden generation, in the minds of New Orleans Creoles, was their own boy, Sidney Bechet.

"Sidney," said one ancient, "had a clarinet all wrapped around with rubber bands, and when he'd begin to play the roaches would all run out of it—but that little devil, just about twelve years old, he could outplay Freddie Keppard!"

"I used to see Sidney around Piron's barber shop," said another. "Now, Piron had a house full of every kind of instrument. So this little boy, he come in one day and pick up the flute, 'What is that?' he ask Piron. 'That is a flute, Sidney,' Piron tell him. So Sidney start right in playing it. Show Piron what *is* a flute. Put that down. Walk over and pick up a saxophone and say, 'What is *that?*' 'That's a new something they call a saxophone, son.' 'Well, it look like a pipe to me, I see if this pipe will make a tune.' And be damn if he didn't start making the thing just talk!"

Jelly Roll, too, was such a "natural," but he was a waif who laid cold plans to conquer the world with "original ideas," whereas Bechet, whose family loved and protected him, wanted only to sing to people: perhaps the difference between the music of these two great Creole jazzmen may be so explained. At any rate, Sidney Bechet's story, as Doctor Bechet, his brother, told it, bears upon Jelly's history because it shows a further blending of Uptown and Downtown and the unabashed emotional flowering of jazz in Sidney's playing.

It is always a hard thing to have a genius right in the family. Dr. Leonard Bechet certainly loved his brother, Sidney, with all his heart (and this heart seems to be as generous as the Mississippi), but he still spoke about this prodigious younger brother with considerable nervousness.

". . . It's like I tell you, I think I could have become a fine musician if I had only kept on," Dr. Bechet began somewhere in the middle of a thought. "I took trambone lessons, but then I got so busy with my inlay work and being a voluntary probation officer, you understand . . ." the doctor's voice trailed off.

"See, my brother Sidney used to hide his schoolbooks when he was real little and go off and play flute. I never knew he was playing, you understand? And at that time I had a clarinet and I put it up on the armoire, because I wanted to give it to him when *I* was ready. I asked my mother did Sidney touch it and she say he did. So I ask him to show me what he could play. He sound pretty good.

"So from then on, Sidney started and I couldn't keep up with him. Sometime I'd look at him and I'd imagine the shape of his mouth just fit the clarinet. Sidney got everything so easy, you understand?" Dr. Bechet had to wipe his eyes before he could continue.

"We had a fine clarinet player, George Baquet,* who taken a great liking to Sidney and showed him a few little tricks on the clarinet. And sometimes, when Baquet wanted to lay off, he used to come and speak to my mother and ask could he take Sidney to play in his place for the evening.

"Well, you know, we were very poor. My father had a little shoe shop one time. Then afterwards he got into a little restaurant and that didn't do so well, so he had to come back with the shoes. Then he did achieve a job in the Mint—nothing so big—but anyhow he worked there awhile.

"He was a Republican and liked politics and helped orga-

---

* George Baquet, Creole, whom Jelly Roll called "the first jazz clarinet."

nize the Citizens League. He had selected friends and he liked to spend a quiet evening with them, playing his flute. He encouraged Sidney in music, but when he thought we kids done wrong, he'd be a little rough. Grab a shoe strap and beat you almost anyhow. My mother used to intercede because she was very soft-hearted, and she'd talk to Sidney, 'My dear child, this, and dear child, that.'

"Now, in our family we kept ourselves nice and always be at home, not running around. We didn't want to jeopardize our family by mixing with the rough element. We worried a lot about Sidney, when he'd be out playing.

"So, when Baquet would come for Sidney, Mother would insist that he be sure to bring the boy back and not lose him. Baquet would promise and he'd generally bring him back about two in the morning. Sidney would bring money home to Mother and tell her don't worry, he was all right. Of course, she'd be worried, but, naturally she would feel, 'Well, that's one time. That's over until the next time come.'

"After I found out other men were so interested in his playing abilities, I hurried and organized a band to keep Sidney. Called it the Silver Bell Band. One time we invited Bunk Johnson to play with the Silver Bell, and first thing you know, it was hard to keep Sidney with us. See, Bunk needed a clarinet for the Eagle Band, and so he enticed Sidney with him and that's how the Eagle Band broke into the Silver Bell.

"Now Bunk Johnson was one of them kind—rough and ready. You understand?" The doctor paused, embarrassed at what he was thinking. He went on apologetically. "Fellows like that, they used to drink a whole lot and we didn't like Sidney being out with them so much, those rough fellows, like Big Eye Louis Nelson and Jimmy Noone. . . ." (Old Big Eye had said, "We never could keep our hands on that Sidney. Regular little devil, always running off down the alley after them little womens.") "Louis and them played that lowdown type of music, when us Creole musicians always did hold up a nice prestige, you understand, demanded respect among the people, because we played nice music. So we didn't like Sidney playing with them.

"The pimp they call Clark Wade, he liked Sidney's music and he bought him fancy clothes. Sidney began to spread out and feel big, because he used to have a bunch of fans that followed him to know where he was going to play. Many nights he wouldn't sleep home. Then he quit school.

"So, you know, I had become a voluntary truant officer, not for pay, but doing what I could in a way to help make things run much better—you understand?—helping people and little kids that goes wrong. Well, I went and saw Captain Pierce and explained I wanted them to put Sidney away in a home or something.

"I told Sidney one morning I was going to take him to work, had a job for him. I had Mother fix him a nice big sandwich and we started out. When we got close to the Juvenile Court building, he began to walk kind of unwilling-like. I walked close to him to see he didn't run away and he went up before the captain.

"The captain said, 'Oh, that's the boy you have the complaint against.'

"I said, 'Yes.'

" 'Sonny, why don't you stay home?'

"Sidney start to tell him about his music and the captain say, 'I would not advise you to let him stay out all night, especially in the district.'

"Sidney told him about how he always goes with some man. Captain Pierce say, 'Well, I want you to do this. Listen to your brother. Go to school. You can go ahead and play music. But try and stay in school. . . . Leonard, it's no use to discourage this boy. He's got some talent. But try to keep him in school.'

"I try to explain this to Sidney, naturally, but not long after, some people come and ask him and my brother, Joseph, to go in a band to Texas. So they went and, Sidney being a better musician, they picked *him* out and kept *him* and he went away with them. From that on, he continued going, going. I reckon I never seen my brother for something like twenty-seven years. . . ."

The boy, Sidney, left New Orleans behind him when he was fourteen, carrying with him all the richness and fire of the pure jazz tradition, unstained by the mire of Storyville and untouched by the conflicts that disturbed other jazzmen. Following his own sweet-singing reed, he wandered across America, astonished New York, charmed Paris, toured Russia, enriched a Berlin cabaret, pursuing his star and ripening into one of the notable virtuosos of our time—the poet of jazz. To the end of his days this quiet, gray-haired man played with the passion of a young man in love with love and life, lending the clear gold of New Orleans style to popular ballads or improvising new melodies in the Creole idiom. He became a national idol of the French, had his own club in Paris for years, and married a beautiful Frenchwoman. At his funeral on the Riviera, a flock of white doves was released by his admirers. His brother, Dr. Bechet, after twenty-seven years, remained astonished by Sidney's talent.

"Baquet and all them helped my brother," he said. "But Sidney was just naturally gifted. He was an entertainment all

by himself. Folks used to say, "Who is that playing yonder?'
And it was Sidney doing all kinds of things with the clarinet
to *soothe* himself, playing over whatever his mind was saying."
The doctor broke off and looked at me with his warm and
agonized smile.

"Now I'll tell you," he said, suddenly casting aside Creole
prejudice, "a person have to go through all that rough stuff
like Sidney went through to play music like him. You *have* to
play with all varieties of people. Some of the Creole musicians
didn't like the idea of mixing up with the—well, with the
rougher class, and so they never went too far. You see, Picou—Picou's a very good clarinet, but he ain't hot. That's
because he wouldn't mix so much.

"You have to play real *hard* when you play for Negroes. You
got to *go* some, if you want to avoid their criticism. You got
to come up to their mark, you understand? If you do, you get
that drive. Bolden had it. Bunk had it. Manuel Perez, the best
ragtime Creole trumpet, he didn't have it.

"See, these hot people they play like they *killing* themselves,
you understand? That's the kind of effort that Louis Armstrong
and Freddie Keppard put in there. If you want to hit the high
notes those boys hit, brother, you got to *work* for that. Of
course, Sidney puts it in *with ease,* but Sidney's different from
all the rest." (Jelly Roll also "put it in with ease." He liked to
play with other musicians who could put it in with ease.)

"Now, I'll tell you another thing," Dr. Bechet concluded.
"When the settled Creole folks first heard this jazz, they passed
the opinion that it sounded like the rough Negro element. In
other words, they had the same kind of feeling that some white
people have, who don't understand jazz and don't *want* to
understand it. But, after they heard it so long, they began to

creep right close to it and enjoy it. That's why *I* think this jazz music helps to get this misunderstanding between the races straightened out. You creep in close to hear the music and, automatically, you creep close to the other people. You know?"

Hot blasts from black Bolden's horn and searing arpeggios from light Tio's clarinet burned away the false metal of caste prejudices and fused tan knowledge with black inspiration. These groups had been separated since their revolutionary Reconstruction days, but the attraction between black people and mulatto was too strong for the dividing lines. When they met again, surmounting age-old fears and prejudices to do so, a flame leapt high into the muggy heavens above Storyville, a flame and a feeling that has made the music of New Orleans important to America and to the world.

Perhaps nothing in human history had spread across the earth so far, so fast as this New Orleans music. Thirty years after its genesis it was as popular and understandable in New York, Paris, Prague, and Shanghai as in its own hometown. Of course, the phonograph record and other means of rapid communication assisted in the diffusion of jazz, but this cannot explain its triumph over other forms of music, which were also broadcast and recorded. The worldwide impact of an expanding American economy undoubtedly lent great (though at times dubious) glamour to jazz in international circles. This, however, would not explain its triumph in America, where the plebeian origins of jazz were familiar to everyone. Jazz is sensual and jazz is African, but so are many other Creole musical styles which have never gained such widespread acceptance. These were all contributing factors but leave the central mystery unaccounted for.

Jazz became many things—frenetic, destructive, hysterical,

decadent, venal, alcoholic, saccharine, Lombardish, vapid—it has enriched stuffed bellies; it has corrupted the innocent; it has betrayed and it has traduced; but, everywhere and in all its forms, something jazz acquired at the moment of its origin has profoundly touched all its hearers. What was this thing that set folks dancing and smiling from the slums of New Orleans to all the capitals of the earth?

"We had all nations in New Orleans," said Jelly Roll. "But with the music we could creep in close to other people," Dr. Bechet added. . . . Jazz was the hybrid of hybrids and so it appealed to a nation of lonely immigrants. In a divided world struggling blindly toward unity, it became a cosmopolitan musical argot. This new musical language owes its emotional power to the human triumph accomplished at the moment of its origin in New Orleans—a moment of cultural ecstasy.

Two neighborhoods, disjoined by all the sordid fears of our time, were forced to make a common cause. This musical union demanded that there be not merely acceptance and understanding, but respect and love on both sides. In this moment of ecstasy an interracial marriage was consummated, and the child of this union still jumps for joy wherever jazz is hot. *Perhaps it is so wherever peoples share their treasures and a truly fresh stream of culture begins to flow. Such moments of cultural ecstasy may occur prior to all great cultural movements just as seeding precedes birth.*

That this black and tan wedding took place in the streets of Storyville, streets thronging with pimps, chippies, rotten police, and Babbitts on a binge, may forever have stained this otherwise lusty and life-giving proletarian art. As Jelly and the others have indicated, Storyville involved all the musicians in

its principal trade. It made them guilty on the very score their
families so feared—dragging the family name in the gutter.
Yet there was a toughness in jazz that laughed at all that, the
toughness of black-skinned Americans like Bolden and Bunk
Johnson who would "kill themselves playing so hard." These
black Americans had no music lessons, no family name and no
stable community life to support them. They were orphaned
by the color of their skins. If they became professional musicians, it was only by virtue of exceptional talent and drive.
"You got to *go* some to play for Negroes," said Dr.
Bechet. . . .

Johnny St. Cyr, Jelly Roll's favorite guitarist, belonged to
this group even though he had Creole blood. "A man around
my color just didn't score with the Creoles," he said. Besides,
St. Cyr's widowed seamstress mother raised her family in the
slums "back of town." At fourteen Johnny "took up the plastering trade" and began to play guitar on the side. Years later
in Chicago he became the star guitarist of hot music, recording
with Armstrong, Morton, Oliver and all the best bands. Depression brought him back to New Orleans and his old trade
of plastering. In the normal course of things, he played weekend dances and ran a spare-time auto-wrecking business. A
big, rangy, philosophical working stiff, he had his own views
on jazz:

"A jazz musician have to be a working class of man, out in
the open all the time, healthy and strong. That's what's wrong
today; these new guys haven't got the force. They don't *like* to
play all night; they don't think they *can* play unless they're
loaded. But a working man have the *power* to play hot—
whiskey or no whiskey. You see, the average working man is

very musical. Playing music for him is just relaxing. He gets
as much kick out of playing as the other folks get out of
dancing." (Here St. Cyr has clearly stated the African feeling
about music—music as a *source* of energy, rather than a *demand*
for it.) "The more enthusiastic his audience is, why, the more
spirit the working man's got to play. And with your natural
feelings that way, you never make the same thing twice. Every
time you play a tune, new ideas come to mind and you slip
that on in."

St. Cyr's credo brought back the beautiful lines of Jim
Robinson, black New Orleans trombonist . . . "If everyone is
in a frisky spirit, the spirit gets to me and I can make my
trombone sing. I always want people around me. It gives me
a warm heart and that gets into my music . . ."

Yes, here was the African tradition speaking—music as a
release of vital energy in repeated rhythmic figures which call
for an infinity of variation. Music for the blacks was not pri-
marily an avenue of self-advancement, as with the Creoles,
but, first of all, sheer, unadulterated joy. "As the saying goes,"
Johnny St. Cyr said in his warm, velvety voice, "back in those
days we didn't make a lot of money, but we had a lot of fun."

Johnny went on to develop his theory of jazz and it was
quite apparent that he agreed with Jelly Roll on every important point. What Jelly Roll had said was New Orleans jazz
theory.

"In New Orleans we had a system of playing, so as to get all
the sweetness out of the music. We play the first theme *mezzo-
forte,* the second very soft, and the last time we play the second
theme, everybody gets hot." (Exactly the plan of Jelly's
records.) "Them times you had to toe the mark. Whatever you
did had to be good. No off-key playing. You had to keep

within the boundaries of the melody, but our old heads had great ability to beautify a number.

"We had our own way of doing. When we'd buy the regular stock arrangements, we would familiarize ourselves with the melody and then add what *we* wanted till we sounded like we had special orchestrations. Then we'd cut off the names at the top of the music in order to throw everybody off scent. It used to make the music publishers so mad they wanted to tear up the sidewalk. But what could they do . . . ?" Johnny's laugh rattled the windows.

Black and tan musicians were driving the music publishers crazy, as they pooled their ideas and played them hot, but at the personal level, old prejudices operated. . . .

"I guess the most popular trumpet player with the mulatto race was Keppard," said Johnny. "He was brown-skin man, light-brown, but, when you come darker than Keppard, you didn't score with the mulattoes at all. They wouldn't invite us to none of their entertainments; they just wouldn't affiliate with dark people. Wouldn't intermarry. They were actually more prejudiced than many white people back in that time.

"Maybe you don't believe that," said Johnny sincerely, "but it's true. There were mixed neighborhoods of colored and white where we all got along just like one race of people. The white lady and her husband next door used to set on the steps of our house and talk to my mother and stepfather. I even had a cousin married to a white woman and had two children by her. It wasn't until 1902 they began that segregation outfit; then it got so bad around here it made a fellow want to go North if he had the chance."

Jelly Roll had preferred to remember New Orleans in the days before "they began that segregation outfit," yet he had

left town earlier and younger than almost any of the other
Jazzmen. Never once did he mention this problem, nor did he
once refer to his Negro status. His attitude made it impossible
to ask him the question that Johnny St. Cyr answered readily.

"What about segregation in the tenderloin district?" I
asked. "Was there a Negro section?"

"There was. Uh-huh."

"Was it pretty strictly enforced?"

"Yes it was."

"A colored man couldn't go to the white houses?"

"No. That's right. It was only forced on one way, though.
White man could go to *Negro* houses."

"Yeah?"

"That's the bad part about the South! Should be, if going to
be segregation, be complete segregation."

"Tell me, did any colored man you ever know of ever go to
these highclass houses?"

"Well, not that I *know* of—none ever *frequented* those highclass houses."

"But that was a privilege *some* of the musicians had?"

"Well, yeah; the musicians had more of an opportunity than
anyone else, that is, in the colored race, to go to these houses.
But I don't *know* that they could go there as *guests*. If they was
a piano player like Jelly Roll Morton or Tony Jackson in there
playing, an ordinary musician could go and set side the piano
and chat with *them,* in between numbers. . . ."

"So those piano players were the boys who frequented those
houses the most?"

"Yes, they were," and Johnny went on, "and they made the
best money. Nothing but money men come in those highclass
houses and they just as soon tip you a five-dollar bill as a

dollar, if they was in the mood and the music was good. So a piano player knock down around fifteen and eighteen dollars a night and not have to work too hard. They were lone wolves; every penny come in, *they* kept. That way they made better than us boys in the bands. That was Jelly's class. . . ."

Here Jelly Roll, the lone wolf, found his road. Piano keys opened doors into a white world where the other boys in the bands could not follow. This bordello world gave him money and fine clothes and raised him above his brother musicians. His notoriety set him apart from the common musicians of Storyville. The Frenchman's, not 25's, became his hangout. And this was why few of the boys in the bands remembered Jelly Roll in his New Orleans days.

"Those fellows you been talking to didn't know Jelly," affirmed Bunk Johnson, who started working in the district in 1897. "See, Jelly played only in white houses in those days. *They* couldn't play there. But him and Tony Jackson did. They'd have Tony one night and Jelly the next. Albert Cahill, Freddy Washington, Harrison Ford, and Jimmy Arcey played those places, too. All of them boys always wore fine clothes, had plenty money and plenty diamond rings.

"Jelly was one of the best in 1902 and after that," Bunk went on. "Noted more so than Tony Jackson and Albert Cahill because he played the music the whores liked. Tony was dicty. But Jelly would sit there and play that barrelhouse music all night—blues and such as that. *I know* because I played with him in Hattie Rogers' sporting-house in 1903. She had a whole lot of light-colored women in there, best-looking women you ever want to see, strictly for white. . . . Well, I was playing with Frankie Dusen's Eagle Band on Perdido Street and sometimes after I'd knock off at four in the morning

Jelly would ask me to come and play with him. . . . He'd play and sing the blues till way up in the day and all them gals would holler, 'Listen at Winding Boy!'

"He was really a ladies' man, really stylish. But, even when he dress up, he *still* look like a kid . . ."

One can almost hear what they said behind the back of this handsome young mulatto, dressed in the best, wearing diamonds, as he strolled down Iberville Street. The jazzmen didn't say it to his face, for Jelly could back his brags with plenty of money, plenty of red-hot piano and, when necessary, a "hard-hitting .38." Still they could hardly love him, for Winding Boy had moved into "higher circles" leaving his fellow jazzmen behind, yet carrying with him the music that had cost them so much.

This music had all the pretty octoroons calling out, "Here comes Winding Boy!" It won him recognition on Basin Street, a half-world, to be sure, but still a white world, rich and power-filled, where notoriety compensated an orphan for the loss of his family and for the painful memories of his mulatto childhood. Basin Street seemed a possible avenue of escape from a confining Negro status; at any rate, the kid piano wizard accepted this way of life—gambling, prostitution, dope-peddling, pimping—without reservations. Fifty years later he still reveled in his Basin Street memories. Things never again looked quite so rosy.

It would have been instructive to chat with some of the "inmates" of those sporting-houses along Basin Street, but the paint was peeling from those antique sybarites. The windows were boarded up and no one knew the addresses of Lulu White, Josie Arlington, and the other madams of Jelly's young days. There is a little book, however, which has conserved the feel, the style, the smell, and the lingo of those prim bawds. *The Blue Book,* a directory of the tenderloin, printed for the convenience of tourists and on sale at Storyville bars for twenty-five cents, carried ads from every madam of reputation. "Read what this little booklet has to say," the editor suggests with candor and modesty, "and if you don't get a 2–1 shot it ain't the author's fault." While *The Blue Book* can no longer guide us directly to guaranteed satisfaction, a few excerpts reveal the purlieu where Jelly Roll got his standards and his purple prose.

GYPSY SCHAEFFER

To operate an establishment where everyone is treated exact is not an easy task, and Gypsy deserves great credit. Gypsy had always made it a mark in life to treat everyone alike and to see that they enjoy themselves while in her midst.

There are few women who stand better with the commercial people than Gypsy, who has always kept one of the best and most refined houses in which a private man may be entertained by lots of handsome and well-cultivated ladies. A visit once will mean a long-remembrance and friendship forever.

What more can any sane person expect?

BERTHA WEINTHAL

While still young in years, Bertha has, nevertheless, proven herself a grand woman and has also made 'good' as a conductor of a first-class establishment.

The word of 'able' is portrayed to the full when the name of Weinthal is mentioned.

If it were in my power to name Kings and Queens, I would certainly bestow the title "Queen of Smile" on Bertha.

Her 'Chateau' is grandly equipped and lacks nothing to make it the finest in the world. Pretty women, good times and sociability has been adopted as the countersign of Miss Weinthal's new and costly home.

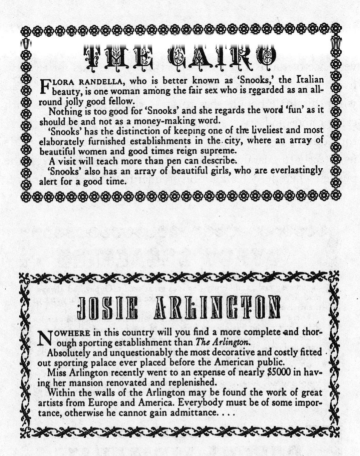

THE CAIRO

FLORA RANDELLA, who is better known as 'Snooks,' the Italian beauty, is one woman among the fair sex who is regarded as an all-round jolly good fellow.

Nothing is too good for 'Snooks' and she regards the word 'fun' as it should be and not as a money-making word.

'Snooks' has the distinction of keeping one of the liveliest and most elaborately furnished establishments in the city, where an array of beautiful women and good times reign supreme.

A visit will teach more than pen can describe.

'Snooks' also has an array of beautiful girls, who are everlastingly alert for a good time.

JOSIE ARLINGTON

NOWHERE in this country will you find a more complete and thorough sporting establishment than *The Arlington*.

Absolutely and unquestionably the most decorative and costly fitted out sporting palace ever placed before the American public.

Miss Arlington recently went to an expense of nearly $5000 in having her mansion renovated and replenished.

Within the walls of the Arlington may be found the work of great artists from Europe and America. Everybody must be of some importance, otherwise he cannot gain admittance. . . .

Jelly Roll's piano made him a person of "some importance and "gained him admittance" at fifteen. The "jolly good fellows" who ran these palaces haggled for virgins, used them, then threw them into alleys where they were free to sit naked behind their crib doors available for twenty-five cents to any customer. "Fun" was a money-making word; the girls provided the "fun"; the madams, the pimps, the police, and the politicians collected the money. Heroin, sadism, assassination—anything went if you had the price.

No matter how tough they might pretend to be, this cold-blooded world must have deeply wounded the young musicians who were sensitive enough to create jazz. "Poor Alfred Wilson, he smoked so much dope till he died . . . Tony Jackson, he drank himself to death . . . Freddie Keppard, the damn fool, he was a hog for liquor and it killed him . . . Buddy Bolden blew his brains out through a trumpet and died in the insane asylum . . . I just don't like to be out after dark any more"—these epitaphs could be many times multiplied.

Ferdinand Morton, however, thrived. He eschewed the vices of his associates and cultivated their business acumen. He learned to drink moderately. And he worked hard. If, by playing the lowdown blues, Morton could pick up a dollar Tony Jackson scorned, he was ready to oblige. If the white customers wanted a laugh, he had ready "some sensational trick and surprise effects." Whatever he played, however, it had to be good and it had to be Morton. He had nothing but scorn for brain-pickers and imitators.

The musical currents of Uptown and Downtown came together, joined in Morton's piano. He retained his Creole technique and, unabashed by the hot playing of the black Americans, his composer's mind brought all the voices of the band under the control of his two perfect piano hands. Outcaste and intellectual, he felt none of the finicky reservations and fears of the mulatto, nor suffered from the undisciplined anger and melancholy of the rejected black. Creole finesse and American release were of equal value to him. As his compositions began to flower within him alongside the boundless ambitions of youth, he became the master of New Orleans music. Others it mastered, but Morton, the cool young man with plans and a profound sense of form, had a firm hold on his tiger.

"Jelly Roll played piano all night and practiced all day . . . He never stopped running, always on the go, couldn't seem to rest one place more than a few days . . . He was young, but he was the best pianist we had . . ."

At nineteen young Ferdinand was restless. He could not be content with his music, because jazz for him was power, a way out of a narrow valley of Jim Crow and Creole prejudice. He began to look away from New Orleans, wondering if he had the key to a larger world. After 1904 he was constantly on the prod, using New Orleans only as a base of operations, and nurturing ambitions mortal strange for America's first jazz composer.

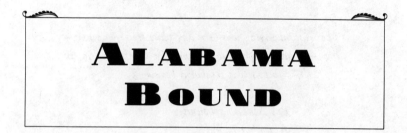

ALABAMA BOUND

The frequent saying was—in any place that you was go-
ing—you was supposed to be bound for that place. So, in
fact, I was Alabama bound . . .

I'm Alabama bound,
Alabama bound,
If you like me, honey babe,
You've got to leave this town.

She said, "Doncha leave me here,
Doncha leave me here,
But, sweet papa, if you must *go,*
*Leave a dime for beer . . ."***

---

* Tune 9, Appendix 1.

A Half-hand Bigshot

●●●I wanted to be the champion pool player in the world, so I left New Orleans, where there were too many sharks, to go to some of these little places where I could practice on the suckers. My system was to use the piano as a decoy. I'd get a job at one of these little honky-tonks along the Gulf Coast, playing piano, then some of the local boys who called themselves good would ask me to play a game of pool. I'd play dumb, until the bets rolled up high, then I'd clean them out. My system was different from most of the piano players I met along the coast—Skinny Head Pete and Florida Sam, they didn't work, because they were kept up by women. From time to time two or three girls fell in love with me, but I didn't pay much attention. I was interested in playing pool.

I made a lot of towns those days learning how to be a
half hand highbor McHenry, Harrisburg, Jackson, Vicksburg, Greenwood, Greenville—but I spent the biggest part of
my time in Gulfport* and Biloxi. Biloxi was quite a prosperous little city and a great summer resort. A lot of millionaires
used to make it a kind of headquarters during the winter
season because the weather, the fishing and the oysters was all
fine. Many times I played for big parties of the men who ran
the shrimp and oyster boats. But somehow or another I had a
kind of a yen to be a halfway smart guy. Since then I have
realized that these smart guys were much worse off than I was.
But I didn't see that then.

All the smart guys wore overalls and a flannel shirt, busted
open at the top, with no tie. From that dress you was considered a sharpshooter. One of these sharpshooters named Harry
Dunn was a very nice fellow that liked music and taken a
liking to me. He was a tall, lanky, light-complected fellow
and considered the best Georgia Skin player in that section.
He'd clean up on those turpentine men whenever they would
come to town for payday, because Georgia Skin was their main
game. Of all the games I've even seen, no game has so many

---

* Bunk Johnson ran into Jelly at this time . . .
   "I played with him in Gulfport, Mississippi, round in 1903 and
1904. He was real young, then, but he was a really good piano man.
Had lots of work at the Great Southern Hotel playing waltzes and rags
for the white people. Him and me played a date at the Busy Bee Park
on Labor Day. I remember it because the longshoremen had two parades—one for the union men and one for the boll weevils, the scabs."

cheats right in front of your eyes, and it would have taken a
magician to catch Harry.

"Some day I'm going to make a gambler out of you," he
told me. And, of course, that interested me because I wanted
to have the other young fellows of my class beat. So Harry
taught me some holdout tricks, meaning that you are sure to
win if you get the works in, but very dangerous if you can't get
the cards back into the deck for the next deal. He taught me
day by day until one time he decided to make a payday at a
railroad camp at Orange, Mississippi. What Harry meant by
"making a payday" was that he was going to win all the money
from the people that had worked for it.

I will always remember Orange, because it almost meant
fatal to me. Orange was a little bit of a place close to the
Alabama line—had a log cabin and two or three houses was
all. Harry took me along as his little brother. "I want to let
you see how these things is done, because showing you without the actual experience wouldn't do no good. These holdout
tricks in Georgia Skin take a lot of nerve."

That's what Harry told me, but he also knew that, by me
being able to play piano in the sporting-houses, I always had
some kind of money. I tried to convince Harry that I had a lot
of nerve and could do these tricks already, but he told me to
stay out of the game. However, I secretly decided to get some
experience, and that I did.

After we got to playing in this little bit of a camp at
Orange, I noticed that there were three jacks together, and
I swung out and kept those three jacks. The next time the
deal went around, one jack fell and I said, "That's my card"
and I picked up the jack. That meant I had all four jacks—

but they didn't know it. So I told the boys, "All right, get down on this card." "Getting down" means to put some money up. They put down their bets and, because I knew I had the best card, I said, "Roll up and make it easy on yourselves." And when we rolled up, I began taking in money so fast it was a shame.

Then one of the camp men picked the deck up and turned it over before Harry could do anything—he knew I had those three jacks and didn't know how to get them back in the deck. So, since I had won on the jack and they couldn't find the other three, the suspicion was right on me. A fellow pulled out a great big pistol and he said, "You either come in with my money or off goes your head."

Harry began to beg them, "Don't hurt this boy. He's only a young brother of mine and don't know what he's doing. I'll assure you I'll give you back all the money you lost on this deal." So, when they started claiming money, the one that had lost three dollars, he's say ten and all of them the same until it taken all the money I had in my pocket, all I had won and practically all Harry had won to straighten the thing out. Then, although a certain suspicion fell on Harry, he told me, "You stay out of the game. Let me play these boys and maybe I'll be luckier than you." Then he began to flip the cards and sing,

I'm gonna get one and go toreckly!

Bop! a card would hit.

I'm gonna get one and go toreckly!

Another card would hit.

> *My baby is down and out,*
> *So I'll get one and go toreckly.**

"You want anything on that tenspot . . . ? All right, king, come up there. Ten dollars more will catch the king. Okay, boys, it's a bet."

> *If I can make this one last,*
> *If I can make this card last,*
> *I'm gonna get one and go toreckly. . . .*

"Eight more dollars on the eightspot. . . . Let's make it sixteen. Nobody standing here but you and I. I got the ace—it's better than your eightspot, what do you say? Twenty dollars more. Okay? Bet . . ."

> *I'm gonna get one and go toreckly.*

The eightspot fell and Harry taken all the money and we finally got out of that place safe.

So I didn't do so good gambling, but beat up on the pool players and got me a few clothes and decided I'd hit the road for a while, trying out the women. Those days I would land in some little town, get a room, slick up, and walk down the street in my conservative stripe. The gals would all notice a

---

* Tune 10, Appendix 1.

new sport was in town, but I wouldn't so much as nod at anybody. Two hours later, I'd stroll back to my place, change into a nice tweed and stroll down the same way. The gals would begin to say, "My, my, who's this new flash-sport drop in town? He's mighty cute."

About four in the afternoon, I'd come by the same way in an altogether different outfit and some babe would say,

"Lawd, mister, how many suits you got anyway?"

I'd tell her, "Several, darling, several."

"Well, do you change like that every day?"

"Listen, baby, I can change like this every day for a month and never get my regular wardrobe half used up. I'm the suit man from suit land."

The next thing I know, I'd be eating supper in that gal's house and have a swell spot for meeting the sports, making my come-on with the piano and taking their money in the pool hall. The police would be unable to pick me up for vagrancy, because I had me a residence in that town with a loving babe that really liked the way I could play piano.

One of my instructors at the pool table was a very black gentleman, named Lily White, whom I later wished I had never met. We started out from Biloxi together and he convinced me that there wasn't any use to pay train fare; we could ride the train free. I tore both the knees out of my trousers taking my first free ride, but the next one I made successfully. It was a deadhead, an empty mail car. When we reached our destination and got off, Lily White heard someone coming and said, "Look out, let's run," which I refused to do. Up came a guy with two big pistols and carried us on down to the jail.

They claimed we had robbed a mail train, and, when we proved out of that, they gave us a hundred days on the county gang for carrying weapons. It seems that Lily White had a big razor up his sleeve.

When the inmates on the gang saw us, they hollered "New meat in the market!" Then they jumped on us and took our money and cigarettes. I didn't have but one thing in mind—how to get out of there the quickest way I could. It was said that whenever anybody got a hundred days on the gang, they wasn't no more good ever afterwards. I knew if I didn't get out of there, I would ruin my hands and never be able to play again. So I got some money from the outside and bought food for everybody and that way I made plenty friends. Then I watched my chance. We used to travel about eighteen miles from camp to where we worked on the road. I studied the route and picked me a piece of woods where I figured I could lose myself. Then, one afternoon about dusk, I fell over the side of that wagon and started running.

They had a system there of sending a prisoner to catch a prisoner and the one who did the catching got a lot of good time added to his record. The man they sent after me could really run, but I managed to keep ahead until we neither one of us could run no more—I guess it was some miles I kept in the lead—and then I picked up a big log and turned around and told him I was going to die before he'd get *me* back. I couldn't hardly talk, my throat was so dry, but I guess that man must have understood me, because, when I began to make my advance with that log, he backed away and left me alone. I went on a few miles further through the woods and just fell down somewhere, finally, and slept. The next day I stole some clothes off a poor farmer's wash line, walked into Mobile to a gal's house I knew, fell down and slept for a week. . . . That cured me of riding the railroad without paying my fare for quite a while.

Those Battles of Music

●●●It was about that time, in 1904, that they announced the piano-playing contest at the World's Fair in St. Louis. I was a half-hand bigshot on the piano around Mobile and the girls were willing to finance my trip. I had decided to go until I heard that Tony Jackson was going to appear at the contest. Of course, that kind of frightened me and so I stayed in Alabama. Later on I heard that Tony Jackson hadn't gone and that Alfred Wilson had won, which disgusted me, because I knew I could have taken Alfred Wilson. So I kept on traveling around the different little spots, singing my new tune. . . .

. . .

> *I'm Alabama bound,*
> *Alabama bound,*
> *If the train don't run, got a mule to ride,*
> *Just Alabama bound.*

> *Well, that rooster crowed,*
> *And the hen run around,*
> *"If you want my love, sweet babe,*
> *You've got to run me down . . ."*

I'd play it and the girls would do the high kicks and say, "My, my, play that thing, boy." And I'd say, "Well, I'll certainly do it, little old girl." That's the way we used to act down in Mobile around St. Louis and Warren, part of the famous corner. I will never forget that place because if it hadn't been for some of my piano-playing friends, one of those guys would have knifed me right in the back. I had cleaned him playing pool and he had the knife right on me. Said I only used the piano as a decoy, which was true; and, of course, he had it in his mind that I was kind of nice-looking. I suppose he was jealous of me. Imagine that! But he wasn't such a good-looking fellow, himself. Had some awful rubber-looking lips, I'm telling you. So I said,

> *Alabama bound,*
> *Alabama bound,*
> *One of them good-looking girls told me, "Baby,*
> *Come on and leave this town."*

I always had an inkling to write a tune at most any place I would ever land. So when I hit Mobile in 1905, I wrote *Alabama Bound* and all my friends considered it very good.

There was Charley King from Mobile, Baby Grice and Frazier Davis from Pensacola, Florida; Frank Racheal, supposed to be the tops from Georgia; and Porter King, a very dear friend of mine and a marvelous pianist now in the cold, cold ground, also from Florida. Porter King was an educated gentleman with a far better musical training than mine and he seemed to have a yen for my style of playing, although we had two different styles. He particularly liked one certain number and so I named it after him, only changed the name backwards and called it *King Porter Stomp.*

I don't know what the term "stomp" means, myself. There wasn't really any meaning only that people would stamp their feet. However, this tune became to be the outstanding favorite of every great hot band throughout the world that had the accomplishment to play it. Until today, it has been the cause of great bands coming to fame and outstanding tunes use the backgrounds of *King Porter* in order to make great tunes of themselves.* In 1905, the same year as *King Porter* and *Alabama Bound,* I also wrote a number called *You Can Have It, I Don't Want It,* a tune which was the first hit of Mister Clarence Williams. He got the credit for it, although I happened to be the one that taught him how to play it.

You may wonder why I didn't copyright my tunes in the old days. Well, it was not only me, but many others. The fact is that the publishers thought they could buy anything they

---

* As any student of jazz knows, this pride of Jelly's in his *King Porter Stomp* is warranted by its great importance in the development of jazz. Benny Goodman, for instance, used *King Porter* as a theme for a number of years. Tune 11, Appendix 1.

wanted for fifteen or twenty dollars. Now if you was a good piano player, you had ten jobs waiting for you as soon as you hit any town, and so fifteen or twenty dollars or a hundred dollars didn't mean very much to us. (Those were wonderful days. I would really like to see them back again, because, if I make ten dollars today I think I've got a great day.) So we kept our melodies for our private material to use to battle each other in battles of music. The men who had the best material in these battles were considered the best men and had the best jobs, and the best jobs meant, maybe, a hundred dollars a day. So we didn't give the publishers anything, but they said, "We know where to get tunes," and they would steal our tunes and come out with them anyhow.

By now I had developed to be a pretty good pool player. But one day a gentleman cleaned me out and I learned I had been playing the original Pensacola Kid. He thought I looked pretty highclass and agreed that if I would help him pick out some clothes he would show me how to improve my game. We both caught on very fast and a pool table began to look as easy as a piano keyboard to me. So I decided to try what I could do in New Orleans. In the latter part of 1905 I came back into town, met the good players and defeated them.* That made Winding Boy into a hot sport in New Orleans. My tunes had become to be very well known. My services were in demand.

---

* Johnny St. Cyr said . . . "Yes he was a *very* good pool player. Played for real *money*. He was in the class with Pensacola Kid, couldn't beat him but he could give him a hell of a game . . . Jelly Roll was on the hustling side. He'd gamble, play pool, play piano—I have even known him to hop bells in a dull season when they close the dance halls down."

Fortunately, I was popular right at that time, because some guys were going hungry.

There was a big slump in business; they was handing around drafts that were supposed to be as good as a dollar but weren't. The work in the highclass mansions fell off and so I had to take gigs and small-time band jobs. It seemed tough at the time, but, looking back now, I know that a depression was a good break for me, because I learned the band business.

Some guy would come up to me and say, "Winding Boy, there's a parade coming up in such and such a club. Do you want the job? It means five dollars for the leader and two-and-a-half apiece for the men." So I would elect myself leader and go around and get me a band. That wasn't much trouble, because the boys knew there would be plenty to drink even if the pay wasn't nothing.

All we had in a band, as a rule, was bass horn, trombone, trumpet, an alto horn and maybe a baritone horn, bass, and snare drums—just seven pieces, but, talking about noise, you never heard a sixty-piece band make as much noise as we did. Sometimes I would play trombone, sometimes bass drums or sometimes the snares, but it really didn't matter; the main part was the swell time we had—the girls giving us the hurrah when we passed, the boys getting drunk and picking up the horses, and the fights which we enjoyed watching. Sometimes the big organized bands would get the jobs—fellows like Emmanuel Perez or Buddy Bolden—and then they would always arrange to meet and have a battle of music in the streets. Those battles of music were something that has never been seen outside of New Orleans. In fact, we had the kind of fun I don't think I've seen any other place. There may be as nice a fun, but that particular kind there never was anywhere else on the face of the globe. Rain didn't stop nobody. It never got cold enough to stop nobody. We musicians stayed there because we felt it was *the* town.

I might name some of the jazz musicians I heard around that period, because these boys taught everybody the style that has now spread New Orleans music all over the globe. . . . Papa Tio, who taught all the best clarinet players in New Orleans, was not a hot man himself. He played straight classical clarinet, sometimes at the Opera House, but he and his son Lorenzo Tio taught Omer Simeon (my favorite of all clarinet players), Sidney Bechet, Pops Humphrey, Albert Nicholas, George Baquet, and Big Eye Louis Nelson. These were the men who taught all the other guys to play clarinet. George Baquet was the earliest *jazz* clarinetist. He played with Bill Johnson's Creole Band, the first jazz band to tour East out of New Orleans, but now—he ended as a corn-fed player in a Philadelphia movie house. Lorenzo Tio came along next. He taught the New York boys all they knew about jazz, used to play on a riverboat running from New York to Albany, drank too much whiskey and caught a cold and died in New York. He was a real swell Creole and wore his high-top shoes till the day he died.

I guess the best trombone players were Frankie Dusen, Eddie Vincent, Kid Ory, and Roy Palmer. Roy, who was no doubt the best who ever lived on the hot trombone, was a funny guy, very ugly and very good-natured and never on time. His main idea was not the trombone, but to be a first-class auto mechanic, and he was always so greasy on the job that, in later days, we used to pull the curtain so you could only hear the trombone and not see him. Every time you wanted to have Roy play a job, you would first have to find

him; you'd look for a sign in a window that said "Music Taught On All Instruments"—that was Roy, although he couldn't play anything in the world but a trombone; and you would always have to help him get his old, beat-up trombone out of hock. Even then he wouldn't play anything but little short jobs, because he wanted to get back to his mechanic work. He was the idol of George Bruneis, the original trombone with the New Orleans Rhythm Kings, and the best white trombone I ever heard. Of course, George was just a kid back in 1908.

To recount some of the other fine instrumentalists I came to know back at that period—there was Dink Johnson, Joe White, Hilaire and D. D. Chandler (he was the best and played mostly with Robechaux) on drums. There was Bill

Johnson, Ed Garland, Billy Marrero and Pops Foster on bass fiddle. Bud Scott was, no doubt, the great guitarist, although Gigs Williams and Buddy Christian could fake when the music wasn't too hard. Then on trumpet there was Buddy Petit, Mutt Carey, and later on Oliver, but, at the period I'm talking about, the great man was Freddie Keppard.

I first heard Freddie Keppard in 1907. He wasn't well known at the time because he wasn't playing in the tenderloin district. Freddie thought my playing was different and he was crazy about the *Indian Blues* I had just wrote. This tune enticed him to play in my style and in a year he had a big reputation and the women were swelling his head. He became to be the greatest hot trumpeter in existence. He hit the highest and the lowest notes on a trumpet that anybody outside of Gabriel ever did. He had the best ear, the best tone, and the most marvelous execution I ever heard and there was no end to his ideas; he could play one chorus eight or ten different ways. Freddie was a very fine fellow—with plenty of cheap notoriety—always was after women and spent every dime he ever made on whiskey. In the end he died broke in Chicago.

It was under Freddie Keppard in 1908 that there happened to come into existence the first Dixieland combination. Freddie was playing at the time at a big dance hall called the Tuxedo, located in the tenderloin district on Franklin Street between Customhouse and Iberville. Billy Phillips' joint was close by and it created such a scandal when Lefty Louie's gang out of New York killed him that business fell off in the place for a while. At that time Freddie had seven pieces—violin, bass, drums, guitar, trombone, clarinet, and trumpet. To save money he dropped the violin, bass, and guitar—and added a piano. This was the first Dixieland combination: five pieces,

composed of Edward Vincent—trombone, Freddie Keppard
cornet, George Baquet—clarinet, D. D. Chandler—drums,
and Bud Christian—piano. Then I wish you could have heard
those boys ramble on.

Whatever his pet prejudices, Jelly Roll never lost sight of
his main point: hot jazz was the creation of New Orleans
Negroes. In his view "the light, two-beat jazz" which has
come to be called "Dixieland" was the creation of the Keppard
combination. One can understand his insistence on this seemingly small point when one remembers that the all-white Original Dixieland Jazz Band of 1917 (by chance the first band to
record jazz) is generally reckoned the originator of "Dixieland." And in this lies the reason for Jelly Roll's telling this
circumstantial tale of Keppard's all-Negro Tuxedo Band,
which antedated the white group by a decade.

The Lion Broke Down the Door

●●● **T**hose years I worked for all the houses, even Emma Johnson's Circus House, where the guests got everything from soup to nuts. They did a lot of uncultured things there that probably couldn't be mentioned, and the irony part of it, they always picked the youngest and most beautiful girls to do them right before the eyes of everybody. . . . People are cruel, aren't they? A screen was put up between me and the tricks they were doing for the guests, but I cut a slit in the screen, as I had become to be a sport now, myself, and wanted to see what anybody else was seeing.

All the highest class landladies had me for "the professor," if they could get me—Willie Piazza, Josie Arlington, Lula White, Antonia Gonzales, Hilma Burt, and Gypsy Schaeffer, the biggest-spending landlady. Their houses were all in the same block on Basin Street, stone mansions with from three to seven parlors and from fifteen to twenty-five women all clad in evening gowns and diamonds galore.* The minute the button was pushed, that meant a new customer was in and the girls came in the parlor looking like queens, "Why hello, boy. Where you from?" Then I would hit the piano and, when I'd played a couple of my tunes—"Got some money for the professor?" If the guests didn't come up with a dollar tip apiece, they were told "This is a highclass place. We don't want no poor johns in here." Matter of fact, no poor men could even get in those mansions. The girls charged high and made from twenty dollars to a hundred a night.

Oftentimes the girls would ask me to perform my *Animule Dance*. I wrote this in 1906 and ten thousand has claimed it; it's never been published and it never will be, because nobody can do it but myself . . .

> *Ladies and gentlemen, we are now in the jungles.*
> *Every one of you are animules.*
> *You should be walking on four legs,*
> *But you're now walking on two.*
> *You know you come directly from the animule famulee.*
>
> *Yes, we're right here in the animule field.*
> *And I want to tell you people with clothes on*

---

* Jelly Roll added, "There was a *Blue Book* with all the information about the tenderloin district. My name was in that book which they now call *The New Orleans Guide*." (See Interlude 2, p. 129.)

You have tails just the same.
But you wear clothes and you can't see them . . .
    Way down in jungle town
    For miles around . . .
They used to give a ball every night at the animule hall.
The band began to play, they began to shout.
You'd laugh—Haw-haw-haw—Lord, till your sides
    would crack.
    How they'd call them doggone figures out!
    The monkey hollered, "Run, I say!"
    The wildcat did the bambochay;
    The tiger did the mooch;
    The elephant did the hooch-ama-cooch;
    The pan'ter did the eagle rock and began to prance,
        Down in the jungle,
        At that animule dance.

Well, the lion came through the door,
Ugh, you could tell that lion was posilutely sore.
"Let me in the hall." "What you gwine do?"
"I'm gonna break up this doggone animule ball.
    Yes, don't you think I want to dawnce?
    Give me one more chawnce . . ."
    The lion give a roar,
    Broke down the door,
    Broke up the animule ball.
The monkey hollered, "Run, I say!"
The wildcat did the bambochay;
The tiger did the mooch;
The elephant did the hoocha-ma-cooch;

The pan'ter did the eagle rock and began to prance,
In the jungles,
At that animule dance. *

Then I'd carry on some of my scat . . .

Bee-la-bah-bee-bah-a-lee-ba.

People believe Louis Armstrong originated scat. I must
take that credit away from him, because I know better. Tony
Jackson and myself were using scat for novelty back in 1906
and 1907 when Louis Armstrong was still in the orphan's
home.

Those days I hung out at Eloise Blackenstein and Louise
Aberdeen's place—the rendezvous of all the big sports like
Pensacola Kid, who later came to be the champion pool player
of the world. Bob Rowe, the man who didn't know how many
suits he had, and his wife, Ready Money, were regulars, also
the Suicide Queen, who used to take poison all the time. Tony
Jackson also hung out there and was the cause of me not
playing much piano. When Tony came in, the guys would tell
me, "Get off that piano stool. You're hurting the piano's
feelings."

---

* Jelly Roll never entered the "highclass mansions" as a customer.
Instead he sat at the piano and watched the "animules" dance, perhaps
dreaming of the lion breaking down the door. In Danny Barker's wonderful biography, he describes a barrelhouse called The Animule Hall,
where lovers of the blues and mayhem gathered to dance and to brawl
until the police wagon came to take the survivors to the pokey.

One day we were all up at Lulu's saloon. Pensacola Kid was playing Buster Brown for ten dollars a round and they asked me to keep the game. In came Chicken Dick, the Uptown roughneck, and started yelling, "Keeping the game, hey, little boy? You don't know what you doing. *I'm* going to keep game." He hit me hard and I fell on the table with my hands on some balls. I hauled off and hit him with a pool ball and he jumped like he was made of rubber. Then I laid into him with more balls and some billiard cues and they finally had to haul him out of there. That gave me a name. "Don't fool with Winding Boy. He like to kill Chicken Dick." I had sense enough to know it wasn't healthy to wear a name like that around New Orleans where some tough guy might decide to see how hard I really was. So I decided to accept Tony Jackson's invitation to visit Chicago.

I went North on an excursion train, landed in Chicago in 1907 and found that nobody in that town could play jazz piano. There were more jobs than I could ever think of doing, but these jobs paid so much less than in New Orleans I decided not to stay. Tony stayed on because he didn't care about money, but liked his kind of diversion and felt more free in Chicago than in his hometown. Myself, I dropped down to Houston, Texas, to see whether they had anybody could shoot a game of pool. I did a good bit of winning and then I started shooting left-handed so I could get more bets. They slipped a shark by the name of Joe Williams in on me, but right at the end of the game I switched over to my right hand and ran the game out. His backer, who had lost heavily, said I was robbing him (which was true), pulled out a pistol and started shooting. Somehow I got under the pool table, but that cured me of playing pool in Houston.

I moseyed around Texas awhile with a new girl in every town, finding nobody could play jazz in Texas. Then Nick, a sporting-life friend of mine, persuaded me to go to California with him. I went along although I knew that Nick wanted to get in with the sporting-women through me. California was a nice place at the time, no discrimination, but I played very little piano except in Oxnard, a very fast-stepping town. In fact, things was so dead that I headed back to New Orleans, stopping off in Texas and Oklahoma to see my young lady friends.

By now I was heating up all the best pool players including all the good cheaters. I played the Pensacola Kid at the Astoria Hotel and somehow all the breaks were with me that day and I beat him. When I turned to get the stakes, the guy holding them was gone. I told the Kid to get that $40 quick or I would knock his brains out with my cue and, quite naturally, the $40 came up fast. The manager told me to stay on out of the place, I was too rough for him. Yes, I had become quite a hard boy by then, in fact so hard that it nearly cost me my life.

I told you that I had known *about* Aaron Harris, but had never personally seen him. Well, Aaron like to play pool and, like many others, thought he could play me for a sucker because I was a musician. So I played this guy every day for $2 a game, and nobody tells me it was Aaron Harris, who at the time had eleven killings to his credit. Finally, I had Aaron down to his last money and he told me, "If you make this ball on my money, I'm going to take every bit of money in your pocket."

I said, "A lot of people go to the graveyard for taking and I've got what it takes to stop you."

He said, "What is that?"

I said, "A hard-hitting .38 Special, that'll stop any living human.* In a minute you'll have a chance to try to take my money, because if I can make this ball, in the pocket she goes."

I raised my cue high in the air, because my taw ball was close under the cushion, and I stroked this ball and into the pocket she went. It was then that Aaron Harris found out he had been playing a shark all the time. For some reason he decided to treat me square, "Okay, kid," he said, "you're the best. Loan me a couple of dollars."

"Now that's the way to talk," I said. "If you want a couple of dollars, I'll be glad to give it to you. But don't try to take anything away from *me*. Nobody ever does."

After he left, Bob Rowe walked up to me. At that time Bob was one of the big gamblers in New Orleans. He wore a diamond stud so big that he never could get no kind of tie that would hold it straight up. When he died some

---

* "It was a law in New Orleans a person could carry a gun if they wanted to—almost. Of course, there was just a ten-dollar fine—so it didn't make very much difference. If they found you didn't have ten dollars, your sentence would be thirty days in jail; but they put you to clean up the market in the morning and there most prisoners would run away."

years ago, he owned strings of racehorses. Bob was a good
friend of mine and he said,   Kid, don't play that fellow no
more."

"Why should I eliminate playing him? He brings me money
here every day. Why should I pass up money?"

Bob said, "You know who you're playing?"

"Certainly I know—he's my sucker, that's who he is."

"I'll tell you his name," said Bob, "and then you'll know
him better."

"Okay," I said, "let's have you divulge it."

He said, "That's Aaron Harris. . . ."

I came near passing out. Aaron Harris was, no doubt, the
most heartless man I've ever heard of. He could chew up pig
iron—the same thing that would cut a hog's entrails to pieces
—and spit it out razor blades. That man was terrible. A ready
killer. I wouldn't be saying this now, but he's dead and gone.
Old Boar Hog killed him.

Aaron pawned his pistol one night to play in a
  gambling game,
He pawned his pistol one night to play in a gambling
  game,
Then old Boar Hog shot him and blotted out his name.

But even Boar Hog was scared to come up to Aaron's face.
He waited till he knew Aaron was unarmed and then shot him
from ambush as he was crossing an alley in the early hours of
the morning.

Well, I knew *I* wasn't no tough guy and I told Bob, "I will
never play that gentleman no more. He can keep his money."

Bob looked at me a minute and then he said, "Why don't you take a little trip to sort of rest Aaron's nerves? He might decide he wanted to discuss something with you."*

I decided that Bob was right and I should travel for my health.

---

* Johnny St. Cyr remembered Aaron Harris . . .

"He was a big man and a real bully, stood six feet, weighed two hundred pounds and would draw a knife on a police officer. He was a bad, bad actor—killed his brother-in-law, and then beat the rap. I heard—I don't know it to be a fact, but I heard that he had some protection from a hoodoo woman. He must had something—a guy could beat a cold-blooded murder rap. Then in later years he slapped Toodlum—he was a banker of the Cotch game. Toodlum and Boar Hog waited for him at the place he always got off the streetcar on his way home and let him have it."

Jack the Bear

●●● You can understand why I was feeling rather jumpy with all the things that had happened recently and so I thought I would travel with someone who could offer me some protection. I left New Orleans with a guy from Jackson, Mississippi, who had named himself Jack the Bear. I found out later he should have called himself Jack the Lamb. He was a little bit of a guy and it seems like he must have stolen his name from some other big guy. Very often the boys, to be recognized as somebody, would use alias names like that.

Anyhow Jack the Bear proposed that we hobo.

I said, "No, I can't hobo. I tried that once. When I got off the train I thought it was slowing down and I fell headforemost and tore the knees out of the trousers of my sixty-dollar, brand-new suit. So I don't have to do that no more."

So he said, "I'll tell you what we'll do. You play piano very well. . . . We can always get plenty to eat if you play."

I said, "Yeah, I can always play up to some food and a place to sleep, there ain't no argument about that."

The first town we hit was Yazoo, Mississippi. Immediately I started playing piano and I made the landlady of the house, so that meant food for Jack and I. Of course Yazoo is one of those little bitty towns with a river running right through it—maybe a pond, I'd call it—and the sporting-houses of Yazoo was kind of cheap. Nothing like New Orleans at all, where the people spent money like water and where I could pick up plenty of money. So one of the local guys realized I was around and it looked like I was going to get into trouble so I told Jack the best thing for us to do was to leave. Somehow or other we got into Clarksdale.

We got into Clarksdale and it looked like funds was growing low. I was a good pool player. In those days I used to play anybody in the pocket. I didn't need no money because I knew I had to win. I went into a poolroom and I started playing a guy for twenty-five cents a game and I beat him several games. I let him pay off and then I had enough for us to eat on. So Jack said, "I know something we can make money on."

"What is it?"

"We got enough to buy some Coca-Cola and a bag of salt?"

I said, "Sure."

Jack the Bear said, "From now on I am a doctor that cures consumption."

The consumption then, they had a lot of it in this country and anybody say they could cure it, boy, could really reap a fortune, there is no argument about that. So we started around and I would knock at the doors. Of course I have always been known as a fair talker and I would ask anybody, the different people that could come to the door, "Have you anyone in your family with the TB's?"

And most of them would say, "Yes." If anyone was puny or thin, they just accepted it; they agreed they had the TB's.

"Well, ladies (or gentlemen, whoever it would be), it doesn't mean a thing at all to me, but I personally know this gentleman has cured so many cases. Now they happened to be in the city, but you people out here in the country may as well take the opportunity. He's got a medicine that only one bottle will cure you. He wouldn't put it on the market for anything. But he will be glad to let you have one. There is nothing as good and it only costs a dollar a bottle."

We had just ordinary bottles, any kind we could get hold of, big ones, of course. There wasn't nothing in them to hurt nobody, nothing but salt and Coca-Cola. Somehow or other we sold one of these to a poor family and the child died, so we caught the next train out to Helena, Arkansas. We didn't have a chance to reap no harvest, because we didn't have the nerve. We had made just enough for our train tickets.

Going up on the train, Jack the Bear had some kind of a fake pin in the lapel of his coat, and everytime he would get to one of those real simple colored people who had on any kind of a pin, he would walk up to him and cover the pin with his hands and say, "I got you covered now. If you can't tell me the secret oath of the fiftieth degree of this order, I will have to remove your pin. You are really violating the lodge rules, and I will have to have some money not to condemn you. . . ."

From time to time Jack would pick up a couple of dollars doing that kind of thing.

Anyway, we got into Helena, Arkansas, across the river. I

started playing pool and I beat a few of the supposed-to-be sharks around there, left-handed. So they had a lot of stool pigeons around and the blue suit I had on, it was getting greasy then because it wasn't pressed up so much and, by wearing the same suit all the time, I guess it had a bad odor. So a fellow, one of these stool pigeons, marked chalk on my back. That was to designate to the policemens that I was a stranger in town and a shark.

Pretty soon a policeman tapped me on the shoulder, said, "Where did you come from?"

I wasn't so afraid of policemens, because I had seen so many of them in New Orleans and I knew policemens was just another kind of man, in a sense. But I always knew I had to respect authority, and I respected him very much. If I hadn't respected him, it would have been very, very bad for me, because I had learned it didn't take them very much time in shooting you down.

So I told him that I had come from Clarksdale, which didn't mean a thing. I told him that a little down the line I came from Yazoo. So he said to me, he said, "I want you shuck-sharks and crooks to get out of town."

I said, "I am very sorry, but I'm a musician."

He said, "A musician don't mean anything down in here. We put more of *them* in jail than anybody else, because they don't want to work."

I said, "Did you say leave town?"

He said, "Yes."

I said, "Well, that will be my next move, because I don't intend to do anything but play music."

There was a boat leaving for Memphis very shortly. I believe the boat's name was the *Natchez* and it was no doubt the best boat on the river. Man, they had roustabouts on that boat they beat with whips to make them move up faster. They bring down the whip and those boys would holler, "Yes, Cap'n— boss, we comin' up with it." Those guys believed it was still in slavery times.

We got into Memphis, all right, which Jack was supposed to know all about. He was going to take me around and introduce me to the different personnels of Memphis. But the big, lying dog—I found out he hadn't ever been to Memphis before. So, anyhow, after I was in Memphis, safe and sound, on the shores of Memphis, Tennessee, I decided to go to this Beale Street I had heard a lot of talk about. I first inquired was there any piano players in the city and they told me that absolutely the best in the whole state of Tennessee was there. I asked them had they heard about Tony Jackson, Alfred Car- roll, Albert Wilson, or Winding Boy, and they said they had never heard of them guys. "Them guys wouldn't be able to play with this fellow, Benny Frenchy, the best in the whole state." Well, that kind of frightened me and I wouldn't even try to touch a piano until I could hear Benny Frenchy.

This guy, Benny Frenchy, was playing in a place on Beale Street, near Fourth. Nothing went into that place but pimps, robbers, gamblers, and whores—it's really a shame to think of some of those environments I drifted into—which it was run by a white fellow who was the tough guy of Memphis, Ten- nessee. When the police picked up some of his visitors or hang-arounders or the gamblers that gambled in his place, why, that man would walk into the police station and say, "Turn these people loose and don't bother none of the people that hang around my place," and the police department didn't have any trouble at all in getting these prisoners out immediately.

It seems like Benny Frenchy had certain days he came to the place and he was a natural drawing-card. The bunch would come up from the honky-tonks, with tough killers hanging around and prizefighters of a low caliber that would probably kill you for an argument. When Benny would show up, there would be a type of those lowclass women and some that was a little better class. They would have a special way of dancing when he played and I never seen that dance before or since. They would run right directly up to the wall and with a kind of little bitty shuffle and clap their hands together and kick back their right leg. And they'd say, "Oh play it, Benny, play it."

Well, there was this piano right in the Monarch. Benny Frenchy was playing it. All those lowclass whores were doing that dance. I was talking to the fellow who was running the dice game on the daytime watch. I didn't even know who I was talking to, only that he was the gentleman that ran the games. I said to him—it was Bad Sam, only I didn't know who it was—I said, "Who is this fellow?"

He said, "This is Benny Frenchy."

I said, "*I* never heard of him."

"Where in hell you been, never heard of Benny Frenchy?"

I said, "What is he? Supposed to be good?"

He said, "He is the best in the whole state of Tennessee."

I said, "Why, that damn fool can't hit a piano with a brick."

So he said to me, he says, "Can you play?"

I said, "Well, I'm not supposed to be good, but if that is playing I can beat all them kind of suckers."

He hollered to Benny, "Wait a minute, Benny. There's one of them little upstarts around here, thinks he can play. Would you mind lettin him get down there to show what he can do?" And he says to me, "Will you play?"

I said, "Sure, there is no worry about playing with a palooka like that. Why, certainly."

Bad Sam said, "Okay, Benny, here is a little bum thinks he can play piano. Let him try his hand. See what he can do, because, if he can't play, I'll kick him in the ass."

There was a kind of chill came over me when he said that. Bad Sam was a very tough man, but I didn't know it at the time. I found out later he was really the toughest Negro in Memphis, no doubt the toughest man in the whole section, black or white. And he had Sean Mahoney backing him up with plenty money.

I happened to be there personally one day when a man came in the gambling room, selling chickens. Bad Sam was back there with his two pistols and this guy came in hollering, "Chickens."

Bad Sam told him, said, "Say, listen, I'm losing a whole lot of money here. I just lose a bet and I told you about that hollering 'Chickens' and I ain't gonna tell you no more."

And the guy hollered "Chickens"—very soft. Said, "Get your chicken sandwiches."

When he said that again, Sam told the boys, "Wait a minute," and he walked from behind the gambling rack. Then—I actually seen him do it—he drew back his right hand and hit that man on the jaw and broke his jawbone. His jawbone came through the flesh. I actually seen that. So you see, Sam was a very tough man.

Well, when Bad Sam said that to me, this supposed-to-be-tough partner of mine, Jack the Bear, he didn't seem so very tough, he didn't open his mouth. But courage came to me because I knew that no matter how I played I could beat Benny Frenchy because he couldn't play at all. I got up a lot of courage and I said, "You won't kick me in the ass, because I can beat this palooka."

And Bad Sam said, "He's a game kid, all right, so let him go down."

Well, I sat down and began to play the New Orleans *Naked Dance*. All the girls begin to do high kicks and they told me, "Oh play it, mister, play it. Play that thing, boy." Of course I never was a great singer, but I could do better than now. I told 'um I certainly would and then sung something like this:

> *All that I ask is love,*
> *All that I want is you,*
> *And I swear by all the stars*
> *I'll be forever true.*
>
> *All that I seek to know,*
> *All that I want above*
> *All that I crave in this wide, wide world,*
> *All that I ask of you is love . . .* *

I swung out on that number in my style and, when I looked around, Benny Frenchy was standing all by himself looking like he wanted to put a knife in me; Bad Sam was sort of

---

* Composed by H. Ingraham and E. Selden, copyright by Shapiro-Bernstein, Inc., 1908. Lyrics reprinted by permission.

smiling in his deal and all them little whores was running
directly up to the wall and kicking back in that funny little
Memphis dance. Man, I brought the house down with that
thing. Don't you believe me? Think I'm kidding? I brought it
down, man. After that Beale Street belonged to *me.*

As usual, of course, there was trouble with jealous people.
One night when I was playing piano at Bad Sam's I happened
to look around and see a fellow coming at me with a knife—it
seems this guy's girl had taken a liking to me. I pulled a beer
bottle up off the piano and told him, "Come on with your
knife. I ain't scared of you." Of course, nobody can go up
against a knife in the hand of a man who know how to use it,
but, luckily for me, Coon Cant George, one of the dealers,
walked in right then, pulled out that big .45 of his and the
gentleman with the knife faded.

My first real job in Memphis was at the Savoy Theatre
operated by Fred Barasso, where I replaced the legitimate
pianist. Barasso was planning the first Negro vaudeville circuit
to play the four houses in Greenville, Vicksburg, Jackson, and
Memphis. He asked me to go out in the number one show.
That was the reason I stayed on in Memphis for some time and
happened to meet Handy, who had just arrived from his hometown—Henderson, Kentucky.

The one who introduced me to Handy was a guitarist named
Guy Williams. Guy had a little blues of his own he was always
playing, named *Jogo Blues.* This man later joined Handy's band
in 1911 and in 1913 Pace and Handy published the *Jogo Blues*
under the same title and then later changed it somewhat to
make the *St. Louis Blues.*

At the time I'm speaking about, in 1908, when Handy and
his band was already playing Sundays at Dixie Park in Mem-

phis, I requested them to play the blues and Handy said that *blues couldn't be played by a band!*

This is what Handy, who was introduced by Ripley on the radio as the originator of jazz, stomps, and blues, told me. I know his musical abilities because I used to play in his band from time to time. In 1908, Handy didn't know anything about the blues and he doesn't know anything about jazz and stomps to this day. One of my protégés, Freddie Keppard, the trumpet king of all times, came to Memphis on an excursion from New Orleans. I had him and his band play my *New Orleans Blues* and *that* was the first time Memphis heard the blues by an orchestra. So much for Mister Handy.

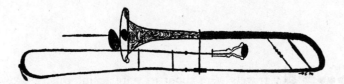

Can't Remember All Those Towns

●●●**M**y travels were about to start again. Buster Brown and Alto Lane, a couple of the hottest sports New Orleans ever produced, came to Memphis broke. At that time a lady friend was helping me along, so that I was able to stake the boys in the enterprise they had in mind, which was to take the dice game at the Monarch saloon. This was a very, very difficult thing to do, because in Memphis you shot dice out of a leather horn with a string across the top to prevent the real experts from setting their shots with their hands. You were also limited to three licks with that horn. But Buster and Alto figured they could beat it. All they had to do was to substitute their loaded dice while *they* was shooting and then remove them when their three licks was over. You might think I was crazy to help them, but I did. They was my friends and they was so down on their luck that they was taking their baths by going down to Father Mississippi and washing their feet occasionally. Well, I staked them to a roll and warned them not to try their loaded dice during Bad Sam's watch at the dice table; told them they'd better go while Frazier Davis was on duty. Bad Sam had an eye like an eagle, and, if he caught them, they would just die on the spot. So they heeded my warning, walked into the Monarch past all those iron bars and those guys with guns in their bosoms, stepped up to the dice game, looking so much like a couple of broken-down roustabouts that nobody ever suspected them, and just naturally cleaned up. It makes me feel chilly right now to think about it. But those boys were artists, and they had all the nerve in the world. Just about daybreak that morning they tapped on my window, gave me my cut of the money and caught the first boat down the river.

Myself, I was glad to get out of Memphis with the number one company on the Benbow circuit a few days later. The band consisted of a drummer and of me on piano. Buster Porter was the main comedian, until he was later replaced by Stringbeans and Sweetie May; Edna Benbow sang the blues; Will Benbow was the straight man and manager. The show was a hit and we toured for two years, although I quit from time to time because I could make more money catching suckers at the pool table. There are two incidents of this tour I want to tell you about, the type of thing that unfortunately does happen in the South. I was an actual witness.

When we came to Greenwood, nobody was on the streets. They told me some white fellow had wanted to horsewhip a colored boy, so the colored fellow wouldn't stand for this and shot the man. Then they lynched the colored boy. Just like that. I heard all about the thing, which had happened just before we came to town. The colored in Greenwood didn't seem very scared. They thought it was an even break. The colored boy had killed a white boy and then *they* killed the colored boy.

Later on in Biloxi I came in view of another lynching. This fellow, Henry Lyder, was lynched for attacking a white girl. Now you know yourself that a lot of these rapes is lies. But plenty of them is truth. In this case the people I talked to in Biloxi felt it was the facts. It seems that most of the people of Biloxi, white and black, were satisfied; they seemed to think Lyder had really attacked the girl.

Will Benbow's show played Louisville, Winston-Salem, Richmond, Chicago, Washington, Philadelphia, Baltimore, Kansas City, St. Louis—I can't remember all those towns.* Finally, in Jacksonville my girl friend, Stella Taylor, got dissatisfied and so I quit, too. I sent my trunks with all my clothes to New Orleans and just kept a blue suit, which needed pressing. I took it to a shop on Pearl Street near the railroad station and, as I had some business to attend to, asked the man

---

* By this time Jelly Roll's story began to move so fast that we gave up trying for exact chronology. That he really covered ground the old master of Harlem piano, James P. Johnson, testified . . .

"First time I saw Jelly was in 1911. He came through New York playing that *Jelly Roll Blues* of his. He was, well, he was what you might call pimping at the time, had that diamond in his tooth and a couple of dogs [prostitutes] along. That diamond helped him in his business, you know—it made some of these gals think he was a bigshot. Of course, Jelly Roll wasn't a piano player like some of us down here. We bordered more on the classical theory of music."

for a pair of pants to wear. He gave me an old pair, torn and full of holes. When I went back to get my suit, this guy drew a baseball bat on me and forced me to leave without my suit.

I went back to the hotel and somehow Stella and I got into a quarrel. The way those things go, we said things we both regretted later on, among which Stella told me she had found a guy she liked better than I. It so happened that I knew the fellow; he was a supposed-to-be pool player. I looked this gentleman up in a pool hall and just naturally beat him to death playing pool and took every nickel he had in the world. I told him I hoped he would have a nice time with Stella, who was a girl with very expensive habits, I'm telling you. Then I walked off and left him.

I just hung around Jacksonville, might have been a couple of months, feeling low on account of what had taken place between me and Stella. I even bought a trombone and practiced awhile. Then I heard that Billy Cassans was putting together a show in Memphis and I decided to join him, which I did. We went on tour and in this show I acted as straight man to Sandy Burns, the blackface comedian and the first eccentric dancer in the United States, and it was through him I happened to get the name, Jelly Roll.

One night while working ad lib on the stage, doing comedy,* Sandy said to me, "You don't know who you're talking

---

* About Jelly's talent for comedy, his old friend Reb Spikes had this to say . . .

"I met Jelly in Tulsa, Oklahoma, in 1912 and we had a show. Jelly wanted to be a comedian. He thought he was a funny man and, my God, he was as funny as a sick baby. He never made nobody laugh. He'd to." I said, "I don't care." Right there we had a little argument and I finally asked him who was he? He said he was Sweet Papa Cream Puff, right out of the bakery shop. That seemed to produce a great big laugh and I was standing there, mugging, and the thought came to me that I better say something about a bakery shop, so I said to him that he didn't know who *he* was talking to. He wanted to get acquainted, and I told him I was Sweet Papa Jelly Roll* with stove pipes in my hips and all the women in town just dying to turn my damper down! From then on that name stuck to me and was the cause later of one of my greatest numbers to be called the *Jelly Roll Blues*.

In those days I had the bad habit, which I never broke entirely, of being a big spender when I had money. Well, the show stranded me, broke, in Hot Springs, Arkansas. So when Sandy proposed that we accept an offer and go to the Pastime Theatre in Houston, I decided that since I was a straight man, I might as well be the best straight man on earth.

We took Texas that year—Dallas, Denison, Cuero, Yokum, Brownsville (where I saw a bullfight), San Antonio, and more towns I can't remember. Every place I looked up the piano players, and they were all terrible. In fact the only piano player in Texas I remember was George W. Smith, who gave up the

---

black up (he was very light, you know) and come out and sit at the piano and tell jokes and play some rags and nobody ever laughed and so one day I told him to cut out the funny crap and stick to the piano crap and he'd do all right."

* Jelly roll—a folk term of sexual reference which antedates Morton's rechristening. See Tune 12, Appendix 1.

piano when he heard me and moved to California to make his living as a trumpet player.*

I tried to organize a stock theatre in Houston, but relatives ruined it. So I took the money I had left and bought a tailor shop and went after the tenderloin trade, since I was a part-time piano player in a couple of the best houses.

I was sitting in my tailor shop one day with a great big cigar in my mouth and my feet on the desk—those days I thought in order to be a big businessman you had to have a big desk—when Anna Mae Fritz (later in the movies) came in with my girl friend, Rosie. Anna Mae and I had an argument and I slapped Rosie in the mouth and said I would murder her if she didn't do like I told her. Later that day Detective Peyton came into my place and threatened me. I pulled the big gun I kept in my drawer and told him not to come any closer to me. "I heard you say the chief of police can get you out of anything," I told him, "but he can't get you out of where I'm going to put you, because I'm going to put you in the ground."

Peyton backed on out my tailor shop, but he was a tough guy to beat (I always heard he was the instigator of the famous Houston riot), and he laid for me. He ordered two very prom-inent pimps, Black Dude and Macbeth, friends of mine, to get on out of town because they didn't have a job. They came to me for help and I turned my supposed-to-be tailor shop over to them (the whole thing had cost me twenty-five dollars), so

---

* "George Smith is frank to admit that Morton carved everybody, including himself. The thing that stuck in Smith's mind was the way Jelly played *Jelly Roll Blues* and that specialty, *The Lion Roared and Broke Down the Door*." —*Downbeat,* April 1938.

that when Peyton saw them they could say they were in business. Peyton worked them over until they told him I had made those arrangements. Next day Peyton came in my place and all he said was, "Jelly Roll, you've got to shut this place and blow town."

I was tired of Houston anyway. There wasn't any decent music around there, only jew's-harps, harmonicas, mandolins, guitars, and fellows singing the spasmodic blues—sing awhile and pick awhile till they thought of another word to say. So I said, "Okay, Peyton, goodbye to you and your ratty town. I'm going North."

Jelly Roll Blues

●●●It was along about that time that the first hot arrangements came into existence. Up until then, everything had been in the heads of the men who played jazz out of New Orleans. Nowadays they talk about these jam sessions. Well, that is something I never permitted. Most guys, they improvise and they'll go wrong. Most of the so-called jazz musicians still don't know how to play jazz until this day; they don't understand the principles of jazz music. In all my recording sessions and in all my band work, I always wrote out the arrangements in advance. When it was a New Orleans man, that wasn't so much trouble, because those boys knew a lot of my breaks; but in traveling from place to place I found other musicians had to be taught. So around 1912 I began to write down this peculiar form of mathematics and harmonics that was strange to all the world

For a time I had been working with McCabe's Minstrel Show and, when that folded in St. Louis, I began looking around for a job. My goodness, the snow was piled up till you couldn't see the streetcars. I was afraid that I'd meet some piano player that could top me a whole lot, so I wouldn't admit that I could play. I claimed that I was a singer. At that time I kinda figured I was a pretty good singer, which was way out of the way, but I figured it anyhow. Well, I was hired at the Democratic Club where they had a piano player named George Reynolds. He was a bricklayer trying to play piano. He couldn't even read music. In fact, none of the boys couldn't read much and so it was very tough for them to get those tough tunes. They bought sheet music just to learn the words of the songs.

This George Reynolds, that couldn't read, played for me while I sang. Of course, George was a little bit chesty, because all the girls around were making eyes at him (he was a fairly nice-looking fellow); but I thought, if this guy's the best, the other piano players must be very, very terrible. So I asked George to play me one of the numbers I was going to sing. He played it, although he didn't seem very particular about doing it. I told him, "One of these parts here you don't play right. I'd like a little more pep in it." I forget what tune it was, some popular number of that time.

"Well," he said, not knowing I could play, "if you don't like the way I'm playing, you do better."

"Okay," I said, "if you don't play my tunes right, I can play them myself." So I sat down and showed him his mistakes.

Immediately he had a great big broad smile on his face. Seeing that I was superior to him, he wanted to make friends with me. I didn't object and we gotten to be friends right away. He asked me did I read music. I told him a little bit. So he put different difficult numbers on the piano—he thought they were difficult, but they were all simple to me. I knew them all. By that time he started getting in touch with the different musicians around town that was supposed to be good and they started bringing me different tunes. They brought me all Scott Joplin's tunes—he was the great St. Louis ragtime composer—and I knew them all by heart and played them right off. They brought me James Scott's tunes and Louis Chauvin's and I knew them all. Then Audie Mathews (the best reader in the whole bunch) brought me his *Pastimes* and I played it. So he decided to find out whether I could really read and play piano and he brought me different light operas like *Humoresque*, the *Overture* from *Martha*, the *Miserery* from *Ill Travadore* and, of course, I knowed them all.

Finally they brought me *The Poet and the Peasant*. It seems like in St. Louis, if you was able to play this piece correctly, you was really considered the tops. The man that brought it was the best musician in town and he hadn't been able to master this piece. Well, I had played this thing in recitals for years, but I started looking at it like I hadn't ever seen it before. Then I started in. I got to a very fast passage where I also had to turn the page over. I couldn't turn the page, due to the fact I had to manipulate this passage so fast. I went right on. Audie Mathews grabbed the tune from in front of me and said, "Hell, don't be messing with this guy. This guy is a shark!" I told them, "Boys, I been kidding you all along. I

knew all these tunes anyhow. Just listen." Then I swung the
Miserery and combined it with the *Anvil Chorus*.*

You find, though, that people act very savage in this world.
From then on it was George Reynolds' object to try to crush
me. He couldn't do this, but he made things so unpleasant
that I finally took a job out in the German section of town.
The manager wanted a band, so I got some men together,
although there wasn't many to pick from—clarinet, trumpet,
mandolin, drums, and myself. These were not hot men, but
they were Negroes and they could read. They didn't play to
suit me, but I told them if they played what I put down on
paper, they would be playing exactly as I wanted. Then I
arranged all the popular tunes of that time—I even made a jazz
arrangement of *Schnitzelbank*—and we made some pretty fair
jazz for St. Louis in 1912.

St. Louis had been a great town for ragtime for years because
Stark and Company specialized in publishing Negro music.
Among the composers the Starks published were: Scott Joplin
(the greatest ragtime writer who ever lived and composer of
Maple Leaf Rag), Tom Turpin, Louis Chauvin, Audie
Mathews, and James Scott.** But St. Louis wasn't like New
Orleans; it was prejudiced. I moved on to Kansas City and
found it was like St. Louis, except it did not have one decent
pianist and didn't want any. That was why I went on to

---

* Tune 5, Appendix 1.
** For the record, Jelly Roll imitated the piano style of some of these
great old-timers. These remarkable imitations, tossed off casually
twenty-five years later, prove his phenomenal musical memory, for they
faithfully mimic the style of these long-dead pianists, and can be
checked with piano rolls of the period.

Chicago. In Chicago at that time you could go anywhere you wanted regardless of creed or color. So Chicago came to be one of the earliest places that jazz arrived, because of nice treatment—and we folks from New Orleans were used to nice treatment.

Up to this time the published arrangements of hot music were simply a matter of writing down the ragtime tunes played by some theatre band. Then *Jelly Roll Blues* became so popular with the people of Chicago that I decided to name it in honor of the Windy City. I was the only one at the time that could play this tune, *The Chicago Blues*. In fact, I had a hard time trying to find anyone who could take it down. I went to Henri Klickman (author of the *Hysterics Rag* and arranger for the Will Rossiter publishing house), but he didn't know enough. So, finally, I wrote the score out myself. Dave Payton and several more said what I had put down was "wrong," but, when I said, "Correct me then," they couldn't do it. We argued for days and days, but they couldn't find no holes in my tune. Finally, Klickman made an arrangement from my score and the song was published.

Immediately brass bands all over the country took it over and it was considered the hottest band arrangement anywhere. Here's the way we used to sing it at the old Elite Café . . .

> *In New Orleans, in New Orleans, Louisiana town,*
> *There's the finest boy for miles around.*
> *Lord, Mister Jelly Roll, your affection he has stole.*
> *What? No! I sho must say, babe,*
> *You certainly can't abuse.*
> *Isn't that a shame?*
> *Don't you know that strain?*

That's the Jelly Roll Blues.
  He's so tall and chancey,
  He's the ladies' fancy.
  Everybody know him,
  Certainly do adore him.

When you see him strolling, everybody opens up,
He's red-hot stuff,
Friends, you can't get enough.
Play it soft—don't abuse.
Play them Jelly Roll Blues . . . *

The old original Elite at 3445 State Street was the most beautiful place on the South Side and the most famous place in the history of America's cabaret land. The trade was of the finest class—millionaires and good livers. When Teenan Jones, the owner, put his partner in charge of the Elite Number Two, corner 31st and State, this man, Art Cardozier, ran the place right into the deep blue sea. It was an A–number one failure even with space enough to get Barnum and Bailey's Circus in every night, because they used operatic and symphonic musicians, which was considered obsolete in the city of Chicago since the invasion of Tony Jackson and Jelly Roll Morton.

Then Teenan Jones begged me to accept the manager's job. I explained that the only way I could bring his place to fame was if he would turn the cabaret department over to me with

---

* Tune 12, Appendix 1. Lyrics reproduced by permission of the copyright owners, Melrose Music Corporation.

no contradictions. Mr. Jones agreed and I accepted the job as manager.

The first thing was done was to fire all the waiters. Next I fired all the musicians and entertainers, including "Give-a-Damn" Jones, Teenan's brother, who was cashier at the bar. "Give-a-Damn" got his name through an argument, when he stated that he would go to Paris just to buy a drink—which he did, because he didn't give a damn. I came near getting shot, when I fired him, because he was known to be a pistol man.

The first sign was put out Thursday. On Sunday there was two policemen holding the crowd back. The entertainers were highclass, and the band, the second Dixieland combination in the country, was in my name—Jelly Roll Morton and His Incomparables. It consisted of myself on piano, Menns on drums, Henry Massingill on trombone, Horace George on clarinet and John Armstrong on trumpet. We were the hottest thing in Chicago those days. In fact I got the offer to go with Vernon and Irene Castle, the great ballroom dancers, on their European tour, but I turned it down because I felt that I was very permanent at the Elite (I have since learned there is nothing permanent in the entertainment business), and I was making $50 a week when everyone else was making about $17. Anyhow, Jim Reece Europe went on that tour, took my clarinet player, and they featured my *Jelly Roll Blues* all across the continent. . . . (Isn't whiskey a wonderful thing at times!)

To show you how that job had me tied down, one night a very beautiful woman offered to take me to California and backed her proposition by filling my hat with money. I said I was very sorry; it looked like all the money in the world to me, but I liked Chicago. Then some history fell on me that caused me to change my mind. It was all through relatives.

My brother-in-law, Bill Johnson, had gone into Freddie Keppard's Tuxedo Band to play bass fiddle, and, as Bill was a very, very good-looking boy in those days and all the girls taken to him and those bad chords on his bass fiddle and that song he sung . . .

> Let me be your salty dog,
> I don't want to be your man at all . . .

he taken over the Tuxedo Band. So Bill heard about California from me and he wrote my wife* and she financed a trip for the five pieces plus guitar and bass. On entering Los Angeles, the Tuxedo Band made such a tremendous success that the Pantages Circuit signed them immediately. They toured the country as The Original Creole Band over what was the largest circuit in the world at that time, finally landing at the Palace Theatre in New York. This was in 1913, long before the so-called Original Dixieland Band was thought of.

It was known that no act played the Palace Theatre in New York for more than one week, but the Original Creoles played for weeks to standing-room-only.

Later at the Grand Theatre in Chicago they took the town over and caused John Armstrong, my trumpet player, to quit.

Armstrong came from Louisville. I had tried to teach him

---

* Anita Gonzalez, Bill Johnson's sister, whose sudden appearance in this story is somewhat explained by the chapter that follows.

New Orleans style, but he was stubborn. Well, when he heard Freddie Keppard, hitting those high C's, F's and G's as clean as a whistle, he got ashamed and refused to play any more.

There was no limit to how Freddie could go. Louis Armstrong has never been in his class. Among trumpets I would rate Freddie first, Buddy Petit second, King Oliver third, and then comes Armstrong, all very great men. Freddie would agree with me. He was a real Creole, about my color, Creole accent, a good spender, wore plenty nice clothes, had women hanging around all day long, liked to drink a lot* (all the band drank up everything they could find), and he talked so big that people misunderstood and thought he was egotistical. This caused the break-up of this great band in the end.

They were always in an argument on account of Freddie's big talk. He would arrive at rehearsal an hour late and say, "Let them wait for me. The band can't play till I get there." Morgan Prince, the comedian with the band, was not a Creole and he took Freddie seriously. In one argument he hit Keppard across the head with a cane and that started the breaking up of

---

* "A quart a day?" said Johnny St. Cyr. "That was at the beginning. But Freddie Keppard graduated from that. Man, when I was in Chicago, Freddie would drink all day. He'd go in the local union when it open at one o'clock and start off with a pint of white lightning. Sit down and play hearts to round five o'clock and by that time he done drank up two pints. He'd go home and eat—he kept a gallon or two at home—and he'd lounge around there and drink up a pint and then he'd take a pint with him at night. His average was about a half a gallon to three quarts a day."

the band. I don't know when it happened but I understand that was the beginning of the end.*

Anyhow Keppard certainly finished *me* at the Elite. Business went to the bad and, as I did not wish to stay on and not satisfy everybody, I hit the road again.

---

* "Freddie was very cooperative with his band," said Johnny St. Cyr, "except for that independent Creole way of his. He always kept his own band and never had many engagements outside of them. His band would have been the first to record, but the boys didn't want a percentage deal and held out for a flat fee. Freddie plain refused, said he wasn't gonna let the other fellows hear his records and catch his stuff. That way they missed out being the first jazz band to record and the chance came to a white band—the Original Dixieland."

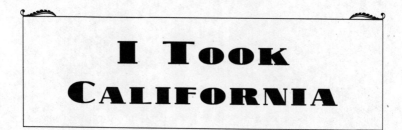

I Took
California

The Cadillac in Bloom

●●●In 1917 I came back into Chicago from a trip on the road. I had been doing a lot of pool playing and I was quite prosperous. That was the year that Blankenship was the champion pool player of America. He came up to the South Side and challenged everybody there, and my friend, the Pensacola Kid, thought he could beat him, but he didn't have the money for the stake. Him and I had been friends for years, so he came to me. . . . "I can beat this guy."

"He's the champion of the world," I said. "He's got to be good to be the champion."

"Jelly, I can beat him, if you'll let me have fifty."

Well, I lent him the fifty and, when that game was nearly over, I thought I wouldn't see it again. Blankenship was almost out and he had left the Kid very hard against the cushion. The Kid needed eighteen balls and the shot was impossible, but the Kid made it to beat the world's champion. After that the Kid left for South America. He went to Buenos Aires to beat all the pool players in South America, which he did. I even remember his address—Sala Hotel, B.A.

By that time I was thinking of leaving Chicago—a different class of people were invading the city at the time. So when a very prominent figure around town by the name of Lovey Joe Woodson came to me and told me they had a job for me in Los Angeles, I didn't even wait to ask him the salary, I was so anxious to get away.

I had a lotta clothes those days, which I packed and shipped. It happened to be summertime and the dust was terrible in that tourist car; I was almost as dusty as a boll weevil when I arrived in Los Angeles. It was a funny situation. They had a brass band to meet me at the station, but, when I got off covered in all that dust, the newcomers that didn't know me asked was that the hot Jelly Roll people had talked so much about? "The first thing this guy needs is go to the cleaners. He's got a dirty suit of clothes on."

Well, that suit was terribly dirty, but, when I left Chicago, it was swell, a brand-new suit. Anyway, I thought my trunks would be there that night when I had to start work; but they were delayed three or four days and I had to wear that dusty suit on the job. People thought it was strange that I had come to L.A. with only one suit, and so I was under very, very tough criticism from the beginning. Of course, after my trunks got there, I turned the town out. They thought I was one of the movie stars, I had so many clothes.

On my opening night they had to have the police department to stop the crowd, because I had been pretty well advertised. Then the movie-star trade began, and we didn't have anything but movie stars at the Cadillac Café long as I stayed there* until my argument with Bright Red.

Bright Red, I'd known since she was a kid. She was born and raised in Chicago, where she had learned the art of the average entertainer—that is, when she got a big bill as a tip, to switch it and put a small bill in its place. Those days I never looked at the keys, I always watched the entertainers. For every move they'd make, I had them, whether they were singing or whether they were stealing. So, when Bright Red went south in her stocking with a ten-dollar bill, I demanded from the boss that she come up out of her stocking. The boss says, "I'll pay the ten dollars."

I said, "Don't pay it. I want to make her come up with it. You will only encourage her to steal further."

Bright Red didn't like the idea that I had caught her stealing and she decided to try a little undercover work. She sent to New York for the pianist Hageman. One day, when I walked into the Cadillac to get my meals, I saw somebody at the piano and I say, "Is that Hageman?" He say, "Who's talking?" I say, "Jelly Roll." "Gee, I'm glad to see you." (I'd

---

* Bill Johnson played with Jelly Roll during this period. When interviewed he was manager, counterman, dishwasher, and cashier of a café at the corner of Forty-fifth and Central in L.A. He told me in his dry and humorous way . . .

"You could go by a house where Jelly Roll would be playing and you'd know it was him because nobody did and nobody does play just like him. He wasn't afraid to admit it, either . . . 'Nobody playing piano I can't cut,' he used to say. The thing was he really could do what he said. He was the best, the very best."

always thrown a lotta work his way, so naturally he's glad see me.) "What you doing here?" I say. "I'm gonna work here."
"You mean at the Cadillac? That's strange. They didn't tell me anything about it. I'm working here."

I asked the boss what kind of tricks he was pulling and he said I was hard to get along with, not realizing that I was right and Bright Red was wrong—"So I sent and got somebody as good as you." I told him, okay, I would close his joint in two weeks.

It might not have been two weeks, but it wasn't more than two and a half.

There was a roadhouse out in a little place called Watts, about nine or ten miles from Los Angeles. The colored owner, George Brown, wasn't doing any good, so, when I offered to come out there, he immediately accepted. I told him I didn't want to open until he notified Hollywood that I'd be working there. We had invitations printed and, my opening night, all Hollywood was there. That ended the Cadillac. They kept on going down and down until they had to close. Then another friendship landed me in trouble.

Willie Taylor, considered one of the greatest violinists in the United States, came to town and I gave him a job in my band. After Willie came in, he decided to take the band away from me, outtalked George Brown, and did take the band over. When I left there, he brought Hageman in as pianist, and I told him I would close *him* up right away. By that time the Cadillac was sure I was the man, so I took over half the business, went back in there with a four-piece band and ran George Brown out of gas. Took all the movie-star trade away from him. Then Brown moved a half a block from the Cadillac (that was on Central between Fifth and Sixth) with his eight-piece band and did fairly well from the overflow trade, but it wasn't long till all the movie stars drifted back to us and Brown cut his band down man by man until he had nobody left but Hageman. Finally he let him go and closed the place. That left me with George Brown as a real enemy from then on.

The Cadillac was again in bloom. Of course, the musicians couldn't play the tunes we could in New Orleans; they didn't have the ability. So we had to play what we could—*The Russian Rag, Black and White, Maple Leaf Rag, Liza Jane* (a little comedy song, the whole Coast went for that), *Daddy Dear, I'm Crying for You, Melancholy Baby*—these were quite prominent in 1917, if I don't get the years mixed up. Then I wrote a tune and called it *Cadillac Rag* that we used to do with a singer.

I often seen my brother-in-law, Bill Johnson, who was so crazy about California, and I would constantly ask him where Anita was, but he wouldn't never tell me. Finally I runned up on her old lady, her mother, and she says, "Oh my, how Anita would like to see you!"—and she got me in touch with Anita. Anita had bought a saloon business in a little town called Las Vegas, Nevada, and she had made a lotta money. When her mother notified her I was in L.A., she came up to see me and we got back together. She said she should let the saloon go unless I decided I liked Las Vegas. So I tried Las Vegas a while, but it was too doggone cold in the winter and too hot in the summer. We turned the place over to Bill Johnson and, when we saw him next, he was riding in a McFarlan automobile, which they was plenty high those days.

Anita decided to stay in Los Angeles. She bought a small hotel on the corner of Central near Twelfth and named it The Anita. By that time I had several little businesses branching out, myself. I had a little dance hall, but because you had to

close a dance hall at twelve o'clock, I went partners with Pops
Woodward, the trombone player and we opened up the Wayside Park at Leek's Lake* out in Watts County. There we
could stay open all night. Wayside Park is the place King
Oliver made much fame in later when I introduced him there
in April, 1922.

A very, very funny incident occurred at this time. Bill
Johnson and I decided to bring a real New Orleans band to the
coast in order to build Leek's Lake up. We sent home for
Buddy Petit, Frankie Dusen, and Wade Waley. We knew
they would arrive in the antiquated dress habitual to New
Orleans musicians, their instruments all taped up to keep
them airtight and Waley's clarinet in his back pocket. So we
decided to bring them in town secretly.

Bill and I met them at the station in his long McFarlan and,
sure enough, they were wearing those boxback coats and those
trousers, so tight you couldn't button the top button. We
asked them where were their instruments? Buddy's cornet was
in his suitcase. Part of Dusen's trombone was wrapped in
newspaper and Waley's clarinet was in his pocket. We were
afraid somebody would see them and think they were downs,
so we rushed them to the tailors and put them in some decent-
looking clothes. Man, they wanted to kill us for making them
change their suits, which they thought was very, very much in
the mode.

---

* Reb Spikes said . . .

"I built up Leek's Lake out in Watts. Made a pile of money, too.
They call it Wayside Park today, but it's still Leek's Lake to me."

But, man, those guys could really play. Petit was second only to Keppard on the cornet, had tremendous power in all registers and great ideas. He was a slow reader, but if the tune was played off first, he would pick up his part so fast no one knew he couldn't read. And, as for Dusen, he was the best there was at that time on trombone. So we had a very hot five-piece band and made plenty money—$75 a night and the tips doubled the salaries.

But those guys couldn't get used to all that money. They used to bring their food on the job, just like they was used to doing in the lowdown honky-tonks along Perdido Street. Here they'd come every night to this Wayside Park with a bucket of red beans and rice and cook it on the job. (Man, I wish I had some of that stuff right now. The best food in the world!)

So anyhow, Dink and me got to kidding the boys about this, because, as a matter of fact, this cooking on the job made us look kind of foolish. And Buddy and Frankie blew up, threatened to kill us. Next day, they left town, without notice, and went back to New Orleans. Which shows you never fool with a New Orleans musician, as he is noted for his hot temper.

Wayside Park did so well and I made so much money that I came into possession of a gambling club, next door to Anita's hotel. I put Zack Williams in there to run it for me. Zack was the first fellow to play Tarzan in the movies. He was a big, black fellow, must have weighed three hundred pounds, and he was very expensive help. He used to demand a dollar and a quarter steak every morning and my wife used to cook them for him. But money was no object. In fact I used to keep the top tray of my trunk full of bales of bills—ones, twos, fives and tens in bales. Once I told a fellow I had a trunk of money and just opened the trunk to the top tray and he nearly passed out—he thought the whole trunk was full.

Anita and I were getting along swell. She had three or four fur coats and I had plenty clothes, plenty diamonds. It's a day I'd like to bring back. I never realized how happy I was until after I left her. There wasn't nothing under the sun that I wanted during that time that I didn't get, but two things. One was a yacht and the other was a cow. After I looked up the price for yachts, I said I couldn't handle one; the upkeep was too tremendous. But, outside of that, everything was swell.* We moved out of the hotel into our own apartment so that Anita could look out for her mother. There was nothing too good for that old lady and she realized it. When she asked for the best apparels, she always got them. Anita loved her mother very much and I thought an awful lot of the old lady myself.

Of course, Anita was devoted to me more so than to her mother. If I told her to do something, she listened to everything I said and she respected me as her husband, as few women today respect their husbands. Aside from that, Anita

---

* "The period was one of Jelly's happiest and most prosperous. He could have his big car and his diamonds, and could keep his music just as a sideline for special kicks while he made his real money from the Pacific Coast 'Line.' As one friend put it, 'You don't think Jelly got all those diamonds he wore on his garters with the $35 a week he made in music.'

"But whether Jelly was really 'one of the higher-ups,' as he claimed, or just a procurer is immaterial, for . . . Jelly loved music and played . . . not because he had to, but because of the immeasurable pleasure he received. . . ." William Russell, *The Needle,* July 1944.

was a very beautiful woman and she dressed very handsomely with plenty diamonds to elaborate the condition. I couldn't wish for a finer woman than Anita. In fact, I don't believe there was ever one born finer than Anita and I know I've missed an awful lot by leaving her. It was all a mistake, but nevertheless it happened, as I'll tell you.

America went into the war and they wanted me to register, even offered to make me an officer, but I said I wouldn't be no better off as a dead officer than as a dead private. I tried to stay out of it, like most musicians, and played lots of benefits and they didn't draft me, until just before the Armistice. Business was booming, so much so, till George Brown, who was now a big politician, came around and said, "If you'll put up $600 and your partner $600, I'll kick in the same amount and we'll control this campaign and run this town to suit ourselves." I told him that I wasn't so interested in running the town as in making some money, and that caused him to deepen in his anger toward me.

One day I got a telegram in Frisco, where I had gone on business, that Zack had lost the $2000 roll of my gambling house. I came home and fired Zack Williams, but that wasn't the end to the mess. The police were making trouble about the license for Anita's hotel, and I couldn't help her because she was accusing me of another woman. She wouldn't even talk to me. One morning I found her and her mother with their bags packed.

"What's the matter?"

"I'm going to Arizona. I've bought a restaurant out there. You want to come along?"

I didn't want to lose Anita and I went with her. But that restaurant business didn't last her long. She got fooling around

with some phony gold stock and lost everything she had made and in a few months we moved to Frisco, where we opened The Jupiter.

I ran the entertainment with a ten-piece band and ten entertainers and Anita handled the bar with ten waitresses and we did a great business. It was *too* good. Soon the manager of the place across the street had us in trouble with the police. He had it fixed so we couldn't get hold of a license for dancing. I fooled around and spent a lot of money. Then I wrote a letter to the police department and showed them my open mind. In a couple of days Anita and I followed that letter to headquarters.

They kept us waiting for a couple of hours and by then our Creole was up. They didn't know Anita had a pistol in her pocketbook when they called us in. The police chief slapped the letter down on the table—"Do you know this hand?"

"Yes, it's mine," Anita said.

"Who dictated it?"

"Me," I said.

"You haven't the intelligence to write a letter like this."

"Say, I was going to school before you left Ireland," I told him and he began to rave. He touched a button under his desk and you never saw so many six-footers in your life, popping in through all the doors. I began to get scared, but still thought I'd better keep talking. "Looks like you plan to mob somebody."

"Shut up before you get your head knocked off. You're too smart. That's why you're in trouble."

"We're not in trouble. We're being molested and we're going to fight for our rights." That's what Anita told him, sitting there cool with that gun in her pocketbook. She was a

wonderful woman. But it didn't do any good. Nothing helped.
We spent fifteen hundred dollars for an attorney who wasn't
worth a dime. He told the commissioner, "Now, Mister Commissioner, this is a nice boy and I want you to give him a
chance."

"I don't want no sympathy," I said, "I demand my rights."

The commissioner looked at me—"You heard what the captain said, boy. We'll close you down if you allow dancing." I
guess what worried them was that my place was black and
tan—for colored and white alike.

The night prohibition came in, the police told me it was the
penitentiary for me if I sold liquor. From then on the police
would hang around the door of The Jupiter and annoy the
patrons with uncalled-for remarks—"Why do you come here?
What's your name? Don't you know this place is likely to be
raided any time?"

I finally told them they would have to get on away from my
premises and, I was so angry, they moved on. Then that
doggone captain made a stoolie out of one of my waiters,
named Frenchy; paid him to plant a bottle of whiskey in the
slop barrel, but that fool went and got drunk at a bar owned
by a friend, told this friend I was going to be raided, and the
friend tipped Anita off.

Anita found the whiskey and hid it. Just about that time,
in came the police captain and said, "You're under arrest,
because you're breaking the law."

Now I was getting so hot that I was just about ready to
shoot somebody with that left-hand-wheeler of mine and I told
that police captain, "Who said so?"

"I said so."

"Well, your word's no prayer book," I said and began to feel for my gun, because I had decided to go down fighting. Just then Anita kicked me under the table.

I hollered, "Why are you kicking me under the table?"

Anita began to laugh and I began to laugh and that policeman must have thought we were both crazy. He said, "Boy, they're going to find you in a ditch dead some day," and he dashed to the place where he thought the liquor was hidden and, when he didn't find it, he began to raise hell. He asked all the customers why they came to a place that was raided all the time. Anita just laughed at him, gave him a drink, and asked him to come back anytime.

Business got bad then and Anita wanted to forget The Jupiter. But I got mad and insisted we hold on to the place. I even arranged for John Taylor, the toughest guy in Frisco, to hang around and protect us. He had beat up the police chief, so I figured he could help us. But Anita managed me, the way she always did.

Diamonds Pinned to My Underwear

●●●She left Frisco one night and went to Seattle without telling me that she was leaving. Then she wired me to come on and join her or she would go on to Alaska without me. That scared me. I was afraid I could never find her in Alaska, so I left The Jupiter just as it was and caught the next train for the state of Washington. Anita met me with a smile, "I didn't want to go to Alaska, baby, just wanted you here."

On the streets of Seattle I ran into Ed Montgomery, an old New Orleans sporting-life friend. Ed was now a big-time gambling man and he brought me into those circles and I started losing money. About the time I got down to my last dime Will Bowman asked me to bring a band into his cabaret in Vancouver, Canada. I sent for Padio, my trombone-playing friend who lived in Oakland. (Poor Padio, he's dead now, never got East so none of the critics ever heard him, but that boy, if he heard a tune, would just start making all kind of snakes around it nobody ever heard before.) I also brought in Oscar Holden, who was no hot man, but played plenty straight clarinet. I had good men, but somehow that cabaret didn't do so good. Folks there didn't understand American-style cabarets. So I took a trio into the Regent Hotel—Doc Hutchinson out of Baltimore on drums and Horace Eubanks,* a beautiful hot clarinet from East St. Louis, who had learned from New Orleans men. It cost my boss $5000 to get Horace across the border, but he was worth it. The Regent did a hell of a business and the other places started ringing hot men in.

Patty Sullivan, the Regent owner, was a big-time gambler. He used to take me along on his trips as a front man—I guess you might say he used me as a decoy the very way I used my piano in my pool-playing days. One trip I left Horace in charge of the band. That fool pulled his stand way up high, pointed his finger at the drummer and hollered, "You the first man to go. Don't miss that beat. All right, boys, let's go."

The drummer threatened to leave, so I had to demote Horace. He took the whole thing as a joke, "If I'm going to be a leader, I'll be a leading son-of-a-gun!" he told me.

Horace had a lot of good offers and pretty soon he quit us. This time I had a hell of a time getting his replacement across the Canadian line. The opposition came from the Canadian Musicians Union. I realized I had to break down these barriers, so I called up Weber, who was president of the union, and threatened to have all the Canadian musicians thrown out of

---

* Jelly Roll later used him in a recording session. See Appendix 2.

the U.S. if he didn't let me alone. He became very nice after
our conversation. Things went well until summer, when busi
ness slacked and I began gambling again.

One night through my boss, Patty, I got hooked up in a
game with some of the biggest gamblers in the country—
Nigger Nate, Chinese Smoke, Guy Harte, Russell Walton,
and Blackie Williams. The smallest bet on the table was $100.
I lost $2000 before I knew what happened. They broke me and
I was sitting there wondering what to do when Bricktop came
in. I asked for a loan and Bricktop said, "All I've got is $10
and I wouldn't loan it to my mother."

Finally Patty gave me $5 and let me ride on his money. He
hit eighteen straight licks and I stayed with him till I had my
$2000 again, when I began to bet for myself. At the end of the
game I had $11,000. A little guy named Jimmy had cleaned
everybody else completely out—and that meant he had to pack
his winnings off in a suitcase; those guys carried their money
in bales.

Anita, who had been running a rooming-house, was feeling
restless, so we sold out, put all our cash into diamonds and
hopped on a boat for Alaska. I wore diamonds pinned to my
underwear all that summer and it was a wonderful vacation. I
got so high on one occasion that I nearly fell into the ocean,
which would have been very bad for me and those diamonds,
as I had never learned to swim. I and Anita were getting along
very, very fine, it seemed to me, but I must not have understood so well.

One night in Tacoma she drank some Worcestershire sauce
with a little whiskey as a chaser and all of a sudden picked up
a great big steak platter and busted it over my head. It took
several strong men to keep her away from me. I got the feeling

she was mad enough to kill me. Next day she was all right, and said she couldn't remember a thing about what she'd done.

We decided to split up for a while. Anita wanted to go back to Los Angeles and I had an offer in Casper, Wyoming. I played a big barn of a place there. Business was bad. The thermometer went down to 45° below and I left for Denver. I played gigs for a time, made some new friends, among them Andy Kirk from Newport, Kentucky, and then ran into my old pal, Gouldstucker from Pensacola. He introduced me to Ben Cooper, the big gambler in that territory, and by May I had lost my $20,000 and all my diamonds. That morning a wire came from Anita in L.A. . . .

NAN AND DAD BOTH AT POINT OF DEATH. MUST UNDERGO OPERATION IMMEDIATELY. COME HOME.
ANITA

I became frantic. I had just thirty cents in my pocket and was ashamed to wire for money. So I decided to hobo. Luck was with me in the shape of a man who wanted me for a dance. I demanded a five-dollar deposit, jived the expressman to haul my trunks to the station by telling him my money was up-town, checked them through to Los Angeles and, when the train pulled out the Denver station, I was riding the blinds. The railroad police put me off at Colorado Springs. I played up some meals on the piano, caught another freight to Pueblo and then another on into L.A. By the time I got home, everybody was well again and I was so mad I raved and hollered and left the house.

. . . Fooled around and organized a band and we played

dates in the Imperial Valley as far south as San Diego. Had a nice set-up at the U.S. Grant Hotel, at least I thought it was okay until I heard their white band was paid double what my boys were getting. Then I pulled my band out of that joint with no notice!

My old friend Bob Rowe put me onto the horses. Before I knew it, I owned one, a nag named Red Cloud. The owner told me, "Red Cloud is the fastest racehorse in the world. You can blindfold him and he can outrun anything on the tracks, by feeling his way along." The truth was that horse couldn't outrun me; he wasn't even a good mule and the officials wouldn't permit him on the track because they claimed I wasn't feeding him. So I had to forget old Red Cloud and the former owners had to forget the $400 they wanted me to pay.

The horses had taken me to a little place called Tia Juana on the borders of Mexico, where I got a job in a place called the Kansas City Bar. Tips ran as high as forty and fifty dollars a night. An old friend, a Negro millionaire out of Oklahoma, owned the place and I taken a fancy to him. I wrote a tune and named it after his bar—*The Kansas City Stomps.*

There was a very pretty little waitress at the Kansas City Bar and I dedicated a new composition to her. This was *The Pearls,* consisting of several sections, each one matching the other and contributing to the total effect of a beautiful pearl necklace. There are very, very few pianists, if any, that can play *The Pearls,* it being the most difficult piece of jazz piano ever written, except for my *Fingerbuster.*

But this good thing had to come to an end. The owner was a very unfortunate gentleman, even though he did have a million dollars. It seems that he had murdered his partner before he left Oklahoma and so the authorities caught up with him and, with all his millions, he had to go to jail for twenty years.

The tracks were treating me very dirty these days and, somehow, my luck in California was running out, due mostly to the moves of my old enemy, George Brown. Some woman in Pasadena was arrested for stealing her employer's furniture and, when the police asked her who was her boy friend, she named me. Down at the jail, when I actually met the woman, she admitted she had never seen me. One of the police told me that it was George that had helped to frame me.

One afternoon while I was playing pool, a policeman named Bobo stuck a gun in my side and told me I was under arrest. I would find out what for in jail. That was on a Monday—I remember it well, because the charge was murder. The day before an old groceryman had been killed on Fourteenth and Central, and the eyewitness, a maid, described somebody who looked exactly like me. This time I had no alibi, but, fortunately, when the maid saw me, she said I was not the man.

Again I discovered that it was George Brown, the half-hand bigshot, who was responsible for naming me. I walked into his place that evening with my hand on my gun. I told George off and I was about to draw, when Bill (Bojangles) Robinson walked in, laid his hand on my arm and said very quietly, "Jelly boy, what's the matter with you? You must be going crazy."

Bill led me out the door and took me home to Anita. A couple of days later, when we were on our way to a show, a cop stopped us and Anita was so rattled by this time, she yelled, "We're going to the theatre, can't you leave us alone."

That cop turned out to be an old friend who just wanted to say hello, and we apologized. But, somehow or another, that was the end of California for me.

It actually came about this way. I was in the music-publishing business with Reb and Johnny Spikes, whom I had met on the stage in the old days. Johnny played piano, and Reb, sax. They could read, but had no ideas. Occasionally I condescended to play with these cornfed musicians. Two of our early tunes became big hits and made the Spikes brothers famous. The first, *Someday Sweetheart*, was my idea and the second, *Wolverine Blues*, was my tune.

The basis of *Someday Sweetheart* was a tune I had learned from an old racetrack friend of mine named Kid North. The Kid at the time was working partners with Bob Rowe, handling his horses for him, as Bob was always kinda sickly. He helped Bob build up the horse, Crowfield, to make an awful lot of money for them both. Kid North was used to money and he was a swell dresser, always wore his clothes very tight across the chest and his word was—"I wouldn't give a dollar and a half for a diamond as big as anybody's hat." He was just a funny sort of guy. He lived in a little house all by himself that he kept to invite the girls to—that is, until he married a beautiful girl named Helen. He particularly named this place of his the Lion's Jaw.

"When they go into the Lion's Jaw, they're cinched," he used to say. "I never let um get away."

So Kid North played a little piano. To tell you the truth about all he could play was this one tune . . .

> *Tricks ain't walkin' no more,*
> *Why they're passing right by that whore,*

I've never seen things so bad before,
'Cause tricks ain't walkin' no more. . . .

Since the Kid knew that I was a writer and we had been friends for quite a while, he told me I could have that tune. As you can see, a part of it was taken for the basis of *Someday Sweetheart.* Of course, my name doesn't appear on that song, but I'm not jealous. I hope the boys write ten million other ones like it, but, since this story is for the Archives where you're supposed to give the facts, the truth may as well come out. The song was practically wrote at the time Reb and I were working together in a cabaret in Oakland, but they left my name off it.

I'm not sore, but I did get hot about how they handled *Wolverine Blues,* which they misnamed because it is not a blues. I first wrote *The Wolverines* in Detroit in the early days.* It was just one of those things that float around in my head and one day, when I sit down at the piano, it comes out of my fingers. The first strain was for trumpet (the basis of one of these new tunes of today, *Flat Foot Floogie*), then the trombone strain,

---

* Johnny St. Cyr remembered Jelly playing *The Wolverines* in New Orleans in 1906. Of course there are two sides of this story; Reb Spikes recalled Jelly's temperament with a chuckle: "He was the most jealous man ever lived. That's when he was funny. When he'd get jealous, he'd hear a piece and say, 'They're stealing that from me. That's mine' or 'That guy's trying to play like me.' Jelly was so jealous he once sued ASCAP. Everybody laughed at him. That was the only time he didn't listen to us. Imagine that—suing ASCAP! Got to think of the other side of it, too. In a way Jelly was right. Colored man can't get a break in this music game. White guys got it all sewed up. Closed corporation."

then I made a harmony strain for the trio, then I found that a
clarinet strain would be very effective, and in the last strain I
put all the instruments in the band together and made the
piano sound as much like a band as possible. The tune got to
be famous around Chicago and Melrose wrote and offered a
$3000 advance for it. Somehow the Spikes brothers got the
letter and jumped up and wrote some words and published my
song as written by Spikes-Morton-Spikes. Right there we had
an argument, because they just wanted to drag me over the
fence, to tell the plain truth. I decided to go on to Chicago and
demand that the tune be changed over to my name, when
Melrose published it. On account of all the things that had
happened around L.A., Anita urged me to leave. So I packed
up and caught a train and since then I never seen either Los
Angeles or Anita again.

Mama Nita

As a composer of melodies, Jelly Roll Morton always remained a Creole, his right hand stroking the treble clef with the intense feeling of a guitarist, evoking bright arpeggios and languorous bursts of song. One of the tenderest of his Creole tunes he called *Mama Nita;* its theme is sensual, yet gentle, reverent, and sad.

Anita Gonzalez, for whom he named the work, was a New Orleans Creole, older than Jelly, always well-to-do and, according to rumor, the person who paid for the diamond in his front tooth. Jelly Roll said, "Anita was the only woman I ever loved." The years have deprived her story of tenderness, and there emerges clearly the man for whom love was a threat and for whom women, especially those he loved, were almost enemies. . . .

. . .

Most everybody, said Anita Gonzales, thinks I met Jelly out
here in California, but the truth is I knew him from New
Orleans. I didn't know at the time that he had any family
because he said he was a foundling from a Catholic home. I had
six brothers and I was the only girl. Jelly used to come over
and see me, making like it was to visit my brothers. I never
give him a second look because he wasn't decent. Used to play
piano in a sporting-house.

When I met him again in California, I didn't know it was
the same man. My brother, Dink Johnson, introduced us again
and then we got together. For a while we were very happy.

I bought a hotel here in Los Angeles, but Jelly was very
jealous and that made things tough for me. Whenever the
front bell would ring, I would have to go to my room so
nobody could see me. He wouldn't let me walk in the hallways
or make up the beds or wait on the customers. So we had to
hire a chambermaid and a clerk. That didn't pay and we sold
out.

Afterwards Jelly and his band played up and down the coast
at dances and cabarets. I went on every job with him. He made
me sit right by the piano and not move or tap my feet or
nothing. And he wouldn't let me dance with anybody. I didn't
want to dance, because I loved him very much. But Jelly was
so jealous he wouldn't have anybody around us, he wouldn't
even ask a man up to dinner.

In my day I was a good ragtime singer and I was always
wanting to sing with the band. One night, playing for Patty
Sullivan's Club in Vancouver, the girl singer got sick and,
before Jelly could stop me, I went up and started singing and
dancing. Right there Jelly quit playing and, because he was

the leader, the rest of the band stopped playing, too, but I kept straight on with my song. When I finished, there was stacks of money on the floor. Jelly was furious. He dragged me outside and made me swear never to sing or dance again, but don't think he hit me. Jelly was a perfect gentleman.

You married? I wonder if you can say the same thing, because there's very few that can.

Well, we had a misunderstanding and he left for Chicago in 1922. He told me, "Baby, I don't think I can live away from you. I'd want to die first." He said he would send for me and I waited. Then he wrote to me that he had a thousand dollars and when he got two, he'd send for me. Then he got sick. He never did send. He went and took up with another woman. But I was the only woman he ever loved.

INTERLUDE THREE

Hello, Central, Give Me
Doctor Jazz

Five years was a long time in the young life of New Orleans jazz. Between 1917 and 1922, while Jelly Roll played around with "the higher-ups" of the West Coast, he lost touch with the ripening company of New Orleans hot musicians, a subtle human contact broken and never quite renewed. Not that his music lagged behind theirs—as a composer, he was absolutely pre-eminent for a decade more. Yet his was a lonely eminence, for the boys in the bands were beginning to express emotions which Jelly Roll did not share, because he had not shared in their common experiences.

On November 14, 1917, the mayor of New Orleans closed down Storyville on orders from the secretary of the navy, who apparently considered the tenderloin a sort of domestic torpedo aimed at the underbelly of the armed forces. While the madams removed their girls into better neighborhoods and quietly resumed trade, honky-tonk business slumped and the jazzmen were on the street. Many dropped out of the music business for good. Some went back to their old trades for a bit—"I just went on back to plastering. . . ." "Picked up my cotton hook and right down on the river again. . . ." Others swung on board the steamers of the Streckfus Excursion Lines, playing in those highly disciplined but red-hot bands that informed every town along the Mississippi of the new American music. ·

As the red lights went out in Storyville, the money and the glory finally departed New Orleans. The grand procession of wedding-cake riverboats and snake-hipped lumber rafts had long since petered out into a trickle of drab barges. The railroads had put the Crescent City and her river on the antique list and had elected Chicago, the rail hub, capital of the great valley. So the word went down the line—"Man, Chicago is the money town, and listen, you can be a man in Chicago." Eventually most competent jazzmen caught the northbound Illinois Central.

The shift of New Orleans musicians to Chicago was only a grace note in a big movement. The factories and mills of

war-time America needed fresh supplies of labor and for the
first time were hiring great numbers of Negroes. Those factory
whistles cried freedom to the black masses down in Dixie,
impoverished by sharecropping and segregation. They left
their mules in the cotton rows; they ceded to Mister Jim Crow
his unpaved back alleys. And, unmoved by either the promises
or the threats of their white bosses, who, suddenly concerned
for their health, told them they would die of homesickness in
cruel, cold Yankeeland, they headed North in one of the remarkable migrations of human history. In five years a half
million Negroes moved North, one-tenth of them settling in
Chicago's South Side.

Thus the jazzmen of New Orleans found in Chicago an
audience of newly independent Negroes, fresh from South
U.S.A., hungry for Southern Negro music and able to pay for
it. Negroes with cash money in their jeans every Saturday
night, Negroes who were called Mister and Missus every day
in the week—when these folk heard the triumphant and happy
New Orleans marches leap out of the trumpet of King Oliver,
when they heard their own deep song, the blues, voiced in
gold by a big band, they began to shout. From that moment
jazz was no longer a New Orleans specialty; it became the
music of the whole Negro people, asserting their new-found
confidence and reflecting, presently, the novel ironies of their
harsh lives in city slums and heavy industry. So The Royal
Garden, Dreamland, The Pekin, The Elite and other gaudy
Southside ginmills and dance halls rocked to the stomps and
blues of Oliver and Keppard, Dodds and Bechet, Perez and St.
Cyr.

All this loud, happy music, especially the charming ringing

of the cash registers, did not fail to attract the attention of other Chicagoans.

At the fringes of the South Side crowds stood a gang of music-hungry, life-hungry white kids. Mezz Mezzrow, who was one of these white urchins, has described how he felt the first time he heard New Orleans music—"That was my big night, the night I really began to live. . . . My mind kept telling me that this was where I really belonged. I had found my utopia and I began scheming to come back every night, including Sundays and holidays. . . ."*

These Chicago high-school kids hung around the bandstands of the South Side, soaking it in, then went and tried the jazz idea out for themselves, as the white New Orleans Dixielanders had done a few years earlier. They did well; not only were they talented, they were the right color. Maybe the blacks played jazz better and hotter, but when you looked up on the bandstand you wanted to see a bunch of nice-looking white guys. So, as soon as white bands could play jazz, they tended in most cases to get the big hotel bookings. There were still jobs for the colored combinations, but within a few years Bix Beiderbecke, Benny Goodman, Gene Krupa, Eddie Condon and their followers would have the money and the fame while old Doctor Jazz died hard in Atlanta and his boys were still scuffling in the honky-tonks.

In later years, some of the lesser Chicagoans even learned to draw the Jim Crow line, refusing to sit on a bandstand with

---

* Mezz Mezzrow and Bernard Wolfe, *Really the Blues* (New York: Random House, 1946.)

the very Negro musicians from whom they had learned the business. Whether Jelly Roll suffered this affront, he was too proud to say. He confined his criticism of the Chicagoans to their frantic jam sessions which he felt had cheapened jazz. . . . "Some people play like they want to knock your eardrums down."

As the sweet orchestral crying of the blues filled the smoky air at the Royal Gardens, another group of musicians sat at ringside tables, some puzzled and not yet sure what to do, others making hurried notes. Here were the fly boys of the burgeoning entertainment industry . . . the band leaders trying to keep track of King Joe and King Louis, who played different trumpet choruses every night just to baffle them. Eddie Cantor sat there, banjo-eyed—near neighbor to Al Jolson, who was picking up what he could. Remember Jolson later made a million-dollar success out of *The Jazz Singer,* a picture without a note of jazz in eight reels? Paul Whiteman, of the king-size orchestra, held court there. In a couple of years he would crown himself King of Jazz by adding a couple of bored hot men to his elephantine band.

The Victor and Columbia Gramophone companies had not yet sent official scouts (they were much too dignified to notice jazz in the early 1920's) but their outriders, the scouts of the smaller companies, hovered in the offing . . . Ink Williams, then of Paramount, later to own a catalogue of thousands of tunes, one of which he composed . . . The Melrose Brothers, in for publishing hot tunes in a small way, bringing a recording machine to capture those hot choruses of Louis Armstrong's . . . Jack Kapp, scout for Vocalion, later president of Decca. This crowd stayed close in to the bandstand, excited by the music, knowing a good thing, eager to make a dollar.

Back in the shadows sat even more blasé white listeners, gentlemen who traveled in casual but wary bunches, wore sharp clothes and snap-brim hats, bulged at hip and armpit, and drank only "the amber." This music suited them fine. It said, The world is a screwy place, but who the hell cares? It was lonesome. It was frantic, this New Orleans hot stuff, especially the Dixieland variety, and it went down with them, for gangsters, too, are outcasts. Besides, they had a proprietary interest: they owned or protected the joints that the hot men were packing with customers.

Most old-time Chicago jazzmen remembered working for Capone or one of the mobsters. They recalled that it was often unhealthy to quit one of those jobs, if the boss said stay. They told about the trumpetman on a job where business was good. A bid to Hollywood came. The boss said "No" and the horn-blower stalled the offer for six months. When he was finally allowed to resign, the mobsters presented him with a diamond-studded watch. As he was packing in his hotel room, two of the gang came by, beat him up, and retrieved their sentimental memento. His wife, who had been slapped around a bit in the fun, at last understood why a bodyguard always sat with her when she visited her husband on his job.

This is not an unusual story in the world of jazz. In this period gangsters operated many nightclubs where hot music flourished, indeed they were its most loyal patrons, keeping the great hot men working while the tides of the entertainment business shifted and changed. Too much has been written about jazz as the direct reflection of the post-war, prohibition era, and too little about the extra-musical influences upon it—the Procrustean demands of the music "business," the gangster control, and the power of certain figures who went into the "legitimate" music business when the rackets got too hot.

This subject used to send Jelly Roll into a passion, but he never forgot himself so far as to name names. Of course his annoyance had nothing to do with truth or beauty. He simply could not compete with these Chicago higher-ups in the rackets, and this he apparently discovered on his arrival. The town was sewed up tight and his familiar sidelines were out. For the first time in years Jelly Roll was forced, to his great annoyance and to our good fortune, to devote himself exclusively to music.

Jelly Roll never accepted such limitations with good grace. As his Chicago publisher put it, "Jelly Roll was not a good old-time Southern darkey like Joe Oliver." He must have talked back loud and long to the racketeers. If they were too fond of his music to kill him, they were not so charitable as to allow him to make his mark in the ginmill circuit. The word went around town that it was unhealthy to work with Jelly—a band leader whose ambitions extended beyond the music stand. The way the boys in the bands put it—"That Jelly Roll is too *notoriety*." So Jelly Roll Morton, who organized some of the finest recording and touring bands of the '20's, never held an orchestral job in Chicago.

Still Jelly must have smiled to himself that May evening of 1923, when he hit the windy city on the lake. Everywhere he went he heard New Orleans jazz rolling like sweet thunder. His riffs, his ideas—Keppard's ideas—Bolden's drive—the march tunes that set you dancing in the street—the lazy sweets of the blues out of the cornucopias of horns—the bands were really fine. King Oliver's, Cooke's, Jimmy Noone's and lots more were playing good music and established in the best

places. Jelly lay low and listened, according to habit, looking
for his angle, planning how he could start at the top where he
belonged. He needed money right away for new clothes and to
send for Anita.

. . . Jazz might be a big business at last, with maybe millions in it. The Melrose Brothers must have thought so or they
wouldn't have wired such a big advance for *The Wolverines.*
And they were playing *The Wolverines* all wrong, with a heavy
old-fashioned street-band beat. . . . Jelly thought of the shifting, dancing cross-rhythms of his new compositions. He could
show them all how. Writing the music down, organizing it,
systematizing it, selling it so the whole world could play New
Orleans style—that was the way to cash in and lead the pack.

Jelly's grin grew wider as he stood at the entrance of the
Melrose Brothers Music Store. . . . "There was a great big
banner hung out front—

WOLVERINE BLUES SOLD HERE

—and I could hear one of the Melrose boys trying to play my
tune. . . . He was clunking those feet so loud you could hear
him clear across the street.

"Naturally, Mr. Melrose was very, very glad to see me. I sat
down and started plugging *Wolverines.* Soon we had musicians
hanging around and before long the crowds were stopping
traffic."

. . . Jelly Roll made his entrance into the Melrose establishment so dramatic that Lester Melrose still remembered it
vividly after twenty-five years. "A fellow walked into our store
with a big red bandana around his neck and a ten-gallon
cowboy hat on his head and hollered, 'Listen, everybody, I'm

Jelly Roll Morton from New Orleans, the originator of jazz!'
He talked for an hour without stopping about how good he
was and then he sat down at the piano and proved he was every
bit as good as he claimed and better. That was when Jelly Roll
got his start."

Jelly Roll, on the other hand, felt this moment had "made"
the Melrose Brothers.

"The Melrose boys had been trying to get into the music
business for some time," said Jelly. "They had worked hard
with *Sugar Babe,* but it had not been a success. With *Wolverine
Blues* they made enough to get them started. So we were in
business together for some years . . . I even had to teach
Melrose how to play because he couldn't do much more than
plunk away in F sharp. . . ." It was Jelly's idea that one
should be an accomplished musician or at least a person of
some talent to succeed in the music business. It continued to
be his feeling that if you created the music, you should also
reap the profits. No matter how often or how stubbornly life
showed that these were simple-minded notions and that he was
wrongheaded and immoral to cling to them, he never could
give them up. Naturally, his stubborn refusal to accept and
appreciate the business order of things caused him to be misunderstood and even disliked.

In his eyes the Melrose Brothers were a couple of nice young
fellows from Kentucky who needed a break. Lester had tried
out for catcher on the White Sox, but, failing there, had gone
to work as a $10-a-week clerk at Marshall Field's. Walter, who
took after his mother and liked to play piano, found his metier
when he rented a garage-front across from the Tivoli Movie
Palace and started a little music store, calling Lester in to help.
Jesse Crawford used to tip the boys off about the tunes he

planned to feature on his organ program; thus they stocked up
and sold what they stocked. One day Ted Lewis told them
about the new Negro music and they began hanging around
the South Side, looking for their opportunity. They claim to
have been the first to suggest King Oliver's band and the New
Orleans Rhythm Kings to the Gennet Record Company. "The
records sold like crazy," which caused the Melrose boys to
become very, very interested in jazz. It was at this moment
that Morton galloped into their store.

"Those Melrose Brothers just had a little old dirty shop until
Jelly came along. His tunes made them millions," one old-time
Chicago musician observed. "After Melrose began publishing
those numbers for Jelly Roll and other colored artists, he began
to click," said another hornblower who was there and saw what
he saw. When I quoted these remarks to Lester Melrose, he got
mad. "Listen, mister," he said with the veins standing out on
his heavy neck and his face flushing with rage, "Jelly Roll
wouldn't have been nothing if it hadn't been for Melrose. We
made Jelly and we made all the rest of them. We made the
blues. After all, we are here and where are they? Nowhere."

Certainly time and tax assessments argue that Lester is right.
The Melrose boys had comfortable homes and fat bank accounts;
they had got somewhere. Bunk Johnson died in poverty down
in New Iberia—Louis Nelson, on charity in New Orleans
—King Oliver without a dime in Georgia—most of the blacks
who created jazz died broke or had to quit jazz to keep from
starving to death—that's "nowhere." Even the great Ellington
band never had a long-run radio show in the great days of radio.

It was more profitable to publish and own music than it was
to compose or play it—Jelly Roll was beginning to see that.
Therefore he resolved to throw in his lot with the Melrose

boys. The money was in records, sheet music and band book-
ing—and great musicians like Oliver weren't making it. You
had to be in business. Like so many blacks up until recently,
Jelly Roll felt he needed a white man, like Melrose, to talk for
him in business deals. In the twenties, blacks still did not
know business and business did not know them, and go-
betweens were often useful. There were some legitimate record
producers, like Frank Walker of Victor, who were truly devoted to black music, and did a great deal to sell the tunes and
talent of the black ghettos to the record companies, linking
the folk-jazz half-world to the super-respectable and stuffy
world of the music business.

Although the big corporations were slow to respond ("Victor's manager threw me out of his office when I first proposed
the hot idea," said Walter Melrose), they took a firm hold on
the jazz field when they did enter it. Thus, when King Oliver
and Jelly Roll Morton encountered the Melrose boys and the
Melrose boys went to the record companies, the first step in
the ultimate big-corporation control and exploitation of jazz
had been taken. As the years rolled up the profits, the Melrose
boys, in their turn, began to have a grievance.

"I never got paid a penny of salary from the big companies
as a talent scout," said Lester Melrose. "I took my chances on
some of the tunes I recorded being hits, and I wouldn't record
anybody unless he signed all his rights in those tunes over to
me." (Until a short time ago this was the accepted, if not the
completely open, practice of the record industry in dealing
with rural or black artists, who seldom even knew what a
copyright was. Even Jelly Roll said, "I never paid attention to
copyrights those days because I had a thousand great ideas and
I knew I could always come up with new material.")

Lester went on, "Well, I reckon I own about three thousand tunes, most of them blues"—this gentleman who couldn't read or perform or even sing a note of music—"and you know what those so-and-so's did to me?" Lester's voice rose in a wail, "I sold one thousand and four hundred tunes in my catalogue to a certain music corporation and they never paid me a nickel. Now they just laugh at me when I call them!"

The Melrose boys were only little fish in a shark-infested sea. Nevertheless, Jelly Roll mistook them when he saw them as "nice polite Southern boys who needed a break." While he was "helping" them, they were helping themselves to large slices of his tunes. In return, Walter Melrose explained with the myopic self-importance so familiar to his trade, "We did a lot to build him up. We published his tunes. We got him a Victor contract. And he lived off his royalties," adding, "I'll have to hand it to him. That guy was prolific. He could go home and produce overnight."

Jelly Roll was thirty-eight in 1933, an old man in the jazz field, but he turned out new compositions with the fire and energy of a youngster. During the next decade he composed and arranged almost a hundred original works of jazz* in which the New Orleans idea was, for the first time, set forth clearly in musical notation. Not only did he compose hits, but many of his compositions became standard in the jazz repertory, the whole mass of his ideas forming the basis of the universal hot language, intoned by every band and written by all arrangers. The trouble was, perhaps, that he never let anybody forget that.

* See Appendix 1.

"Jelly Roll was a man," said one of his old Chicago friends, "who could talk himself right into a million-dollar proposition and talk himself right out again. Jelly Roll," the speaker paused and smiled, "of all his mother's children, he loved Jelly Roll the best. I remember one incident at the Melrose Music House. Jelly Roll was playing one of his latest compositions—a very good number—and he look over at Melrose and ask him, say, 'How you like that one?'

"So Melrose say, 'That's good, Jelly.'

" 'Good, hell,' Jelly Roll say, 'That's perfect!' "

"About that time another guy walked in; he knew Jelly good, wanted to get his kicks and said, 'Jelly Roll, they tell me you're the best stomp player in town.'

"And Jelly Roll tells him, 'The best in town—I'm the best in the world!' Funny part, Jelly was the best we had, even greater than Oliver in those years of the '20's, I'd say, but talk like that made him unpopular."

If Jelly's Creole swagger bothered his familiars, it made Southerners like Melrose a shade more than uncomfortable. As dry-spoken Walter expressed it, "He was a poor salesman for himself. A fine guy, but he talked too much." So both the brothers Melrose deprecated Jelly even as they praised him; and they praised him in such contradictory ways that they might have been describing two musicians. Lester, the completely unmusical blues magnate, described Jelly Roll as a superior folk artist with a low level of musical literacy.

"I believe he overshadowed Oliver in his time," said Lester. "Old Jelly was a good orchestra man, but he couldn't write music [not so!]; we had to have an arranger take down his stuff. Jelly led the way on account of his piano, the best at the time we ever heard, and we heard them all. No piano player could touch him in his years from 1923 through 1928. Then he left us and went to New York, got around those high-falutin' guys and got away from his original way of playing." Actually Jelly's piano style never changed basically during his whole career, except that in later years it became simpler and closer to the style of the folk blues.

More musical than Lester, Walter Melrose wrote off his sense of obligation to Morton in another way. According to him, Jelly Roll, while prolific, was not an innovator. "Jelly Roll could write music, don't let them kid you. He made his piano copies and we turned them over to Elmer Schoebel and Mel Stitzel to orchestrate. Sales on those orchestrations, particularly *Milneburg Joys,* were really terrific, because the New Orleans Rhythm Kings played the tune and *they* were big all over the country. . . . But, so far as Jelly Roll originating anything, he didn't do that. All Jelly did was to come along and write additional numbers in the style that goes back to Scott Joplin in the '90's. Scott Joplin was his God; and, really, things like *Maple Leaf Rag* and *Grace and Beauty* were his models. Jelly always worked with two twelve-bar strains, modulating into trio, just like Joplin. . . ." There is just enough truth in this observation to make it plausible. Jelly Roll's music, like all early jazz, reflects the influence of Scott Joplin; but it is astonishing that Melrose, after living off Jelly's brilliance for years, would deny the important differences. As I listened to his sour comments, my dislike of this man grew.

"Jelly was a prolific writer," Walter Melrose went on drily. "And his numbers, some of them, did pretty well." (This is rather faint praise from the publisher of twenty-six Morton tunes, among them: *King Porter Stomp,* Goodman's big hit,

Dead Man Blues, Oliver's big hit, and *Milneburg Joys*, everybody's big hit.)* "He never was able to get a band together
and get the bigger jobs. So far as how he rated, well, Joe
Oliver was the most important musician in Chicago between
1921 and 1930. Joe was more the old Southern-type nigger.
Like Handy. Didn't want any trouble with anybody."

As he reached out for status, Morton had printed cards,
reading, *Jelly Roll Morton, composer and arranger for Melrose Music Company*, but Walter hastily denied the tie-up. "Oh no, *of
course* he didn't work for us. He used to come around sometimes to talk about numbers. That's all."

So drily and coldly Walter Melrose summed up his rela-
tionship to his star composer. The heartbreaking part of all
this is that Walter was the nearest thing Jelly had to a friend.
"When I came to visit Ferd in 1925," said his sister, "Melrose
was the only friend he had in town. At least he was the only
person Ferd took me to see."

Two years had gone by and still things had not panned out
so that he could send for Anita. Morton had fallen ill. Unable
to endure his loneliness, he sent for his younger sister to come
and nurse him. Yet even this member of his family he kept at
a distance.

"I never did find out what was the matter with him," she
recalled. "He put me up with some folks he knew and kept on
living in an old flat at the Baldwin Apartments. He had written he needed a nurse, but he would never let me come to his
room. Seems like he didn't want me to see and know anything.
All I know is he went out to work at some nightspot—I don't

---

* See Appendix 1.

know which one or what he did there because he never took me on the job—and come right back home and get in bed and sleep all day. He said his nerves were shot to pieces."

Somehow of all the stories about Morton, this anecdote of his sister's is the most shocking and melancholy. His pride would never allow him to admit to any woman, not even his sister, that he had not achieved the impossible goals he had set himself. He could not permit even his sister to come close and comfort him. Yet he trusted no woman out of his sight. His young sister spoke of her Chicago trip with bitterness.

"I thought he was sending for me to show me a nice time in Chicago," she said. "But I didn't get to see nothing much except what he wanted me to see. He demanded that I be home at eight or nine o'clock, told me I was too young to be out in Chicago at night. A whole lot of New Orleans musicians were in town, but Jelly never seemed to go around them. About all he would do was take me riding in his old piece of a Marmon car that wasn't running half the time. And, once or twice he came by and played for me. Of course, I just loved to hear him play. But I thought it was a mighty funny sort of visit. . . . I remember one thing he told me, 'There's only two of you left in the family down home. Stick together. Remember, you must take the bitters with the sweet.' "

If any man ever lived who knew how to produce the sweet out of the bitters, it was Jelly Roll Morton. During these lonely years in Chicago when he was trying to scrape together "that second thousand" so that he could send for Anita, he set down in notes the flower of his compositions, realizing at last the musical plans that had taken form in his mind in

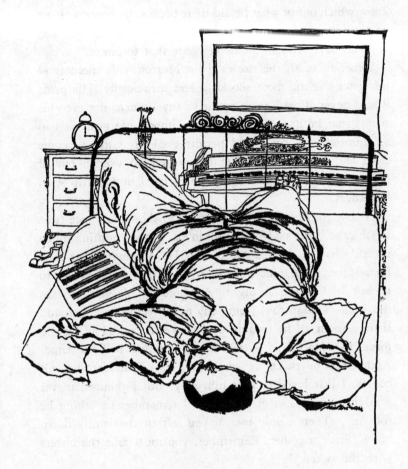

Storyville, and by organizing and leading Jelly Roll Morton and his Red Hot Peppers, he produced the finest recordings of New Orleans music ever made. There may be more deeply emotional and moving jazz records than *Black Bottom Stomp, Doctor Jazz, Sidewalk Blues, Grandpa's Spells, Shreveport, Turtle Twist,* but none more subtly designed and brilliantly executed, none with such a rich rhythmic and harmonic texture, none touched with such true fire. All these tunes and more he recorded for Victor and other recording companies. He was much sought after, much respected, and well paid. In these sessions, Jelly Roll, an equally remarkable composer, orchestral leader and pianist, purifies and extends New Orleans hot tradition, while strictly abiding by its canons. His records outnumber his published compositions almost two to one, but, with a half dozen exceptions, all are his own tunes, a recording career topped by no one in jazz except the redoubtable Ellington. From the very first session these discs exhibit a harmonic finesse and a rhythmic variety which outshine those of other leaders and arrangers of that day.

In these records Morton was faced with a twofold problem, somewhat unfamiliar to composers in other fields. In order to speak his musical thoughts clearly, not only did he have to write the music and assemble men who could play together with the virtuosity and the imagination that his New Orleans compositions required, but he also had to discipline a roomful of temperamental Creole virtuosos. In all these respects this loneliest of the lone wolves, this friendless, sick, and almost paranoid man measured up. The men who played with him on those early Victor recording sessions never forgot.

Omer Simeon, born in Chicago of New Orleans Creole

parents, instructed on the clarinet by old Lorenzo Tio himself, remembered . . .

"I met Jelly at the musician's union and the first thing I noticed was that big diamond in his tooth. Jelly told me he wanted to use me on a recording session. I knew he was a bigshot and one of the pioneers of jazz, so I was real excited. 'You're going to compete with Benny Goodman. In fact, I believe you're better than him.'—That's what Jelly always told me." (Indeed, Jelly did regard Simeon as the finest of all jazz clarinet players.)

"Those people at Victor treated Jelly like he was somebody special, which he was, being the best in the country at the time in his style, and they paid us boys a good deal over scale to work with him. . . . See, Jelly Roll was mighty particular about his music and if the musicians couldn't play real New Orleans, he'd get somebody else."

It is a very rare experience to come close to the creative process itself. The next few paragraphs bring us very close. In them Simeon and St. Cyr describe the technique by means of which Jelly produced the best-recorded performances in jazz.

"I'll tell you how he was in rehearsing a band," Simeon went on. "He was exact with us. Very jolly, very full of life all the time, but serious. We used to spend maybe three hours rehearsing four sides and in that time he'd give us the effects he wanted, like the background behind a solo—he would run that over on the piano with one finger and the guys would get together and harmonize it. . . .

"The solos—they were ad lib. We played according to how we felt. Of course, Jelly had his ideas and sometimes we'd listen to them and sometimes, together with our own, we'd make something better. For me, I'd do whatever he wanted. In other words I just cooperated with him, where a lot of the fellows wouldn't. It was my first big break."

Giving cues to a roomful of New Orleans jazzmen was just about as risky and sometimes as useless as telling so many bullfighters how to execute their faenas. But in Chicago, at least, Jelly was working with musicians who respected him. Among them was Johnny St. Cyr, the great New Orleans string man who set many Chicago sessions on fire. Johnny felt more independent than Simeon, but his respect for Jelly Roll was no less. Having played with both King Oliver and Morton, Johnny knew which man was more capable.

"Now Jelly was a very, very agreeable man to cut a record with and I'll tell you why. . . . He'd never give you any of your specialties, he'd leave it to your own judgment, say, 'You take a break here,' . . . and 'Clarinet'll take a break here.' That's what cause his records to have more variety than you find on Joe Oliver's records, for an instance. See, Joe, he got on the strictly legitimate side when he got to recording. It had to be just so with him and that cause the men to be working under a tension and they couldn't give vent to their feelings, as they would like to.

"But Jelly Roll would ask me, 'Can you make a break here?'

"I tell him, 'Okay.'

"He say, 'All right, we going over it. Now when we get there, you make the break. Okay, let's take it.'

"Just let your conscience be your guide, see," Johnny went on. "If you sounded good, all right. If you didn't sound so good, he'd say 'Wait a minute, that don't sound so good, see if you can't make something else.'

"You'd try something else and get something that sounded good to him. Or, if you couldn't get the idea right then, why he'd give the break to someone else.

" 'You try it on the clarinet,' or 'You try it on the trumpet.'

"Reason his records are so full of tricks and changes is the liberty he gave his men. Sometimes we ask *him—we* get an idea, see—and we ask him to let us play a certain break, and he was always open for suggestions. . . ."

"Always open for suggestions"—this characterization is hard to associate with Mister Jelly Roll. Yet it is evident in St. Cyr's and Simeon's stories that Jelly knew how to gentle his temperamental New Orleans virtuosos into playing exactly what *he* wanted while giving them full credit as creators of their own solos. Apparently, when the musicians were men whom he could respect, when there was a real bouquet of New Orleans in the studio, Jelly Roll became a great leader.

His records (beginning with his piano rolls of 1920 on to his Victor orchestra sessions in 1929) are always ahead of the best records of other musicians of the same years. A clear conviction emerges from long listening to Jelly Roll Morton—with all his failings and his clichés, he was the most creative and original figure in the golden decade of hot records.

In one important respect, however, Morton fell short of his fellows—he was not moaning the blues, the lost and homeless, the freezing-ground-was-my-folding-bed-last-night blues —he was not protesting against the way things were run, because within himself he accepted Jim Crow, economic inequality, frustration and his own eternal insecurity as part of the natural order of things. In this respect he does not belong in the company of great hot jazzmen. He did not feel the blues, because he always refused to admit he was black and that he was lonely. Yet one of his friends remarked, "Jelly's got no folks and never had. . . . Always said he was too busy to get married."

By the late twenties the golden simoleons began rolling in. His Red Hot Pepper Band often played the best college and hotel dates in the Middle West—one of the first bands managed by the then young but already thriving Music Corporation of America. Victor Records advertised him as the "Number One Hot Band." Royalty checks swelled bigger every quarter as if they would never stop growing. Anita was long gone and New Orleans was buried by the avalanche of time. "Good, hell, you're perfect," those frantic years said to Jelly and to every successful American. Life was a succession of big deals. How big were your diamonds, how thick was your roll, how did the headwaiter treat you? If there were other questions, who should know the answers better than the man leading the jazz band. Night after night, the faces turned toward him, the white possessive faces of the girls, the prematurely gin-ripened and apoplectic faces of college boys; the faces followed him on the bandstand while he called for the answer . . .

Hello, Central, give me Doctor Jazz.
He's got what I need, I'll say he has.
When the world goes wrong
And I got the blues,
He's the man who make me
Get out both my dancing shoes!

The more I get, the more I want it seems,
I page old Doctor Jazz in all my dreams.
When I'm in trouble bound and mixed,
He's the guy that gets me fixed.
*Hello, Central, give me Doctor Jazz.**

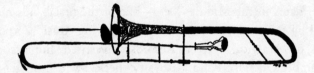

---

* *Doctor Jazz*, by King Oliver, lyrics reproduced by permission of copyright owner, Melrose Music Company, 1927.

THE BITTERS
WITH THE
SWEET

Mabel

One night in 1927 Mister Jelly Roll strolled into the Plantation Club in Chicago and sat back sipping his champagne, absently watching the show. Something about one of the girls, an octoroon specialty dancer, caught his roving eye. He signaled the manager. "Who's the little lady?" he asked. "Oh, that's Mabel, Mister Morton." "Well, you tell Mabel I'm gonna come back in here and kidnap her sometime," and Jelly Roll paid his bill and rolled away down his lonesome road. But the little octoroon wouldn't let him alone.

Her name was Mabel Bertrand. Jelly Roll wrote a tune for her, querulously dedicating it to "Fussy Mabel," yet Mabel, of all who knew Morton, most appreciated and loved him. Born in New Orleans, raised in a convent, she was courted by him at a nightclub table, mighty uncomfortable because she was

nine-tenths naked and knew exactly what this Creole man was
thinking. She married him, although he had sworn he was too
busy ever to marry. She lived with him for twelve years of
poverty and defeat and rejection; and, at the end, she still
loved him.

In the 1940's her face had a little gray and puzzled look,
but, when she spoke of Jelly Roll, the vagueness departed and
her strong and sweet Creole voice, which did not complain,
cried out of a welter of Harlem tenements—"I have been loved
by a great man, I have watched a genius at work in the cold,
lonely hours."

Perhaps this might have sounded melodramatic to plain,
brave Mabel Morton, a good union member, a faithful Catholic, singled out, who knows whether by fortune or misfortune, as the companion of Jelly Roll Morton. She watched his
struggles, she helped as she could, and she was the only one
who cared that he was hurt. So it is Mabel who now will carry
Mister Jelly's story on to its strange and terrifying end . . .

I met Jelly when I was working at the club in Chicago,
Mabel began. As soon as he saw me he said he was going to
kidnap me, but that took some time, it really did.

"You know, I can't make you out," he said. "I've conversed
with you and you have traveled quite a bit, you've had experience in the theatrical business, but you're different, you're
very different. Where are you from, anyway?"

"I'm from New Orleans," I told him.

"What, New Orleans? Where did you live?"

"On Rampart Street."

"Why, we're from the same parish. Did you go to school
there?"

I told him about the nunnery and I told him who my father was. "Why, yeah, I heard of Dr. Bertrand. Now I see how you're different. I see why I can't make any headway with you."

"Not like that," I said. "I'm making okay and I'm perfectly happy. Some make more but their ways are different than mine."

"From New Orleans, well, hey!"

"Yes, from old New Orleans," I told him.

You see, my father was French, said Mabel Bertrand Morton, and my mother was an Indian from Shawnee, Oklahoma. I was born in the French section of New Orleans on Rampart Street where my father, Dr. Bertrand, had his doctor's office. How he happened to meet my mother, he came to Shawnee to learn about the different herbs the Indians knew. He studied all that, then he asked for my mother to travel with him to demonstrate the Indian cures, and from that he fell in love with my mother and he married her. Then she couldn't go back to Shawnee because she lost her membership in the tribe. Anyway she was happy to come with him to New Orleans and live.

My father died when I was very young and I was put into boarding school until I was fifteen. My mother died two years later and left me all alone. . . . In those days I was a real cute little thing—weighed about ninety pounds—and I decided to go to New York and try the theatrical business.

That's just what I did. I came to New York and met a man named Billy Arnat and he taught me to sing and dance. I remember he used to switch me on my legs and say, "Move that right foot, Mabel. It's still in church. It's gotta move, too."

Well, Billy and I worked up an act together and we toured Europe. I had the pleasure on that tour of entertaining Queen Victoria and King Edward at Buckingham Palace. We did our Swanee River routine. I had on a white silk top, a pleated candy-stripe taffeta skirt down to my knees and ballet slippers, and they gave me a bracelet that said, "God be with us till we meet again," but it got away from me.

Billy and I played the "Follies Brassiere" in Paris. We toured Cuba and Mexico. We even went to Hong Kong. Then we returned to the Palace Theatre for an audition and out of there booked the entire Keith Circuit. In the wintertime we played the big theatres in the North and in summer the small theatres upstate.

Now this Billy, he began to insist that I marry him, and I—as he was much older than I—I told him that wasn't no part of our agreement. He could take all the money and pay me my salary, but what chance in life would I have with a man so much older? I was eighteen at the time.

He began to resent any small attention anybody would pay me. Finally, in Oklahoma City, I went to the head chief of the Shawnees and asked for protection. After the chief had talked to Billy and saw Billy wouldn't talk sense, he took me out to the reservation and hid me for a couple of months till the whole thing blew over.

I must admit Billy had been good to me. He used to pay a hundred and fifty for a costume anytime I wanted a new one, and he put three diamonds in my teeth, like the one half-carat Jelly always wore. That was a common thing with theatrical people at the time. Billy had three himself. Baby Cox had one. Butterbeans and Susie had them. Just something of the theatrical business.

Well, I did my tap numbers in a lot of shows after that—
"The Blackbirds" and then, with Florence Mills, "From Dixie
to Broadway." "Shuffle Along," I was in that. Worked in the
7-11 Club. Some summers I toured the South with my own
plantation show, trained my own acts, and helped manage the
show. I did well in the theatrical business, and when Jelly met
me, I had a job in the best club in Chicago.

That evening he asked me over to his table after my number, of course I was very, very much impressed, although I
thought he was just kidding me along. He was very pretty and
he had on the best clothes you ever saw. When he sat down,
he took out three or four thousand dollars and laid it on the
table. I said, "Somebody will stick you up." He just laughed
at me, "Not with this big .45 I have under my coat. Just let
anyone touch it," he said. "Let um touch it, I'm not afraid."

So Jelly wanted to take me out for a drive after work and I
said, "The only place for me is to go home and get a shower
and a rubdown in alcohol and go to bed."

"Aw naw, I'll take you out in my big Lincoln car and let the
cool air blow on you," he said.

I told him, "No, I still have the teaching of my mother. A
man is not going to give me anything unless he's looking for
something in return. That's a known fact. When I'm on the
floor entertaining and you give me money, that's a different
thing; but, when you say you're going to put something in my
stocking, I know you're looking for something in return."

He told me he didn't like for me to be out there dancing in
that short costume of mine in front of all those guys. I told
him that was my profession, so what did it matter to him.

He said, "I'm coming back for you."

I just laughed—"A man making fifteen or sixteen hundred

a day. That's out of the question for you to be interested in a little nightclub entertainer like myself. Why, you can marry almost anybody."

Anyhow, I thought he was just stringing me along. Then I didn't hear from him no more until one night the phone at my hotel rang. . . .

"Hello?"

"Hello, who's this?" I said. I had already taken my shower and was about to go to bed and I had left strict orders no one was to call. I guess he paid the bellhop, maybe twenty dollars—money didn't mean anything to him—and a bellhop will do anything for twenty dollars, practically burn the hotel down.

"Don't you remember?" he said. "This is one of your many admirers. You had an appointment for me to come up tonight."

"You don't have any appointment with me. I think you have the wrong number. What's your name?"

"Jimmy. Don't you remember I was sitting at the table with you tonight."

"Well, let me tell you, Jimmy. I don't know you and I'm very tired and very sleepy and I'm going to bed." And I banged the phone.

Then it rang again and this was five o'clock in the morning. I told him, "I'm going to get in touch with the house detective and I'm going to find out who's allowing you to call me at this hour of the morning."

I could hear him laughing when he hung up. He told me later on he was just trying to test me, every way. If he could have just slipped a fifty-dollar bill in my stocking, he said, we might have had one night of supreme pleasure, but then he would have been gone with the wind.

But sitting there in the dressing room after the show, I used to feel very, very excited. He was very handsome. And the real fact is I was getting tired of nightclub life. And I used to ask myself, "I wonder if he really means what he says. He's probably just kidding me along like all the entertainers he has met. . . ."

So I thought it was a joke, but Jelly was serious. One day I got in his big Lincoln and we just kept on driving until we got to Gary, Indiana, and stopped at a Justice of the Peace and we got married. And he told me then, "Mabel, you know I never married. I don't know what it was about you. I guess I saw I couldn't get you no other way. Now," he says, "I'm going to take you out of theatrical business and you're going to stay out."

Red Hot Pepper

That was in November, 1928, at the sign of Justice McGuire on the highway. Just me and the judge and Jelly Roll. Afterwards we drove to Kansas City and took in the nightspots and different things and I saw that everybody knew him there in K.C. We stayed there a month (Benny Moten was playing there, I remember, at the time) and then drove on into New York, and stayed with friends on 135th Street in Harlem.

In 1929 and 1930 I lived on the road with him. He had a beautiful bus for the band with a sign on the outside—JELLY ROLL MORTON AND HIS RED HOT PEPPERS—but he and I traveled in the Lincoln. I guess the only trouble we ever had was over him going sixty-five around all those curves. That made me very nervous. He used to kid me and say,

"May, I'm gonna leave you at home. . . . Don't you *know* I love myself better than anybody else in the world and I ain't never gonna have an accident when I'm driving the car?" Of course, he never did have an accident; and if a cop stopped him he could smooth-talk his way right out of it just like they were relatives.

Ferd did all his own bookings by letter or in person. Fifteen hundred and sixteen hundred dollars was about an average night's pay for the band and lots of time they would stay a whole week one place. He had his records; he showed them where he was number one hot band with Victor. And when they heard that band, they wanted him back. He had Barney Bigard, Albert Nicholas, Red Allen, Wellman Braud, and other great men long before Ellington and those other bands was ever heard of. They broke all records in Pennsylvania, Indiana, Ohio, the interior of Canada, and all up through the New England states, playing the best places such as Narragansett Pier. In the time I was with him he never went South, I don't know why.

The band all wore black tuxedos, but Jelly Roll wore a wine-red jacket and tie to match, white pants and white shoes. He directed the band himself, used to cut a lot of capers, then sit down at that piano with that great big smile of his, and, I'm telling you, he was a sensation. He never carried a singer with his band. He took the solos on piano and then the rest of the band didn't mean anything. They would just stop dead and all the people would gather around the stand to look and to hear. Jelly had two perfect hands for the piano—not like some players, one hand good and the other weak—he was just as good in the bass clef as in the treble. It was a wonderful thing to listen to him every night.

You see, I was right with him on the bandstand at every date. He was very jealous, didn't like anybody to speak to me—in fact he would get mad at his best friends if they so much as pass the time of day with me, but he wanted me there, dressed my best, so everybody could see me. Sometimes the boys in the band would ask him to let me sing, but he would never allow that. He used to tell me, "After all, I'm the big thing here and it would be bad for me if I shared with you my popularity." To tell you the truth, he was a little too jealous in that way, because after a while I began to want to go on with my professional career.

He was number one hot band then. All the others, like Ellington and Calloway and Basie and those, came up after. Jelly was first. Just like when you plant a seed, the others came along up, but Jelly was first. And he was so well liked by the white people that he never had to play a colored engagement; the colored places couldn't afford him. Only time colored people saw him was when he dropped into a cabaret for a drink, an announcement would be made and everybody would stand up to get a look at him. Really, Jelly Roll didn't like Negroes. He always said they would mess up your business. And Negroes didn't like him. I guess they were jealous.

He was all in diamonds, those days. He wore a ring with a diamond as big as a dime and a diamond horseshoe in his tie. He carried a locket with diamonds set all around it. His watch was circled in diamonds. His belt buckle was in gold and studded with diamonds. He even had sock-supporters of solid gold set with diamonds. Then you could see that big half-carat diamond sparkling in his teeth. That year they called him the diamond king.

Jelly loved to dress so well that he used to pay fifteen and twenty dollars at Kaplan's for his pajamas and underwear. When I met him, he had about one hundred fifty suits, and overcoats of all kinds—some out of this "melton" material, one of beaver, one lined with muskrat and several more. He had fifteen or twenty pairs of shoes and too many shirts and socks and ties to mention.

We stayed at the best hotels and ate the best of food. Jelly liked the best. He would always tell me, "Never mind tomorrow. Tomorrow will take care of itself." So anything I wanted, I could have. He knew all my sizes and he would go downtown and, anything that he saw, irregardless to what it cost, he would have the saleslady put it on, walk around in it, and if he liked it, he'd have it sent. All the years that I lived with him, I never knew what it was to do any shopping. He was marvelous, just marvelous.

Anytime that a person can get up out of bed in the middle of the night and just plunk his hand on a piano and begin to write down something and have a tune, he's wonderful to me. And Jelly used to do that all the time. He made himself one of the greatest musicians by his own ideas. He used to wake up at two or three o'clock in the morning and an idea would strike him and he'd get right by that grand piano. He wanted it to be completely quiet. He'd begin whistling and then go to dotting it down, dotting it down—just an idea in his own creative style. And I've watched him sit up all night there writing out a complete fifteen-piece orchestration for the next night's show.

Lots of times he liked to get in the car and go out in the country, maybe look at an old house or some scenery and he'd write a song from that. He was an artist, just a genius, that's all. They're giving the credit to him now—but then they gave him arguments. They used to tell him he was old-fashioned. Now you listen on the radio and you'll hear how old-fashioned he was—all the big bands using those riffs I heard him work out in the early hours of the morning.

He used to tell his band, "You'd please me if you'd just play those little black dots—just those little black dots that I put down there. If you play them, you'll please me. You don't have to make a lot of noise and ad lib. All I want you to play is what's written. That's all I ask."

Jelly always kept the same band, but along in 1930 he began to have trouble with his men. They thought they were great and knew their instruments and how to make jazz without him. They began getting drunk and wouldn't behave.

Jelly, he was very strict about that. Any man that drank on his stand, he didn't want because of his reputation. And he told them, "If this don't stop, I'm giving up the band, because you can spoil my name and reputation by getting drunk and trying to mingle with the guests on the dance floor. Because I pay higher than any other leader—ninety and one hundred dollars a week, you think you're in demand; but I can get along without you, because I can always play plenty of piano and get good men for recording dates . . . so come on, boys, and stick to those black dots."

Things kept going to the bad. Finally, one day, Garland, the bass player, missed the bus. When he arrived late to the dance, Jelly wouldn't let him on the stand, told him the contract called for fifteen pieces and *he* cause it to be only fourteen. So Garland went to the union and put Jelly up on charges for firing him without cause. Somehow Garland's word took effect and the union said Jelly couldn't use union musicians no more till he paid a thousand dollar fine. By the time Jelly got that fixed, the band was broken up and gone.

He had another disappointment that year. A deal came up for his band to go to Russia. He had the band all set—Bigard, Bechet, and several more. Then they found out they couldn't send any money back out of Russia to their families and so the men refused to go.

Anyhow, we settled down in a nice apartment in New York and Jelly started taking gigs up through the New England states with pickup bands. I think he was also making records for some of these little secret companies and he must have had some sort of business downtown. But Jelly was always very close about his private business. He never told me what he made a year, and he never let me know exactly what was going on. He used to say, "I'm the man of the house. You must depend on me." And I wasn't bothered much because we were living very, very well, like I told you.

I had nothing to worry about—the rent, the electric, the gas, the groceries—he'd take care of all that. He would go to the store and he would order and pay the bill by the week. Anything I wanted, he would have sent. And I had wonderful food for him, because I knew exactly what he liked.

His favorite was gumbo filé. I would get dry bayleaves and grind them up as fine as black pepper—that was my filé, my base. Then I put a big ham bone on to boil and, after while, add the filé. Put in shrimp, crab, rice, and diced ham. Let that cook a while and Jelly used to holler, "Honey, let's go back home to New Orleans."

He loved to eat, but he didn't like parties and things like that at our apartment. *That* he didn't like. Of course, I had a lot of close friends when I was in theatrical business, but it seems Jelly didn't want me to have any company. He'd take me out in the country in his car—like on a Saturday—find an old country place and go out there and stay, lie under a tree and have a big pitcher of lemonade and eat a lot of fried chicken and corn on the cob—that was sport to him—he liked *that*. Of course, we had our friends out in Jamaica, Long Island, who owned their own homes and we used to go out there and stay weekends, but no company in New York.

If I regret one thing, I regret this. He used to tell me that he wanted to build a nice home for me, said, "Just pick the place, in Long Island or Connecticut, and I'll buy a piece of land and build you a home." But I never would. I wanted to stay in town to be close to him. Now I wish I had done what *he* wanted.

Jelly loved to play pinochle. That was his favorite game and I used to get so angry with him—see, I knew he'd leave his office downtown about four and I'd realize about four-thirty or five he'd be ready for his meal. So I'd have it ready. Well, he'd meet someone in the Rhythm Club and they'd begin talking (he loved to talk and argue, especially when they began talking about music) and then they'd get to playin' pinochle. It might be twelve or one o'clock before he'd leave there. And I'd be trying to keep everything good and hot all that time. The chicken would be overdone when he came in and I'd be *so* angry I'd say to him, "I don't think it's fair for me to stand up in this kitchen in this hot weather and try and keep your meal hot, and you don't even come and eat." I said, "Even if you would come home and eat and then go out, I wouldn't feel as bad. But you want me to stay home all the time, and then you do me like that. . . . "

He'd tell me, "May (he called me May for short), I haven't been no place in the world but the Rhythm Club," And I'd have to forgive him because he was really so sweet. Very, very, very gentle and kind. Of course, he was very high-tempered. If you got him angry, that French blood would come up in him and he'd be *plenty* angry, but, even those times, he wouldn't say anything bad, you know—no more than, "I'm getting tired and disgusted." In fact, the only arguments that came up, came up over how I kept his clothes.

He had all those shirts. . . . When he'd go downtown in the morning, he'd wear a white shirt for business; when he'd come home in the afternoon, he'd put on a colored shirt; then, in the morning, another white shirt. And he was very particular. Believe it or not, when he taken a shirt off, he would miss it if I didn't launder it that day. I'd think, "I won't do the laundry today, I'll let it go until next week." Then he would go through the drawer, looking for that particular shirt.

I'd say to him, "What you looking for?"

"I'm looking for that pink-striped shirt."

"It must be in the chiffonier," I'd say, but he'd go straight to the bathroom, find it in the clothes basket. "Is it getting too hard for you to do the laundry?" Jelly would say.

"No."

"May, I'm trying to make it easy on you. Isn't it easier to wash and iron *one* shirt just when I take it off than to wait and let them pile up?"

"Yes."

"You don't have a thing in the world to do but keep my laundry clean. There are a thousand laundries in New York that will do my shirts and won't let them lay around. If I take them there Monday, I can get them Tuesday; but I won't put my shirts in the laundry, because I don't like the way they make them so stiff in the collar. Seems to me you're just a glutton for punishment. When I take off a suit of underwear or a pair of socks, all you have to do is run them through a little Lux—no rubbing and scrubbing to do. You're home here all day and all you have to do is iron them and put them up in the right place. . . ."

He was very strict on that, very strict. His suits, if he taken them off, he wanted them to go to the tailor and be dry-cleaned and right back. The idea was that he wanted every suit there and in the right order. He used to say, "Now when *I* go to my drawers, look at the difference between you and I; I can go to my drawer in the dark and get out any shirt I want, white or colored, any pair of socks, any tie; but you got to tear up *every*thing to find one slip."

That was his way and I couldn't fool him about it or get him away from it. Of course his papers and his music, nobody could touch and I never did. So all the trouble we ever had was about my keeping the laundry *his* way.

You know, I never regretted one day that I gave up the theatrical business to marry Jelly. I used to tell him, "If I was no longer living, I know you would marry again; but, if you die before me, I know I will never marry because I can't *never* compete with you." That's the way it was as long as he was living; he was marvelous to me.

And, really, I will never meet anyone in life that good and that kind. Not only to me, he was kind to the less fortunate. He was always trying to help anybody that wanted to do something in life. He lent lots of money to his musician friends when they was down on their luck. . . . Any place that the Catholic sisters wanted to go, he'd fill up his car with gas and oil and take um. And I remember one time a lady's little daughter died of T.D. of the spine over on the Island and the only thing she could afford was the hearse. Jelly told her:

"Now I don't want to make you feel bad and I don't want you to think I'm trying to be a bigshot, but I want to let you have my two cars for the funeral." So he went to the garage and put his chauffeur at the wheel of the Cadillac and he took the Lincoln and drove those folks to Woodlawn Cemetery and back. My pastor, Father McCann, told me later, said, "Jelly Roll was a nice person to know. He was really kind. We miss him so much."

See, while we were living in New York I brought Jelly into the Catholic Church. He had been *born* a Catholic, but he had let the practice go. And the Father suggested that we be married in the church and *I* wanted that, but Jelly refused. He said we had been married once, so what's the use of doing it over again—we couldn't be separated without the church consent to it, whether we stood up in the church or no. "And we have a license to prove it," he would say and touch his inside coat pocket.

Now I think back, it's a peculiar thing that he always insisted on his carrying our marriage license and wouldn't never give it to me to keep. I used to ask him why couldn't I have it framed and put it up on the wall and he'd tell me, "Look, now, May, the way we travel up in Massachusetts and all that where they have those strict laws about entertainers being really married, I need to carry this license at all times. I'm the man of the house and you just let me bother about these things." So I didn't worry my head about it and let it go. I was just dumb to the fact, that's all I can say now.

At that time, though, what could I think? I had everything

in the world I wanted and I never had any trouble with Jelly and other women. I never heard anything about him and another woman, not even in Harlem, and you know if there had been something I'd have heard it in that place. Anita? I never heard of her till later.

No, the truth about Mister Jelly Roll Morton—the actual facts about Mister Jelly Roll Morton was that he was not what you call a very high-sexed man. No, not a very high-sexed man. It was just once in a while with him. When that mood would strike him, yes, but otherwise he was too wrapped up in his *own* music. Often he told me he had no time for such foolishness; he had other things to think about. He used to go to bed thinking about music and get up whistling, dotting down those dots and poking those piano keys.

At night, after he had his supper, he wanted it perfectly quiet so he could compose. He was a man that worked *all* the time. He was *al*ways busy. And any time of the night an idea would strike him, he get right up and start dotting it down, dotting it down.

All during these years, from 1930 to 1933, after his regular band broke up, Jelly kept busy and made good money playing gigs up through the New England states. But he began to have more and more trouble getting the cooperation of the colored musicians. They wanted to play everything but what he had dotted down. They thought they could bring a bottle of whiskey to the job in their back pockets. All that hurt him. Jelly spoke and preached and did everything he could.

"I want to tell you one thing," he used to say to the boys around the Rhythm Club, "you cannot play around, just because you think you're so great. I'm telling you those white boys are not playing corny any more. They're coming up right

along. I hear them playing my tunes. They're getting the *idea*
of how to play hot. Once they get it, they're going to use it.
Then they're gonna sell *you* for five cents a dozen. If I ask you
now to go out on a gig, it's thirty-five or forty dollars for that
night. But it won't be long till you'll be around the club,
standing on the corner, with your instruments under your arm
and glad to get a five-dollar job."

And that's what happened, just the way he told them. Once
the white boys got the idea of it, they went to town. Like
Benny Goodman. To get the idea, he taken Fletcher Henderson* with him as his arranger. Then Goodman got the idea
and he branched off, because then *he* knew what to do with the
hot idea. . . . Artie Shaw, he taken Billie Holiday with him,
but when he began playing the New England states, he said to
Billie, "You're marvelous. You're wonderful. Nobody can
compare with your style, but they will not book me in the
New England states with a colored entertainer."

Now, my husband didn't feel there was prejudice involved
in the white bands taking jazz over; he felt it was all through
the Negro musicians thinking they were so great, getting
drunk on the job and not cooperating. . . .

Listening to Mabel Morton, it was hard to remember she
was talking about the years between 1930 and 1939, when
most American musicians were on the WPA. Her unawareness
reflects her husband's attitude, for Mister Jelly Roll was the
kind of American who refused to recognize the Depression,
just as he was the kind of black who refused to recognize racial

---

* One of the best black jazz arrangers.

discrimination. He could see this much, however. Friends of Negro jazz like Goodman and Shaw ended up with the best jobs in hot jazz. This is doubtless an ironic end for good intentions since both men stood for mixed bands and against discrimination when such a stand was dangerous, but then old Mister Jim Crow is a past master at irony.

Jelly Roll's whole life was constructed around his denial of his Negro status. He was a mulatto, a New Orleans man, a higher-up, a number one recording artist, but not quite a Negro. Of course this is typical of New Orleans Creoles. Even a younger man, Omer Simeon, the clarinetist, expressed only mild indignation over the operation of Jim Crow in music . . .

"From what I hear"—in his pleasant and husky voice—"colored bands used to play at the Waldorf-Astoria and all the biggest hotels in New York, but then they began to cut that out. I never did figure it out, but I imagine there's prejudice involved. It came more from the proprietor than the public, though. At least, that's what I believe."

Jelly Roll's grandmother, Mimi Pechet, kept her job with the Solaris by being "nice" and being strict with her children; and her grandson, Jelly Roll, could interpret the closing of the Waldorf to his band in only one way—"the niggers acting rowdy." He took out his increasing hysteria on his fellow musicians in Harlem.

"I always called him the Dizzy Dean of Music, he was so belligerent and braggadocio," commented Simeon mildly. "He was a real fanatic over the music. He wanted real New Orleans style and he wanted it played just so. So the boys figured him for a radical. Different arguments came up. And, by him being one of the pioneers of jazz, he'd come right back at them when they disagreed with him. Well, they felt they

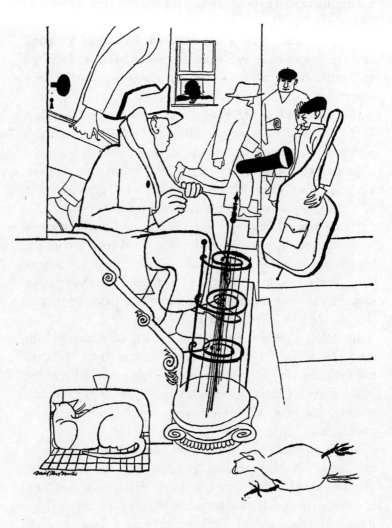

was as big as he was—those that had been in music any length
of time—and so, naturally, he had a hard time keeping the
same personnel.

"It was really a show when Jelly got in an argument," Simeon
chuckled. "We used to all be standing around the Famous Corner at 131st and Seventh and Jelly would be telling what a great
composer he was. So Chick Webb would kid him about his 'old-
fashioned' music just to get Jelly started. I'll never forget Jelly's
favorite expression, 'I'm the master,' he'd say, 'I'm the master.'
And he would tell all the big musicians, 'Listen, fellow, anything you play on your horn, you're playing *Jelly Roll.*'

"Lots of those boys would get hot at that. But, one thing I
always noticed about Jelly, he could back up everything he
said by what he could *do*. . . ."

A few years later Jelly Roll was calling New York "that
cruel city." The laughter of the young Harlem musicians on
the swing kick hurt him cruelly. They intimated that he and
his music were "corny." He could no longer back his brags
with diamonds, for the diamonds had disappeared—Mabel
thinks in 1930, about the time the Red Hot Peppers broke up.
He was no longer the "Number 1 Victor Jazz Artist." When
RCA took over the company in 1930, Jelly tried half-heartedly
to enlarge his band; he tried to play big-band swing, but he
couldn't bring it off; the records didn't sell; soon Victor showed
Jelly the door. The diamond king, the great hot composer, the
lord of New Orleans piano was scratching hard for a living on
the hardest street in the world, subbing for other piano players
who showed up drunk on their jobs, talking up big deals on
windy corners, then watching them blow into the gutters with
the day's newspapers.

MCA had the best jobs sewed up and they wouldn't have
him. ASCAP wouldn t give him a full membership. The goons
who then ran the union had threatened to kill him if he didn't
keep his mouth shut about things that every member knew
went on. The gangsters who operated the big dance mills had
promised to rub him out if he didn't stop trying to hire away
their star New Orleans sidemen. All this Jelly Roll used to
pour out in an angry diatribe, followed by even wilder plans
for revenge—he would sue the American Society of Composers, Authors, and Publishers and expose them; he would set up
an outfit to rival and to ruin the Music Corporation of America; he would expose the Musicians Union and the gangsters to
the United States attorney. . . . The big corporations had
taken over jazz and ruined Jelly Roll, that was his theme, and
he would speak on it for hours. Some of his personal stories
reflected feelings of neurotic persecution, yet, in a larger sense,
the years have shown that Jelly Roll was right.

Jazz became a big business in the early thirties, and Jelly
Roll, who had been a big wheel in 1923, was a small-time
operator in 1933. Every year there was to be less room for the
inspired and careless talent of the past. What the big money
boys needed were efficient music machines who would turn out
every day—quantity, instead of quality. There was certainly
no room for a black man who claimed, with some justice, to
have originated much of jazz.

The economic source of his troubles Jelly Roll would not
recognize—the boom, that had set diamonds on his garters,
was bust. Depression America could afford Jelly no longer, nor
did it care to listen to the joyous and confident music he found
along the shining avenues of his idealized New Orleans.
Ghetto Negroes wanted the real blues which stated their agony

openly. The rest of the country was being rocked into a rosy dream by such ballads as *The Isle of Capri, Night and Day,* and *The Gold Mine in the Sky.*

Jelly Roll had quarreled with the boys in the band and they wouldn't go along with him. They preferred to work for younger, more flexible, more race-conscious, even if less inspired, leaders—leaders who compromised and who got the jobs. Mister Jelly Roll had high-hatted the black world, and now the white world, into which he had entered briefly, closed its doors. He was *out* on the cold dark streets of the Depression holding on to his musical integrity with a fervent Creole pride, and he was all by himself.

Since he could not see where he had been at fault, nor where, in a much larger sense, his culture had failed him, he turned back as he always did to his roots in New Orleans, finding the meaning of his troubles in the childhood fears his New Orleans godmother had given him along with his first diamonds. Morton never felt certain whether voodoo or big business had ruined him; both were mysterious forces which finally overpowered his tiger. Usually he delivered his economic tirade, but once, in a confiding moment of weariness, he told the following fantasy—a poignant story of his final attempt to be a New York bigshot, a story of a voodoo curse that shadowed Mister Jelly Roll along the Great White Way.

It Like to Broke My Heart

●●● **W**hen I was a young man, these hoodoo people with their underground stuff helped me along. I did not feel grateful and I did not reward them for the help they gave. Now, when everything began to go against me, those underground streams were running against me, too.

One day I met a frizzly-haired woman who said she wasn't a fortune teller, but that she could work in those fields. If you wanted anybody killed, you would deposit her fee in the bank and she would go to work. She would buy a package of fine meat, tie it up with strings and throw it in a desolate section. In nine or ten days, this meat would decay and, as it decayed, your enemy would be dying. At the end of ten days, the enemy would be dead and she would go to the bank and collect her money. If the person was not dead, you didn't owe her a thing.

I didn't believe in those things. I didn't pay any attention when this woman told me that somebody was working against me. She said my Lincoln would be stolen. In three weeks it was gone. When they caught the thief, he wasn't even put in jail.

It wasn't long before I wished I had taken this woman's advice. I was in the music-publishing business. Everybody was writing me for bands and for music and for radio programs and I had more work than I could do. I bumped into a West Indian guy who was fooling with the music-publishing business in an office so small you couldn't turn around in it—to get out you had to back back the way you came in. I kinda liked this guy and wanted to give him a break and, besides, as I had decided to form a monopoly and put my money behind a lot of my type bands with the main office located in Los Angeles, I needed a confidential partner to handle the New York end. This guy said he could type and do accounting, so I gave him a break and took him into the firm as a partner, keeping all the property in my name.

I assured him I didn't want to make him an office boy, but the son-of-a-gun was jealous of me. He didn't want to handle the music counter and told me I was high-hat because I kept my door closed. I had to have it quiet for my arranging and composing. I guess he hated me because he was such a poor excuse for talent, himself—if you told him to rhyme "ham," he would say "Pontchartrain."

Many evenings I used to drive him home to Brooklyn in my Lincoln and often he would ask me to wait for him on a certain corner where he would meet and talk with a light-complected old man. Quite often he would have me wait so long that I would grow very impatient. Once I heard this old man tell my

West Indian partner that such-and-such a woman was no good. "Listen," the old guy said, "that woman ain't paid me what she owe me. If it hadn't been for me, she wouldn't have had a quarter. Now she has a fleet of trucks, and is doing business with the subway company. All right, you wait. In a month she won't have anything."

Sometime later on, the West Indian remarked to me that this woman had lost everything she had. He told me the old man had a book like an encyclopedia, full of charms that never fail. If the police caught him with that book, right in the jail he would go. That put me to thinking and wondering if my partner had put anything on me through this old man.

Well, I found out that this West Indian not only couldn't do accounting, he could hardly count on his fingers, much less type. Then I discovered that he was stealing my music and selling it to a big, high-powered firm and I knew I would have to kick him out. "What's the idea of taking my music out of here and giving it to these other companies?" I asked him. "Don't you realize you're selling out for peanuts when I'm trying to go for the millions."

He wouldn't admit to anything. I told him that our contract didn't mean anything if one of the partners didn't play fair. I showed him I had the goods on him. He told me, "Morton, everything in this office is in my name and belongs to me." We started to fight and the super of the building came running and hollering, "Don't hit him in here. He will sue the building." That gave the West Indian a chance to escape, which he did. He hollered back, as he ran away, "Jelly Roll Morton, you will lose everything you have."

That night he tried to get back in the office, but I had beat him to it and changed the lock on the door. He then had the phone cut off—which it was in both our names—and from then on I couldn't get a phone for love nor money. In many ways that was the most peculiar thing that happened to me. I still don't understand why I couldn't get a phone. But the phone business was just the beginning.

I had a young lady working for me by the name of Billy Young. She was an actress friend who was down on her luck and I occasionally was able to give her things to do in the office.* After I kicked the West Indian out, she told me she had noticed that people would come to the door, and stop, seemingly unable to step across the sill; that was strange to her, because formerly a lot of people came to the office. We pulled up the rug near the door and there, underneath, were four different colors of powder—gray, white, brown and pink. We started searching the office. We found powder sprinkled everywhere, even in the woodwork of the desk. There wasn't a piece of stationery that was clean of it.

How we found out the stationery was fixed—Billy was writing a letter and by this letter being to a friend, she had her head in her hands, thinking. When she took her hands away from her face, her cheeks busted out in a horrible-looking rash. She took a drink out of a paper cup at the water cooler and her lips swelled up as big as the bumpers on a box car.

I was getting wise. I realized this was some funny business the West Indian had done and I started out to find the old man in Brooklyn. I knew he was the one. I planned to shoot him on sight any place I seen him, but everywhere I was directed to

---

* One of the things Miss Young did around the office was to sing on a number of Jelly's Victor recordings.

look, he had just moved away. And there was something in my mind that made me want to stay out of Brooklyn.

My bus, which I used on out-of-town dates, was in storage at this time. The garage wrote they had completed about six hundred dollars' worth of work and asked for their money. I replied that when all the work was done I would pay. When all these things started happening I began to worry about my bus and I went down to see about it. The company had already sold it to pay for the storage and repair bills. I asked about my trunk. They said they didn't know nothing about a trunk. This trunk had all my contracts and all my write-ups in it, as well as the world's most extensive repertoire of ten thousand numbers. I sued the company, but they beat my case.

I began to think I had better get some help and that was the reason I attended a séance run by a woman named Madame Elise. She asked me for one hundred dollars and got it. I seen her put her hand on a woman's head and this woman went out like a light and stayed out for thirty minutes. That put a fear into my heart. Then Madame Elise prescribed a bath to this woman, a bath composed of three or four vials of different water and costing twenty-five dollars. I took one of them baths, too, and she told me everything would be better.

Sure enough, OCA got me some bookings through Pennsylvania. I organized a good band and we set out with great hopes and in two weeks we were stranded in a hotel in Washington, Pa. The boys piled up some terrific bills for food and drinks and rent, so, when I left for New York to get some money to bail us out, I had to leave my trunk and my fur coats with the hotel. All my most important tunes and my mother's picture were in that trunk, along with shoes and socks and clothes galore, worth a lot of money. (I never wore shoes those days that cost less than $18; and my socks averaged around $5 a pair.) The hotel also had my raccoon and my beaver coat. When I got back to New York, somehow I just forgot to send for that trunk. I always planned to, but I never could get around to it.

I just wasn't myself any more. I walked around in a stupor. I went back to see Madame Elise. Pretty soon I was bringing big bags of food to her. Then I got to eating there—I don't think her husband liked that. I told her about the condition in my office—how people couldn't walk in the door. She took some turpentine and scrubbed the walls, but this only made everything worse. Then I resolved to take action and to beat the West Indian to death, because Madame Elise told me it would help if I caught him and drew blood. But every time I got to the guy I couldn't raise my hands.

I realize now that she was helping my enemy, the West Indian. I found this powder all in my hats. Every time I would put one on, it felt like I had the Library of Congress on my head. Madame Elise told me to take my handbags and cut them up in small pieces and throw them into the Harlem River, and, like a fool, I did. She personally ordered me to cut up every bit of clothing I had and burn it all. I always had a lot of clothes and the stack I made in my backyard was way up over the top of my head. I poured on the kerosene and struck a match; it like to broke my heart to watch my suits burn.

It seems like I'm still blurry about that doggone thing in New York. I spent thousands of dollars trying to get this spell taken off me, but my luck just got blacker and blacker. I had jobs on jobs offered me, but it got so I couldn't get the men together to make a band. Somehow I never could hold a band together in New York, except for recording dates. The movies called me to Hollywood, but while I was trying to get my men, they decided they couldn't wait any longer and called in Ellington and this was the beginning of his great rise. The Palace Theatre wanted me and I had the same trouble, and then was when Cab Calloway got his start. I joined a show and the show folded. I decided to quit the music business altogether and I started a cosmetic company which lost me the last few pennies I had. Finally I went to the New York District Attorney to see whether he could put the old man in jail to stop him from working against me. He told me there was no law in New York State to prevent people from working in this way. . . .

Mabel Morton confirmed this strange tale in part. According to her, the West Indian was a songplugger whom Jelly took into partnership out of charity. Financed by Morton, the rascal rented the office, installed the phone, even bought the furniture in his own name and, when Jelly threw him out, sprinkled some kind of powder all over the place. Mrs. Morton stoutly denied, however, that voodoo was at work. . . .

I think, she said, it was some kind of a poisonous powder for insects. But I saw it all over the office, some kind of pink stuff. There was a girl drank out of a paper cup and her lips swole up till you couldn't recognize her. And then my husband started to go to fortune tellers. I tried to talk to him and tell him that was all baloney. "You have the wrong idea, honey. It's those people's racket, it's their line, just the same as you're a musician, they'll send *you* to the cleaners."

Which is exactly what happened. Jelly lost everything he still had—his bus, his music, his clothes; a fellow at Victor even ran away with his diamond ring which Jelly had up for a small loan. Besides the one in his tooth, that was the last of Jelly's diamonds and it was the last of him in New York.

A very little time after that in 1935 he told me he was going to try his luck in Washington in the fighting game. He had met a fellow who told him he could make a killing promoting fights, so I was to stay on in New York and look after his ASCAP and Melrose business and he would see what he could do. He wrote me from Washington that they had found a few good fighters, but they wouldn't keep training, drank all the time, and so that went flop and he didn't know what he would do next. I didn't hear from Jelly for almost two years, but I finally located him in Washington and he began writing. . . .

Jelly Roll's penciled notes to Mabel show how the Depression had cracked his confidence. He figured it was everyone for himself in this cold midnight period. It seems pretty clear, too, that he was trying to break it off with Mabel. Once she found him, however, and like a good Catholic Creole, clave to him, refusing to recognize his two years' desertion, sentimental Jelly Roll could not bring himself to speak of an open break. Instead, he wrote in a tender and conciliatory tone, apologizing for his non-support. . . .

Washington, D.C.
Jan. 4, 1937

My Darling Wife:

I received your letter and will say that things have surely runned rotten for you, but we all think

we have the toughest break. Of course, it could be
worse, but it is plenty bad. Have patience and know
we will come out all right. I did not want to write
you until I had something to send you. I feel sure
we will be able to go home for Mardi Gras. Don't
worry. Yours as ever.

Ferd.

But when the brass bands swung out their hot marches and
the Jazz Babies did their Basin Street grinds and the Indians
played their ancient drama in the New Orleans Mardi Gras,
Jelly Roll and Mrs. Morton were not looking on: the middle
of February found Jelly still toughing it out in Washington,
still trying. . . .

Darling Wife

. . . I don't want you to worry. Things are tough
everywhere and we are not the only ones that's
catching Hell. There are plenty worse than us. I
know things will turn out all right. . . . Enclosed
you will find $17. See if you can pay up the interest
on the things that's nearest to be lost. I will send
you something Monday. I thank God I am able to
send you something. Yours.

Ferd.

Another month of striving up and down U Street—another
month of acting up to the part of top composer in jazz on coffee
and cakes in the most class-ridden small town in the U.S.—
the colored bourgeois ghetto of Washington, D.C. . . .

March 16, 1937
Washington

Dear Mabel,

Things has been very bad with me. That is why
you did not hear from me sooner. I have never
thought of giving you up. I am planning to send for
you as soon as I can. Maybe before this week is out.
If not, real soon. Tell Mrs. ————— to let you
have your things and you will pay her the best you
can, because it is so hard on me paying expenses
here and trying to do the best I can to pay there.

Darling, you will hear from me real soon.

Yours,
Ferd.

Probably, Jelly was not much more prosperous than these
letters indicate, but he did not tell Mabel all of his Washington affairs. A rowdy piece of doggerel found among his papers
will explain why. . . .

> *Got a letter from a friend name Young*
> *From his letter got terribly stung*
> *He said, come to Washington, D.C.*
> *To manage club for a woman—do-ra-me,*
> *And said, take the next train and leave*
> *It was cold as hell and I thot I freeze*
> *He met me at the train*
> *In the ice and snow and rain*
> *He said to me I know she will be please*

We sent in the place
And the oil stove hit me in the face   *

The place that so stank in Jelly's nostrils was a nightclub upstairs from a U Street hamburger joint in Washington's colored section. There, as partner to one Cordelia—a lady who apparently had nothing better to do with her money than to lose it in a badly run nightspot, Mister Jelly Roll nursed his sorrows for several bitter seasons, playing master of ceremonies, producing sorry little revues, acting as bouncer on occasion, mixing drinks for important guests, sometimes even cooking New Orleans dishes for his friends. This place was variously called The Music Box, The Blue Moon Inn, The Jungle Inn; every time it failed, Jelly gave it a more primitive name, thus hinting at his low opinion of Washington night-club patrons.

Cordelia was a nice lady in her way, good and kind and generous, but her fuzzy-minded, small-town approach to the business drove Jelly wild. He had big ideas, as always. Sometimes his enthusiasm would carry them both through a redecoration job, a new neon sign for the front door, new acts imported from New York, and a new stock of liquor for the bar. Then Cordelia would balk at a few more dollars for a really good band or she would drop the cover charge for some of her "lowclass" friends or lower the tone of this little bit of old New Orleans in some other way (at least that was his story), and Jelly Roll, King of Jazz, would give up and sulk in a dark corner of The Blue Moon Inn. He and Cordelia might have

---

* From an article in *The Record Changer* by R. J. Carew, 1943.

been redecorating that Washington nightspot to this day, but
Creole forbearance wore thin at last. Mabel Morton was never
afraid to face facts. She confronted Jelly one day in New York.

I said to him in 1937, "Well, what are you going to do? Are
you staying in Washington or are you coming back to me?"
Then he had to break down and tell me the truth.

"I have a little nightclub there," Jelly told me. "I'm in
partners with a woman."

"Oh, I see. So that's it. I thought you were in the fighting
game. Well, then, *I'm* coming to Washington," I said.

"All right, Mabel," he told me.

When I got to Washington, I saw what the situation was.
Of course, nothing was said to me, but you can sense those
things. Well, immediately all the help at the place accepted
me as his wife. They expected some sort of big blow-up, I
suppose, and then nothing happened. Cordelia was very polite
and nice to me and I was the same to her, but I soon saw it was
the wrong spot for Jelly. I told him so. He tried to show *me*
that some of the best people came to his place—doctors, law-
yers and bigshots. "They come, all right," I told him, "and
want the best of everything and then, when their check comes,
ask for a reduction. . . ." Jelly Roll had stocked the bar like
The Jungle Inn was the Absinthe House; you could get any
kind of drink in the world there you wanted. So these Washington folks would lap up all that fine liquor and then scream
about the bill. When an argument would come up, Cordelia
wouldn't back Jelly up, and in the end, she would knock a
couple dollars off the check.

I said, "Jelly, you were running nightclubs when this
woman was ducking the truant officer. Cordelia don't know

how to use her money sensible. She's just running this
place for her friends." Jelly admitted I was right, but he
kept on hoping to make something big out of the place—
which it could have been the hottest place in town if she'd
listened. The people on the city board liked Jelly and had give
him permission to operate the only black-and-tan place in the
city. People who knew Jelly's records would hear about him,
white people from Texas and all over, and come listen to him
play piano all evening. The band would just have to sit
around—they couldn't play nothing anyhow—and those
guests would apologize and explain that they only wanted to
hear Jelly Roll. . . .

Devoted Mabel gently screened out the curses of the young
Washington swingsters shushed by the white folks while old
man Morton played his "corn." Mister Jelly Lord openly expressed his contempt for these "ignorant young rowdies,"
while they repaid his scorn by hating him even more than they
hated the brutal Washington police. When this corny old
handkerchief-head would assert that Count Basie did not know
piano, the atmosphere of The Jungle Inn would be ripe for
murder.

Mister Jelly Roll never bothered his head with these hep-
cats, until his empty bank account at last convinced him that
"swing" might not be so bad as he knew it was. Never one to
do things by halves, he began to preach about saxophone
sections and all the other apparatus of musical display which
shape hot jazz arrangements for a big band. He even set about
writing swing tunes. A sample from *Sweet Substitute* (which he
probably hummed to the fair Cordelia) will be quite enough:

Sweet substitute, sweet substitute,
She/He tells me that she's/he's mine all mine—
Does anything I tell her/him—love is blind—
She's/He's got such loving ways,
My head is in a daze,
My new recruit is mighty cute—
Yes, I'm crazy 'bout my sweet substitute. *

About this same time Jelly suddenly discovered the Depression. His reaction was typical of his fathomless, boundless, limitless, humorless, and altogether Celliniesque ego. He addressed a long letter to FDR outlining a plan which he felt would put every American musician back to work in six months. The plan was to pay off in jobs like a chain letter . . .

Jelly Roll invades Baltimore with government backing, organizes a Jelly Roll hot New Orleans band there, using unemployed Baltimore musicians. This band, naturally, causes a sensation. Turnstiles of the empty dance halls begin to click again; and, while the reinspired Baltimore musicians are branching out, founding yet more hot bands on the Morton principle, and filling more dance halls, Morton himself attacks moribund Philadelphia, lights up cold Quakertown with a magic orchestra, which in turn gives birth to more orchestras, Morton having rolled on, meanwhile, and the Baltimore magic having spread on its own to Annapolis and Hagerstown. So Mister Jelly Roll's progress across America produces a rebirth of the music business, the

---

* Lyrics printed by permission of Tempo-Music Publishing Co., the copyright owner.

orchestras multiplying back down the trail like Schmoos, the unem-
ployment problem for musicians is solved, and more important still, the
people of the U.S., hearing the happy music of New Orleans, forget
their troubles and throw Old Man Depression into the ashcan where
he belongs. The cost of this scheme—merely Jelly's traveling expenses.
He was willing to contribute his time and talent to the cause. . . .

There was something quite disarming about Morton's sin-
cerity. He spoke of himself as an impersonal force that could
be used by the government to lick the Depression . . . How
fine it would have been for all of us if this New Orleans fantasy
could have taken possession of our national music! What a
glittering world of sound and melody would have poured from
our bandstands with Jelly Roll as our conductor, wearing his
wine-colored jacket, smiling that big personality smile, demanding only that we follow those black dots!

While Mister Jelly Roll, hemmed into the obscurity of The
Jungle Inn, was making such bids for attention, real recognition was coming his way without his being aware of it—not
from the big gangsters of music or from the impressionable
throngs of the '20's or from the fancy ladies of New Orleans
pleasure houses—but now from a growing army of young
people who had discovered for themselves that our national
musical idiom was jazz, that New Orleans jazz was the hottest
and that Jelly Roll Morton was one of the hottest red peppers
on the vine.

Hot jazz fans began drifting into The Jungle Inn to watch
in reverence "those two perfect hands." Frightfully serious and
sophisticated jazz critics brought their notebooks and began to
write articles for the little jazz magazines. (The '30's was the
period of the little jazz review.) Jelly Roll now had backing in
his disputes with the "hipsters" and "hot jive boys"; the nick-

els in the jukebox began to fall on his old hits, *The Pearls* and *Wolverine Blues*. Jelly's smiles grew less forced; The Jungle Inn could be almost pleasant with these young people to listen. And he'd play for them by the hour, digging up the fine old New Orleans tunes, limbering up his fingers on the intricate polyphony of his own compositions, smiling, with the world again in a jug and the stopper in his hand, saying to these young antiquarians of jazz—"One of the old ones? Well now, this is no doubt one of the oldest; this one has whiskers . . ."

Although at first Mister Jelly did not appreciate being regarded as a historical figure, feeling that he and his music were both very much alive, he was nothing if not precocious. He had one of those memories that could regurgitate the exact phrases of a street-corner argument twenty years gone; he liked to talk almost as much as to play piano—and he had a grievance. Stimulated by the interest of Washington college professors and their friends, his historical sense began to grow like a liana vine around a palmetto.

The mine was laid and the detonating trigger cocked. A broadcast of Robert Ripley's *Believe It or Not* program in the spring of 1938 touched off the explosion. Jelly, an ardent fan, blew his top as he heard Ripley introduce W. C. Handy (composer of the *St. Louis Blues*) as the originator of jazz and the blues. Mister Handy is a modest fellow and this claim was certainly made for him by a careless Ripley script writer, but Jelly Roll suspected Mr. Handy.

"W. C. Handy is a Liar," was the leading sentence of his letter of protest to the *Baltimore Afro-American*. In a four-thousand-word missive addressed to Ripley (with a copy to the jazz magazine *Downbeat*), a wounded tiger and a polemicist roared.

Dear Mr. Ripley:

For many years I have been a constant reader of your cartoon. I have listened to your broadcast with keen interest. I frankly believe your broadcast is a great contribution to natural science.

In your broadcast of March 26, 1938, you introduced W.C. Handy as the originator of *jazz, stomps,* and *blues.* By this announcement you have done me a great injustice and you have almost misled many of your fans. . . .

It is evidently known, beyond contradiction that New Orleans is the cradle of jazz, and I, myself, happened to be the creator in the year 1902. . . . In the year 1908 . . . I met Handy in Memphis. He was introduced to me as Prof. Handy. Who ever heard of anyone wearing the name of a professor advocate Ragtime, Jazz, Stomps, Blues, etc.? . . . Of course, Handy could not play any of these types and I can assure you has not learned them yet. . . .

Mr. Handy cannot prove anything in music that he has created. He has possibly taken advantage of some unprotected material that floats around . . . This very minute, you have confronting the world all kinds of Kings, Czars, Dukes, Princes and Originators of Swing (*Swing* is just another name for *jazz*), and they know that the titles are deceiving. . . . I would like to put a lie tester on many of these make-believe stalwarts of originality. Mr. Ripley, these untruthful statements Mr. Handy has made, or caused you to make, will maybe cause him

to be branded the most dastardly imposter in the
history of music.

. . . Please do not misunderstand me. I do not
claim any of the creation of the blues, although I
have written many of them even before Mr. Handy
had any blues published. . . . Music is such a tremendous proposition that it probably needs government supervision. . . . There are many who
enjoy glory plus financial gains and abundance, even
in the millions, who should be digging ditches or
sweeping the streets. Lack of proper protection
causes this. . . . I only give you facts that you may
force your pal to his rightful position in fair life.
Lord protect us from more Hitlers and Mussolinis.

Very truly yours,
JELLY ROLL MORTON
Originator of Jazz and Stomps
Victor Artist
World's Greatest Hot Tune Writer

This article rocked the jazz world and put Jelly's name back
in the headlines. There were some who felt that Handy's mild
retort in *Downbeat* was all the answer Jelly's blast deserved.
"Handy could afford to be charitable and slightly contemptu-
ous of Morton, the old whorehouse pianist who seemed to be
trying to loud-mouth his way back to big time, attacking
anyone at all, so long as he attracted attention to himself," one
critic observed. Others, however, saw that Jelly Roll, despite
his bad temper, was substantially right. One of the old originals from New Orleans had stood up on his hind legs and

shouted that his hometown was the birthplace of jazz and that the best of jazz had been made by New Orleans musicians. The more the critics scratched through the old recordings the more they realized that Jelly Roll had told the truth, even if his phraseology was purple.

Mister Handy disposed of, Jelly looked around for another publicity break. He saw that history had put his name back into the headlines, and a passion for history took full possession of him. He sat down at his desk and began an autobiography whose opening paragraphs rolled time back to its very dawn. . . .

> The world was created by the supreme master after working six days and on the seventh day he rested. There were lots of creations that were not known to the greater masses which then lived in the Old World. The New World wasn't known until the King and Queen financed a trip for the great Christopher Columbus to go and accomplish his idea of trying to find a short cut to some other country, which was India. Columbus was lost en route and was almost assassinated for his determination to continue on his journey. Accidentally he spied land after many months journey on the high seas. This was the New World, another of God's creations, a large area of beautiful land, of seas, lakes, rivers, climates, etc., finally known as America.
>
> This land grew tremendously populated and was build up at a tremendous rate of speed. People of every nationality settled in this vast haven. France was the owner of one of the most historical states in

the country, a state named Louisiana. In the southwest central part of this state was the greatest city
in this country, the city of New Orleans. In this
city there was a son born to a family of French
descent, known as La Menthe. The son was named
Ferdinand Joseph La Menthe. . . .

Periods as resounding as these were rolling through Morton's mind when he made his first visit to the Library of
Congress in May of 1938. With his long black Lincoln, his
diamonds, and his highclass clothes he scarcely seemed like a
good source for folklore, but his prose was irresistible. Besides,
as director of the Archive of American Folk Song, I decided it
would be a worthwhile project to discover how traditional
music had influenced an early figure in jazz history.

Mister Jelly Roll, of course, had an entirely different purpose. History had wandered "way out of line." Clearly he felt
it was his mission to set it straight and in doing so to carve a
suitable niche for himself in the hall of fame. At any rate we
agreed on a series of recordings and the one-lung portable
Presto recorder with its little crystal mike was set up by the
piano in the Coolidge Auditorium.

Jelly Roll, unimpressed by the austere setting of the most
exclusive chamber-music recitals in the world, tossed his expensive summer straw on the bench of the Steinway grand,
raised the lid to stash away the bourbon bottle, and then fell
to larruping away at *Alabama Bound* as cool as if guests had
been announced at Gypsy Schaeffer's. The plaster busts of
Bach, Beethoven, and Brahms looked sternly down, but if
Jelly noticed them, he probably figured they were learning a
thing or two.

"This is a little number I composed down in Alabama at one of the early periods, Mister Lomax—around 1901 or 1902," Jelly said. "The frequent saying was that anyplace you was going you was bound for that place. So in fact I was *Alabama Bound* . . .

> *Doncha leave me here,*
> *Doncha leave me here,*
> *But if you just must go,*
> *Leave me a dime for beer.* . . .

The most cynical verse of the blues, intoned in a soft trombone-growl and below it, supporting the clean line of the melody, a procession of limpid chords, balanced, crisp, delicately textured, and tender with color—Mister Jelly grinned at me. He knew what he would find in my face; he'd been "professor" a long time and he knew how to please even a folklorist. The amplifier of the recorder was hot; the needle was quivering with Jelly's arpeggios. I sat down on the floor with the machine behind me—to put the contrivance out of sight—as Mister Jelly was saying, "Now, of course, that will give you an idea of just one of my styles—" his tone was solemn, a mite condescending. I grinned in my turn. It always had helped to sit at their feet; they begin *telling you* at once. "But I believe I might begin at the beginning—" Jelly went on . . .

"That's right, Mister Morton. Tell us who your folks were, where you were born, when, how . . ."

With not a moment's pause—as if all his life he had been waiting for this moment and treasuring up the sentences—

Jelly Roll began to think out loud in a Biblical, slow-drag
beat . . .

> *As I can understand,*
> *My folks were in the city of New Orleans*
> *Long before the Louisiana Purchase*
> *And all my folks directly from the shores of France,*
> *That is, across the world in the other world,*
> *And they landed in the New World*
> *Years ago . . .*

A throbbing stream of tropic chords flowed softly behind
the deep voice, and the husky voice spun out the tale like a
song of Louisiana live-oaks on a lazy afternoon. The warm
magic caught Jelly Roll and lit up the sombre auditorium.
One could feel the back seats filling up with ghostly listeners:
Mimi and Laura in their black shawls, Eulalie holding a John-
the-Conqueror root, Mamie Desdoumes smiling a fuzzy
drunken smile, King Bolden with his red undershirt showing
and his stubby cornet under his elbow, Gypsy Schaeffer in her
notoriety diamonds, Aaron Harris and Boar Hog in their boxback coats and Stetsons, Bad Sam and Benny Frenchy, King
Porter and Scott Joplin, Stavin Chain and Clark Wade, Albert
Cahill and Tony Jackson, a company of young octoroons whispering "Look yonder at Winding Boy"—all these ghosts
leaned forward to listen to Morton tell their story. And in the
front now sat big Ed La Menthe, holding a battered slide
trombone and smiling like he owned the joint. . . .

The next days passed like Mardi Gras. At that time no
precedents or red tape bound the infant folksong archive.

Mister Jelly Roll came to the Library almost every afternoon, driving his Lincoln and finding every visit the occasion for a new, though always conservative, outfit. All this was front for Jelly, I began to perceive, and very thin front, too, for he was at the end of his resources. These sessions were important to him. He was renewing his self-confidence as he relived his rich and creative past for a sympathetic audience that didn't interrupt; he was putting his world in order; but, much more to the point, New Orleans and her boy, Jelly, were getting their hearing at the bar of history itself.

Morton was very polite and kind to me. Although Creole folklore and the street-songs of New Orleans were not in the forefront of his mind, he obligingly recalled them. He performed blues that reminded him unpleasantly of environments where the lice had crawled along his collar. Protesting that the blues were "lowdown, illiterate" music, he nevertheless moaned the blues by the hour, ladling down the cheap whiskey I could afford to buy, warming up his dusty vocal chords and discovering in himself a singing style as rich as Louis Armstrong's. Far from taking all the credit for the origin of jazz, once he got into his historical stride, Jelly Roll generously shared the stage with a host of local stars who played a part in its early days. Best of all, he brought his old friends vividly alive by playing their music in their style in a series of dazzling performances right there on the Library of Congress grand. He re-created the piano styles of ivory wizards a generation dead, re-creations which turn out to match the exact sound of the old piano rolls. To every query his responses were so instant and so vivid with time and place and who was there and what they said that I knew Jelly was seeing it in fancy, as well as in memory's eye. Forgotten by almost everyone, shut out of the great palace of hot music he had planned and built, this tired Creole brought to life again, singlehanded and by sheer energy, the golden period of New Orleans jazz. Since that day Jelly's diamond has glittered in every book and article on hot music.

Till the Butcher Cut Him Down

Mister Jelly Roll tried to give me everything he could remember in the month we spent together, but there was too much to tell. During breaks in the recording sessions, he dictated to my secretary, edging around the desk in pursuit of her, but always urbane, always the gentleman, never breaking the stride of his story. He wanted to tell it all. He repeatedly said he counted on me to write his life story.

We became honored visitors at The Jungle Inn, where Jelly served champagne cocktails and invariably announced—"I have the honor to present the Librarian of Congress."

While U Street patrons stared, we sat in the corner and tried to untangle those years after World War I when Jelly seemed superior to time and lived each month like a decade. Yet we had not worked out a systematic picture for the years after

1921 before both of us had to turn to other things. 1939 slipped away before I was able to call Jelly's place again. Cordelia froze over the phone . . .

"Morton don't work here any more. . . . No, I don't know where he's gone."

Years later Mabel still shuddered when she remembered those last days in The Jungle Inn. . . .

This Cordelia, she never would back Jelly Roll up, said Mabel. He had put a cover charge on The Jungle Inn to keep the riff-raff and the roughnecks out of the place, but she would let them come on in anyhow even when they wouldn't take their hats off. Ferd tried to talk with Cordelia, but she say how could she turn them away when she'd known them from kids up?

One night one of these riff-raff got to acting rowdy and Ferd called him. The fellow then used some bad language. Ferd slapped him. Then he sat down at the piano and began to play and the fellow slipped up behind him and stabbed him. Stabbed him the first time in the head and, when Ferd turned, he stabbed him just above the heart. Then Ferd grabbed him and they went down.

I was back of the bar mixing a Pink Lady when I heard the scuffle. When I come out from behind the bar I couldn't hardly tell which was which, they were so covered with blood. The blood was just gushing out of Ferd like out of a stuck beef. I took a heavy glass ashtray and I struck this young man just as hard as I could in the head. Then we pulled Ferd away—Ferd was on top by then—and Ferd grabbed an iron pipe and was going to kill him, but Cordelia grabbed Ferd and the fellow got away.

Some of these Polock cops they have in Washington came in and we took Ferd to the hospital. I hate that town, everything about it—the way they treated Ferd in the hospital. Took him in there and laid him right under an electric fan and put some ice-water packs on the wound. Said that would clog the blood. I think right there was where he got his bad heart and the asthma—right there in that lousy Washington hospital.

And, you know, that boy that had stabbed Ferd only got thirty days! Cordelia wouldn't prefer charges against him.

It wasn't but a few weeks till that same boy came back up in the place again and started hanging around, full of that cheap wine they call "sneaky pete." Ferd talked to Cordelia but she said she couldn't do nothing against the child of a schoolmate of hers.

I began to talk to him. I told him, "The Jungle Inn is going to be your coffin. You've got to get out of here. They're going to kill you."

He had some big plans for Christmas, to bring in a bunch of new acts from New York, but I talked him out of it this time, I said, "Listen, you've got to listen to me now. This isn't your town. These aren't your kind of folks. Just let them get good and drunk Christmas Eve and they'll come in here looking for trouble and that will be your end."

Finally he said "All right." Two days before Christmas he got his car, packed his trunks, and told Mister Carew* goodbye. We didn't say a thing to Cordelia, we just headed North. It was a blizzard that night—a blizzard when he was coming

---

* His friend Roy J. Carew, who published his last tunes and became his musical executor.

into Washington and one when he was leaving—and we had to take it easy. Coming over that Delaware River Bridge we had to just inch along, it was so slippery with ice. We drove into New York in a snowstorm.

So in January of 1939 Jelly Roll Morton tackled that cruel city again. He gigged out on Long Island with pickup bands. He played personal appearances. Now that Morton was an "important historical figure" the young hipsters at least stared at him respectfully, though they scarcely could listen to the music he played at the jam sessions. Jelly abominated jam sessions; they ran counter to his whole approach to jazz; but now he had fallen low and he had to sit in. The French critics discovered him. Victor reissued some of his old records. A small record company did a small historical album of the best tunes he had cut for me at the Library. Two hot-eyed jazz fans were caught by Washington police crawling into a window of the Archive of American Folk Song; they confessed to an insatiable craving for the records Jelly Roll had made for the Library of Congress. It had already become fashionable to collect early Morton, even while the live man was charging around New York City talking about a big new band, demanding a better rating from ASCAP, arranging to sue his publishers for back royalties, ready to launch a war to the death with his old enemy, MCA.

In September Victor called him in to record some of the best tunes from our already famous Library of Congress session.*

---

* Fred Ramsey, jazz critic, graciously permitted a paraphrase of his notes on this session—the only picture of Mister Jelly Roll in action. It appears in Appendix 2.

Mister Jelly Roll pulled together a band of the most accomplished and temperamental New Orleans men, and in the
tense atmosphere of the recording studio looked not like a
museum piece at all, but like a great orchestra leader. He may
have felt he was back in the business the way he wanted to be
as he heard Sidney Bechet take solos on *Winding Boy,* as his hot
piano paced the men through *High Society,* and as the boys
clowned on the choruses of . . .

> He rambled all around,
> In and out the town,
> He rambled till the butcher cut him down . . .

But Mister Jelly had derided the old butcher for the last
time.

I met him one day on a subway stair in New York and
walked a little way with him. He had to stop every few steps
to get his breath; then, after a moment of coughing, he went
on in a weak voice with his plans for suing ASCAP and breaking MCA. He was often tired, he told me. His composing had
slowed down. "From writing music, playing pool and looking
for spots on cards under bright lights, my eyes is shot," said
a very subdued Mister Jelly Roll. Charles Smith, who super-
vised the recording of his fine piano album, "New Orleans
Memories," recalls that "his fingers were stiff and his heart
wasn't pumping the way it should." But the old ram couldn't
stop rambling no matter how sick and bad he felt. Mabel
Morton recalls his last try. . . .

. . . He was to open at the Golden Gate Ballroom in
Harlem with a band, she said. All the time he was rehearsing
he was getting sicker and sicker. I noticed when he walked

upstairs he breathed very hard and had shortening of the breath. The evening of the opening he was shaving in his tuxedo, and he began having those asthma attacks, one right after another, just like he was pulling his last breath. It was getting on to the hour he was supposed to be at the Golden Gate, and I said, "Ferd, let me call up the manager and tell him that you're ill."

"No," he told me, "no, I'll be all right in a minute."

I could see he was terrible sick. Finally, about 7:30 I got on the telephone and called the manager: "I'm very sorry, but Jelly Roll Morton can't appear tonight. He's having a heart condition, one right after another."

I had two musicians carry him down the steps and put him in the car and I took him to the hospital. I stayed in the hospital till almost three, with no doctor around and the nurse telling me she couldn't give him anything.

But you know, those doctors became very interested in him the three months he was there. Whenever I would come to visit, there were always three or four of them around the bed, listening to his stories. And one time, nearly scared me to death, his bed was empty and I found out they had him up on one of the porches playing the piano. . . . They must have been testing him, because his doctor told me, "Well, I'm going to let him go home now. But I'm going to tell you one thing. Jelly Roll Morton can't play the piano any more. He can live ten or fifteen years longer, but he can't play piano."

At home he began to brood all the time, began to worry. I said, "Why should you brood? Your life means more to you than your music. Perhaps it won't be ten or fifteen

years. Maybe it will be longer. Make yourself satisfied with
the royalties from your music and your records." But Ferd
couldn't get that in his head. He was a man used to making
a lot of money and having a big band and he just kept
brooding.

Wasn't out of the hospital a month and he says to me one
day, "I'm going downtown and make some sides." I tried to
prevent him in every way, but he told me, "Let me take my
own chances," and he went down and he made *Alabama Bound,
Good Old New York* and *Fingerbuster*—he played so fast on that
one, I'm surprised he didn't get a heart attack right there—
and one of his late songs, *My Home Is in a Southern Town*. Me
and Ferd had been talking about going back for a visit to New
Orleans and I guess that's what he had in mind when he
sung . . .

> *Way down South where I was born in a country town,*
> *Where they grow cotton and corn, that's where I am bound.*
> > *Where sweet potatoes grow,*
> > *Beets and turnips make a show,*
> > > *Carrots, mustard greens,*
> > > *Cabbage and string beans.*
> > *Wisht I was there. . . .*
> *My home's in a Southern town,*
> *Where folks never wear a frown,*
> *Everybody's happy both night and day,*
> *The sun is shining down upon the new-mown hay.*
> *Where the folks are really true blue,*
> *There's hospitality on tap the whole year through,*
> *There's where I'm going to make my showing,*

My home is in a Southern town,
  Way down South!
My home is in a Southern town!*

In November of 1940 the news came to Ferd from Los Angeles that his godmother had passed away. He got terribly restless. He was worried because his godfather was blind, and he said anybody could step in and take advantage of the old man. He felt like he ought to get out there and take care of the money and the jewels his godmother had left. And it turned out Ferd was correctly worried. Somebody got in there and got that poor blind man to sign something, which he didn't understand what he was signing, and got away with every penny and every last diamond.

I wondered how Jelly was going to travel without any money, but he showed me. He got his two cars, packed all his belongings in the Cadillac and went and got a big chain and chained it to the rear of the Lincoln and he was ready to start. I asked him to let me go along, but he said, "No, I know my condition. I know if something was to go wrong, you'd have hysterics and it would make my heart attack worse."

The priest came out and begged him, said "Ferdinand, this is November and very bad weather for traveling." Ferd said, "Father, I have just lost my godmother and my old godfather

---

* Lyrics reproduced by permission of Tempo-Music Publishing Co., the copyright owner.

There is simply no way to reconcile this maudlin vision of the South, shared by Foster, by the minstrel show, and by most pop music, with the cruel visage it had presented to Morton and to all his people.

is out in California, blind and helpless. He needs my care. Besides, I've got to find someplace that is better for my health. This place is killing me by degrees, and I understand they have six months of dry weather out in California."

So the priest told him he could not prevent him and he gave him the Papal blessing, blessed both of the cars, and said Godspeed be with him on his way. Then Ferd drove away in his Lincoln, towing his Cadillac, headed for California. That was the last I saw of my husband.

What a man he was to start driving all the way to California in the middle of the winter in two cars! What nerve he had! I was so worried. I read in the papers where a bridge collapsed with a car going over it and I was sure it was him. But the next day I read where that man had a dog with him and so I knew it wasn't Jelly had drowned. When I heard from him next, he wrote from a Catholic church; he was saying his prayers after they had rescued him from a snowstorm where he had seen a woman and her child frozen to death. Next I heard he was in California.

Eureka, Calif.
Nov. 9, 1940.

Well Dearest

I thought I would drop a line, to let you know I am safe.

I started and decided to go west, and, believe me, when I hit Pennsylvania and every state thereafter I met a terrific storm—as follows, Pennsylvania, Ohio, Indiana, Illinois, Missouri, Kansas, Wyoming, Idaho, Oregon, California.

I slid off the road in Wyoming in a sleet storm

and damaged the car a little. The blessed mother was with me and I did not get hurt. I had to leave one of the cars in Montpelier, Idaho, on account of the weather was too dangerous. And the next couple of nights I was caught up on a mountain in Oregon near the town of John Day. The snow was very slippery and deep. The police car had to pull me out and I was not hurt. Yes, the blessed mother really taken care of me in a-many ways in all the storms and danger I had to confront me. I did not get a chance to make many novenas on the road on account of driving all the time, but I said lots of prayers just the same.

I am trying to find some kind of good climate and will soon or I will keep roaming till I do.

I cannot go home [New Orleans] at this time without money, but I will send you there as soon as I can. Give the priests and all my friends my best regards and will always remember you in my prayers. May God bless you and keep you. Yours very truly.

> From a real pal,
> *Ferd J. Morton.*

> Los Angeles, Calif.
> Nov. 13, 1940.

My darling Mabel,

I am here in L.A. I am going to try to make some money so I can send you home [New Orleans], then

I know you will be okeh. I would not think of leaving you in that cruel city . . . The weather is warm here and I feel some better. Even my eyesight have improved a bit . . . I will try and see if I can start making a drive some way. . . .

> Yours as ever,
> *Ferd.*

> Los Angeles, Calif.
> Nov. 20th

Hello Angel

Tell Miss H—— when she asks for me, that I went out of town with some musicians to see if I could plan some way to put a band to work. I will never be satisfied holding my hands doing nothing, because I like to make my own living and, furthermore, I want to make some money so I can pay that back even though they don't expect it. . . . I intend to pay my garage bill, but I want him to pay the damages he did to me, so it will be even.

My godfather told me of many diamonds that my godmother left—all was stolen and not one left. Some of their friends told me the same thing, too.

I am glad you have a nice room and are satisfied. I will try to send you to N.O. as soon as I can get hold of some money, [but] things seem very slow here like New York. Be careful what you say or do.

> Much love & success,
> *Ferd.*

Nov. 28th

My own Mabel

It worries me terribly when I don't hear from you under the conditions I left you under . . . Things seem very quiet here now. I don't know how I will be here, but I will be trying . . . as I want to at least to send you something for Xmas. . . .

One to depend on.
Ferd.

Nov. 30th

My dearest Mabel, wife,

I received your letter of the 26th . . . also inquired at post office for your general delivery letter [but] I guess it is lost. . . . I did not have much of a Thanksgiving so far as fun goes, but I was feeling good account of sunshine and thank God for that. I have been going to church Sundays, but I haven't been going much in the mornings account of terrible headaches. . . . Don't pay any attention to any of those. I never told her no such thing. She ask if you were here and I said no and did not give them any satisfaction. They try to find out anyone's business and start gossiping. Pay no attention to them. As soon as I make some money, you will be gone and they won't know where you passed. I never told anyone you wasn't my wife. Find out the fare from N.Y. to N.O.

Much luck to you, my dear. May God bless you.
Yours, as ever.
Ferd.

P. S. Mrs. ——— has proven to be very rotten all the way through. She is N.G. and I don't owe her anything, I am satisfied of that. . . .

Dec. 28th

Dear Mabel:

Very sorry to hear of your illness, but I haven't been very well at all, myself . . . Please accept this token for your Xmas gift, $15.00. As soon as I make some money, I will send you home. Wishing you every success.

> Very truly yours as ever.
> *Ferd.*

Jan. 6th

Dear Mabel

Very sorry to hear that you have been sick but glad you are better. Xmas week found me ill. Outside of that, I was okeh. Could not eat anything much. . . .

How did you come out with Mrs. V———? Did you get your money or the goods? Tell them please settle up with you. They are no good. As soon as I am able, I will send you home. Enclosed you will find $5. . . .

> Very truly yours,
> *Ferd.*

Jan. 16th

Dear Mabel,

I am writing a letter to Mrs. V———. I want you to mail it from N.Y. and we will see if you get an answer from this and, if not maybe you better place it in a lawyer's hands. Of course, there isn't an awful lot for him to gain, but he may write a letter for you.

I haven't made any money since I've been gone, although I received the ASCAP check. But this town takes money to live, so that is about all gone. I was in hopes that I would have gotten the Melrose check, which is past due. I am now awaiting their answer. This is the second registered letter and no answer from them. If I get the check and there's any real money—two or three hundred dollars—I will arrange for your trip to New Orleans. If you can find a cheaper room with some of your church friends, I would take it. . . . Enclosed you will find $10.

Very truly yours,
Ferd.

Jan. 28th

Dear Mabel,

Your letter was received. I was delayed in answering account of being sick. I am much better now. . . .

I received the check from Melrose. $52.00. I seen a lawyer. He advised me not to cash it, so I will institute suit against them. I was depending on that to send you home. Now I will have to wait a little longer. Thanks for the prayers. . . .

Ferd.

Feb. 22nd

Dear Mabel

Your letter was received but due to illness I was unable to answer until now. Up to now I have had two different doctors. My breath has been very short like when I had to go to the hospital and have been spitting blood and many other symptoms too numerous to mention, but I am some better this morning.

Go to Mrs. V————'s church in Brooklyn across from her house and appeal to the priest that you need your money. Tell the whole thing and ask him to help you get it for you and I think it will help. . . . As soon as I am able I will send you the money to go home.

Regards.

Ferd.

An envelope addressed to Mabel and dated April 26, 1941, contained only the following . . .

. . .

Form 6001

POST OFFICE DEPARTMENT
THIRD ASSISTANT POSTMASTER GENERAL
DIVISION OF MONEY ORDERS

No._____

Stamp of Issuing Office

will write soon

FEE _____

The Postmaster
will insert

still sick.

here _____
the office drawn on, when the office
named by the remitter does not trans-
act money-order business.

Spaces above this line are for the Postmaster's record, to be filled in by him

Application for Domestic Money Order

Spaces below to be filled in by purchaser, or, if necessary,
by another person for him

Amount—

USE *FIGURES,*
DO NOT SPELL _____ Dollars _____ Cents

To be }
paid to} _____
(Name of person or firm for whom order is intended)

Whose
address }
is } _____ Street

City
and }
State } _____

Sent by _____
(Name of sender)

City
and }
State } _____ Street

PURCHASER MUST SEND ORDER AND COUPON TO PAYEE
(FOR FEES SEE OTHER SIDE)

DO NOT RISK MONEY OR STAMPS IN ORDINARY MAIL—BUY A MONEY ORDER

FOR SPEED—Send your money order AIR MAIL special delivery

DOWNBEAT   LOS ANGELES
AUGUST 1, 1941
BURY JELLY ROLL MORTON ON COAST

Los Angeles—A solemn high requiem mass, performed at St. Patrick's Church with the full dignity
of the Roman Catholic ritual, followed by burial at
Calvary Cemetery was the world's parting gesture
to Ferdinand "Jelly Roll" Morton, who died here at
Los Angeles hospital July 10 of heart trouble and
asthma.

One white man was among the approximately
one hundred and fifty people who attended the
church service and accompanied the funeral procession to the cemetery—Dave Stuart of the Jazz Man
Record Shop.

THE CONSPICUOUSLY ABSENT

Notably absent from the funeral of the man who did
so much to bring jazz out of the honkey-tonks and
dives of New Orleans were two of the most successful Negro bandleaders of the day, Duke Ellington
and Jimmie Lunceford. Ellington is appearing at
the Mayan Theatre here in a stage revue and Lunceford is at the Casa Mañana.

Among those present were the members of what
was probably the first Negro jazz band to make
phonograph recordings—pioneers of jazz saying
goodbye to one of their valiant gang—musicians
who played from the heart because they never

learned any other way to play. Kid Ory, trombone; Papa Mutt Carey, cornet; Dink Johnson (Jelly Roll's brother-in-law), clarinet; Ed Garland, bass; Fred Washington, piano; and Ben Borders, drums.

FOUR ALL PALL BEARERS

Four of that famous old band were among Jelly's pall bearers: Ory, Papa Mutt, Washington, and Garland. The other pall bearers were Paul Howard, secretary of Local 767; Spencer Johnson and Frank Withers, all old friends who had worked with Jelly in bygone years.

Reb Spikes, Jelly's old song-writing partner, didn't have a car and almost didn't get to the cemetery. Dave Stuart saw that Reb was about to get left behind and took him out in his car, "Sure appreciated that," said Reb. "Wanted to go as far as I could with Jelly."

Somebody mentioned it would have been a nice thing to have a street band there to march back from the cemetery swinging hell out of Jelly's old songs the way they used to do in New Orleans. The men in Ory's old band decided that was a swell idea and that they would do it next time . . .

> *He rambled,*
> *He rambled,*
> *He rambled till the butcher cut him down.* . . .

Two persons at the funeral knew that something was missing out of the coffin. "I've always lived with diamonds and I want to be buried with them," he had said time and again, but now beneath the cold lips forever sealed, the gold inlay in the front tooth showed a ragged hole. The diamond was gone. It was curious that no one accused the undertaker.

As the funeral procession wound its way through the decorous meadows of Calvary Rest at least one mourner thought of the old French Cemetery of New Orleans and of the tomb of Marie Laveau, scrawled over at midnight with formless, impassioned black crayon appeals to the old voodoo queen. Anita Gonzalez, to whom Jelly had now finally returned after twenty years, looked down at the new mound and shivered, surmising in her dark Catholic soul where the man she had loved had gone.

Jelly was a very devout Catholic, Anita explained, speaking calmly, giving the facts. But voodoo, which is an entirely different religion, had hold of him, too. I know. I nursed and supported him all during his last illness after he had driven across the continent in the midst of winter with that bad heart of his.

The woman, Laura Hunter, who raised Jelly Roll, was a voodoo witch. Yes, I'm talking about his godmother who used to be called Eulalie Echo. She made a lot of money at voodoo. People were always coming to her for some help and she was giving them beads and pieces of leather and all that. Well, everybody knows that before you can become a witch you have to sell the person you love the best to Satan as a sacrifice. Laura loved Jelly best. She loved Jelly better than Ed, her own husband. Jelly always knew she'd sold him to Satan and that, when she died, he'd die, too—she would take him down with her.

Laura taken sick in 1940 and here came Jelly Roll driving his Lincoln all the way from New York. Laura died. And then Jelly, in spite that I had financed him a new start in the music business and he was beginning to feel himself again, he taken sick, too. A couple months later he died in my arms, begging me to keep anointing his lips with oil that had been blessed by a bishop in New York. He had oil running all over him when he gave up the ghost. . . .

Anita looked down at her diamond-studded hands at rest upon her silken lap. Then, with a quick smile, she did not forget to add. . . .

"Be sure to mention my tourist camp in your book, Mister Lomax. Our chicken dinners are recommended by Duncan Hines."

ACKNOWLEDGMENTS
APPENDIX ONE
APPENDIX TWO
APPENDIX THREE

Acknowledgments

Sidney Martin introduced me to Jelly Roll. Charles Smith smiled on the project all the way from the recordings to galley proof. Dr. Harold Spivacke gave official leave to make the records. A rather embarrassed but courageous Kansas secretary transcribed the L.C. series.

Had there been no talks with Creole Paul Dominguez, Leonard Bechet, John A. St. Cyr, Big Eye Louis Nelson, Omer Simeon, and Bunk Johnson, I would never have cared to finish the book. Henry Monette, Amède Colas, and Anita Gonzalez helped to find some lost trails. Courageous Mabel Morton held back nothing and laid the basis for a chapter.

R. J. Amateau did invaluable sleuthing. Hally Wood, Jean Ritchie, and Jean Haydock transcribed miles of tape. Bea

Baron, Ronnie Gilbert, Greta Brodie and, especially, Boots Casetta typed and retyped late and long.

Rudi Blesh's advice, counsel, and back files couldn't have been dispensed with. Roy Carew was generous with time and music.

Elizabeth Lomax and Mary Mahoney showed me where I had gone wrong and put me back on the hard road.

To all these, thanks for Jelly Roll and for myself.

Appendix One

The Tunes

Morton's life story should not overshadow his stature as a musician of great originality and influence. He was probably the first true composer of jazz, able to arrange his compositions in music notation, finally producing orchestrations in correct form for ten and eleven pieces. That the best critics of American popular music already take him seriously and put him among the top rank of the men of jazz is, I believe, only a foretaste of the time when he will stand in the select company of American originals along with Billings, Foster, and Gershwin.

SIGMUND SPAETH, *A History of Popular Music in America:*
"He was unquestionably the best all-around musician produced by the classical period of jazz and his career did not reach its climax until past the middle twenties. . . ."

HUGUES PANASSIÉ, *Jazz Information:*
"Jelly Roll is one of the great figures of jazz . . . a first class composer . . . besides Ellington I don't know anyone who has written so many charming tunes . . . the father of hot piano."

PAUL EDUARD MILLER, *Downbeat:*

One of the ten men mainly responsible for the development of swing music. . . ."

RUDI BLESH, *Shining Trumpets:*

"No other player in jazz history has combined so many rich elements in a piano style. . . . More than any other individual he knew the requirements of jazz. . . . There is not a record of Morton's great period which is not as truly modern as the day it was played . . . he completed an entire period of jazz and marked the path the future could take. Without doubt the most creative figure in jazz."

FERDINAND MORTON:

"Listen, man, whatever, you blow on that horn, you're blowing *Jelly Roll.* . . ."

So it was that Morton used to boast at the hangouts of the hornblowers, and it was hard to prove him wrong. His early tunes were the best of hot compositions and the bands that played them read like a royal roll-call of jazz.

MILNEBURG JOYS, best-known recordings by: *New Orleans Rhythm Kings,* Gennet 5217, 3076; *Glen Gray Casa Loma,* Brunswick 6922, English Brunswick 01866; *McKinney's Cotton Pickers,* Victor 21611, Bluebird 10954; *Bennie Moten's Orchestra,* Victor 24381, Bluebird 5585, HMV 4953; Don Redman, Bluebird 10071; *Dorsey Brothers,* Victor 26437; *Tommy Dorsey,* Victor 26437; *Connie's Inn Orchestra,* Crown 3212, Varsity 8042; *Red Nichols,* Brunswick 20110; *Jimmy O'Bryant's Washboard*

Band, Paramount 12321; *Lil Hardway's Orchestra,* Vocalion 1252; *Kid Rena,* Delta 802; *George Lewis' New Orleans Stompers,* Climax 102.

WOLVERINE BLUES, best-known recordings by: *Jelly Roll Morton* on piano, Gennet 5289, Autograph 623; *Jelly Roll Trio,* Victor 21064, Bluebird 10258; *Louis Armstrong,* Decca 3105; *New Orleans Rhythm Kings,* Gennet 5102; *Jack Teagarden,* Columbia 35297; *Larry Clinton,* Victor 25863; *Bob Crosby,* Decca 2032, 3040; *Benny Goodman,* Vocalion 15656, Brunswick 80027; *Earl Hines,* Decca 577; *Joe Marsala,* Variety 565.

KING PORTER STOMP, best-known recordings by: *Jelly Roll Morton* on piano on Autograph 617, Gennet 5289, Vocalion 1020, Commodore 591; *Benny Goodman,* Victor 25090; *Metronome All Star Band,* Columbia 35389; *Glenn Miller,* Bluebird 7853; *Teddy Bunn,* Blue Note 503; *Fletcher Henderson,* Columbia 1534, 35671, Okeh 41565; *Harry James,* Brunswick 8366; *Erskine Hawkins,* Bluebird 7839; *Claude Hopkins,* Decca 184; *Bob Crosby,* Decca 4390.

These listings barely suggest the extraordinary influence of Jelly Roll's ideas on the whole of jazz. Even more catalytic than the set pieces were scores of charming and original musical devices which he scattered broadcast by playing, publishing, recording, and by touring orchestras. To this musical activity Jelly Roll brought the energy and the passion that marked his whole life. In addition, as a composer he never swerved from a consistent devotion to his special flare. He had something in mind to say to the whole world, something which he could only say in music. A review of his published works shows a consistently productive composer with an unswerving purpose. In 1940 Jelly Roll was completing what young Ferdinand set out to do in 1902.

When this book was first published in 1950, Tempo-Music and Mayfair Music were kind enough to permit the duplication of some of his music in this appendix. Since that time, almost all Morton copyrights have been consolidated under the control of Edwin H. Morris and Company and Peer/Southern Music Publishing Company. For further details, see page 353. In addition, Hally Wood has transcribed a few of the folk songs from the Library of Congress sessions. Special kudos are due to Hally Wood, to J. Lawrence Cook, and to Roy Carew for their sensitive work in transcribing these scores.

1 *Mamie's Blues*—transcribed by J. Lawrence Cook
2 *Winin' Boy Blues*—transcribed by Roy Carew
3 *The Naked Dance*—transcribed by Roy Carew
4 *Buddy Bolden's Blues*—transcribed by Roy Carew
5 *The Miserere*—transcribed by Roy Carew
6 *Indian Song*—transcribed by Hally Wood
7 *C'eté n'aut' can-can*—transcribed by Hally Wood
8 *Moi pas l'aimez ça*—transcribed by Hally Wood
9 *Alabama Bound*—transcribed by Hally Wood
10 *Georgia Skin Game*—transcribed by Hally Wood
11 *King Porter Stomp*—Melrose Music Corporation
12 *Jelly Roll Blues*—Melrose Music Corporation
13 *Frog-i-more Rag*—Morton manuscript.

N.B. Morton's unique ad lib. vocal interpretation has been preserved intentionally in this version, even though at times it may seem at variance with the piano score.

Mamie's Blues

(219 Blues)

Transcribed and Edited by
J. Lawrence Cook

Words and Melody by
MAMIE DESDUME

Arranged by
FERDINAND J. MORTON
(Jelly Roll)

Mamie's Blues

Mamie's Blues

Excerpt from:

WININ' BOY BLUES

Winin' Boy Blues

See that spider climbin' up the wall,
See that spider climbin' up the wall,
Well, you see that spider climbin' up the wall,
Goin' up there to get her ashes hauled.
I'm the Winin' Boy, don't deny my name.

Excerpt from:

THE NAKED DANCE

The Naked Dance

Excerpt from:

Buddy Bolden's Blues

I thought I heard Judge Fogarty say,
"Thirty days in the market, take him away,
Give him a good broom, take the pris'ner away,"
I heard Judge Fogarty say—.

Excerpt from:

THE MISERERE

from

IL TROVATORE

(A Transformation)

The Miserere

INDIAN SONG

Transcribed and edited by Holly Wood

1 This is written longer than the singer actually sang it. Barely anticipate the beat without any hurried feeling and you will have it.
2 Not sung as a full tone change, but more as an emphasis on this beat.
3 Sometimes a G.

Copyright, Tempo-Music Publishing Co.

C'ETÉ N'AUT' CAN-CAN

A This note is hit only slightly before the beat. *Payez* pronounced as two syllables.

MOI PAS L'AIMEZ ÇA

A There is actually more syncopation throughout than can be indicated. For instance, this note might just as well have been written as the last sixteenth of the previous beat. Triplets might be substituted.

B The first voice often came in with the stanza while the chorus voices were still singing their last note or two. An early stage of African polyphony.

ALABAMA BOUND *

The smaller notes, in most cases, deserved more time, but it was impossible to give the tone fractions exactly and split them up into heavily flagged notes. The phrase was different each time. The half-tone and quarter, then, are the value of the complete slur, and not the value of the C alone.

GEORGIA SKIN GAME

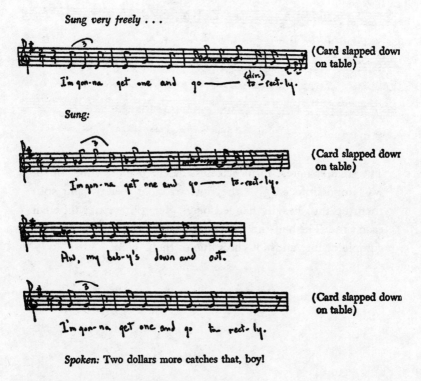

Sung very freely . . .

(Card slapped down on table)

I'm gon-na get one and go ——— (din) to-rect-ly.

Sung:

(Card slapped down on table)

I'm gon-na get one and go ——— to-rect-ly.

Aw, my bab-y's down and out.

(Card slapped down on table)

I'm gon-na get one and go to-rect-ly.

Spoken: Two dollars more catches that, boy!

(Card slapped down on table)

Oh, I'll get one and go to-rect-ly.

Spoken: Three dollars more. Five, I got you on that.
Okay! Bet! Roll up. Okay Roll up here.
Two more on the trey there. Okay! Bet!

Georgia Skin Game

(Card slapped down
on table)

Spoken: Say, you want anything over that tenspot?
Alright, King, come up there.
Ten dollars more'll check the King.
Okay, boys, bet. Okay!

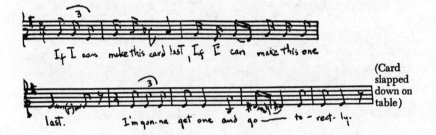

(Card
slapped
down on
table)

Spoken: Eight more dollars up there on the eightspot.

KING PORTER STOMP

King Porter Stomp

285

JELLY ROLL BLUES

Jelly Roll Blues

Jelly Roll Blues

Frog-i-more Rag

By Ferd Morton
Writer of Jelly Roll Blues

Reproduction from Morton's original copyrighted manuscript.

Frog-i-more was composed in 1918 or earlier. At any rate it seems to have been named after a contortionist in a minstrel show with which Jelly Roll toured. This gentleman, who was billed as Frog-i-more, wore a frog costume, and it is likely that Jelly Roll actually played this melody for Frog-i-more's nightly writhings. Jelly Roll wrote the tune down in 1918 in California and his manuscript of the main theme is herewith reproduced with permission of Tempo-Music (copyright owners) as a supplement to William Russell's discussion of the Morton recording.

Comparison of the manuscript with the record shows how Morton played more notes than he usually bothered to transcribe on paper. Nevertheless, examination of this early manuscript discloses a serious composer at work. Says William Russell, most learned of jazz critics . . .

> Jelly Roll had a more formal musical training and background than many New Orleans musicians. Perhaps this fact is reflected in the formal construction of his compositions. At times the close-knit design is marked by an economy of means that amounts to understatement. *Frog-i-more* follows the usual form of Morton's stomps—introduction, a short three-part song form, and a trio section. A definite musical idea is used for each new part. Since the opening idea of the first strain—an ascending succession of seventh chords—does not immediately establish the tonality, a curious effect of an extension of the introduction is created. The contrasting second strain is unusually forceful, employing a repeated note motive and powerful left-

hand bass figures in Jelly's full *two-handed* style. After a modified return of the first strain a characteristic Morton trill bridges over to the trio.

To find a more resourceful imagination and greater skill in melodic variation than Jelly Roll Morton possessed, one can go only to Bunk Johnson. Jelly took great pride in his "improvisations." I was aware that Jelly Roll was not an unqualified admirer of Louis Armstrong, but being particularly an Armstrong fanatic and unable to understand his lack of enthusiasm, I always avoided any argument whenever Jelly brought up the subject of Armstrong. However, Jelly explained to Ken Hulsizer that he thought Louis lacked ability to "improvise *on the theme.*" If anyone should think Jelly's attitude unduly presumptuous let him but listen to the trio section of *Frog-i-more* to discover Jelly's own phenomenal skill in variation. And if one were to study the four different versions of *The Pearls* or the half dozen recordings of *Mister Jelly Lord,* and perhaps also take time to compare some of these variations with the published versions, he would begin to get an idea of Jelly's unlimited imagination and mastery of motival variation, and possibly understand why Jelly Roll had a right to say something on the subject of "improvisation."

The beautiful chorale-like melody of the *Frog-i-more* trio is first played very simply, in a style reminiscent of the sustained trio of *Wolverine Blues.* This first statement, marked "organ chorus" in the Melrose publication, is played entirely in the treble

range. On paper the tune, with its constantly repeated motive, presents a singularly foursquare appearance, but Jelly's performance is a revelation of
rhythmic variety by means of such devices as shifted
accents, slight delays, and anticipations. Of course,
to some of our European-trained "critics" this is
only a bad performance, by a pianist unable to keep
correct time, of a piece any third-grade conserva-
tory pupil could play right off at sight. Curiously,
as raggy as Jelly's performance of this chorale is,
it nevertheless is in perfect *time;* the regular pulse
can be felt throughout with no loss at all in
momentum.

The real marvel of this record, however, is the
final trio chorus. The left hand resumes its regular
beat—and how Jelly makes his old piano rock! Such
final choruses are usually labeled "stomps" in his
published solos, and that is certainly an apt though
almost tame term for the manner in which Jelly
bears down and rides on out.

The melodic invention of this finale is as notable
as its immense rhythmic vitality. Although the melodic developments of the stomp version follow
closely the simple lines of the "organ chorus,"
Jelly's rhythmic impetus and melodic embellish-
ment give the effect of fantastic and frenzied variation. Actually each bar is directly related to its
counterpart in the first simple statement and all of
Jelly's most characteristic and fanciful "figurations"
are fused with the basic idea as though they belonged there originally.

What a contrast to the final choruses of the jumping-jive Harlem musicians who think that to obtain any semblance to rhythmic excitement they must leave the theme and thus become lost altogether. But with Jelly Roll, no matter how exuberant rhythmically or varied melodically the final choruses become, there never is any doubt of their musical logic and that each note grows out of the original motive. Nor is the typical flavor of the unique Morton style ever for a second lost. *Frog-i-more Rag* offers new and most striking testimony of the mastery that placed Jelly Roll in the very vanguard of jazz composers and pianists. . . .

—*The Needle,* July 1944.

During his stay in Washington Jelly Roll acquired the friendship and admiration of a Treasury Department official who plays a very hot ragtime piano. As a sandy-haired youngster Roy J. Carew had, in the palmy old days, hung around The Frenchman's listening to the new and beautiful music Tony Jackson and his protégé, Morton, were riffling out of the piano. This music became Carew's life-long delight and hobby, so that when he found Jelly Roll in difficulty in Washington he set about helping him in a truly practical way. He established the Tempo-Music Publishing Company to protect, publish, and push Morton's uncopyrighted and unpublished works. As Jelly's musical executor he edited the manuscript piano scores here cited and he prepared this chronological list of Morton's compositions:

YEAR	TITLE	COPYRIGHT BY
1915	*The Jelly Roll Blues* (Written in 1905, arranged 1912? First published jazz composition?)	Will Rossiter, Chicago
1918	*Frog-i-more Rag* (Composed 1908)	Ferd Morton, Los Angeles
1923	*Wolverine Blues* (Words by Spikes Bros.)	Melrose Bros. Music Co., Chicago
	Froggie Moore (Part of *Frog-i-more* words by Spikes Bros.)	Spikes Bros. Pub. Co.
	Big Fat Ham	Lloyd Smith, Chicago
	Mister Jelly Lord	Melrose Bros. Music Co.
	The Pearls (Composed 1919—JRM)	"
	Grandpa's Spells	"
	Kansas City Stomps (Composed 1919—JRM)	"
	London Blues (*Shoe Shiners' Drag*)	"
1924	*King Porter Stomp* (Composed 1902—JRM)	"
1925	*Shreveport Stomps*	"
	Tom Cat Blues	"
	New Orleans Blues (Composed in 1902-3—JRM)	"
	Milneburg Joys (with Leon Rappolo and Paul Mares)	"
	Queen of Spades	"
	Midnight Mama	"
1926	*Chicago Breakdown*	"

	Sweetheart o' Mine	"
	(Part of Frog-i-more)	
	Dead Man Blues	"
	State & Madison	Charles Raymond, Chicago
	Black Bottom Stomp	Melrose Bros. Music Co.
	Sidewalk Blues	"
	Cannon Ball Blues (with Charley Rider and Marty Bloom)	"
1927	Ted Lewis Blues	"
	Jungle Blues	"
	Wild Man Blues (with Louis Armstrong)	"
	Hyena Stomp	Melrose Bros. Music Co., Inc.
	Billy Goat Stomp	"
	Windy City Blues (with Peary, Hudson, Raymond)	Denton & Haskin, New York
1928	Buffalo Blues	Triangle Music Pub. Co., New York*
	Ham & Eggs	"
	Georgia Swing	Melrose Bros. Music Co., Inc.
	Boogaboo	"
	Honey Babe	"
	Shoe Shiners' Drag	"
1929	Freakish	Southern Music Co., New York
	Seattle Hunch	"
	Burnin' the Iceberg	"

---

* A great many of these compositions were copyrighted by merely submitting a lead line of melody to the Library of Congress. No known musical score exists for them.

	Tanktown Bump	Southern Music Co.
	Pretty Lil	"
	New Orleans Bump (Monrovia)	"
	Courthouse Bump	"
	Sweet Anita Mine	"
1930	*I Hate a Man Like You*	Ferd Morton
	Down My Way	Southern Music Co.
	Try Me Out	"
	Turtle Twist	"
	Don't Tell Me Nothing 'Bout My Man	"
	Fussy Mabel	"
	Pontchartrain	"
	Harmony Blues	"
	Little Lawrence	"
	I'm Looking for a Little Bluebird	"
	Mushmouth Shuffle	"
	Deep Creek	"
	Red Hot Pepper	"
1931	*Fickle Fay Creep*	"
	Frances (Fat)	"
	Pep	"
	That'll Never Do	"
	I Hate a Man Like You	"
	That's Like It Ought to Be	"
	Blue Blood Blues	"
	Dixie Knows	Melrose Bros. Music Co., Inc.
1932	*Gambling-Jack*	Southern Music Co.
	Crazy Chords	"
	Oil Well	"
	If Someone Would Only Love Me	"
	Low Gravy	"

	Mint Julep	"
	Strokin' Away	"
	Each Day	"
1933	*Jersey* (Joe)	"
	Sweet Peter	"
1934	*Mississippi Mildred*	"
	Primrose Stomp	"
	Load of Coal	"

. . . .

1938	*If You Knew How I Love You**	Tempo-Music Pub. Co., Washington
	*My Home Is in a Southern Town**	"
	*Sweet Substitute**	"
	*Why?**	"
1939	*We Are Elks**	"
	Good Old New York	"
	We Will Never Say Goodbye	Paul Watts
	I'm Alabama Bound	Ferd J. Morton
	Wining Boy (*Winin' Boy Blues*)	Tempo-Music Pub. Co.
	I Thought I Heard Buddy Bolden Say (*Buddy Bolden's Blues*)	"
	Don't You Leave Me Here	"
	Mr. Joe	"
	The Crave	"
	The Naked Dance	"
	Sporting-House Rag	"
	Animule Dance (song)	"

---

* All the above were transcribed from the Library of Congress recording sessions and copyrighted by Tempo-Music Publishing Co.

1940	*Original Rags* (Joplin-Morton)	Tempo-Music Pub. Co.
	Big Lip Blues (song)*	"
	Get the Bucket	"
	Shake It	"
	Dirty, Dirty, Dirty	"
	Swinging the Elks	"
1942	*The Fingerbreaker {Fingerbuster}*	Roy J. Carew
1944	*Creepy Feeling*	"
1946	*Frog-i-more Rag* (renewal)	Estate of Ferd J. Morton
1947	" (published)**	Roy J. Carew
1948	*Honky-tonk Music*	Tempo-Music Pub. Co.
	Mamie's Blues (Desdoumes-Morton)**	"
1948	*La Paloma into Blues***	Estate of Ferdinand J. Morton
	Aaron Harris (*Bad Man Song*)	"
	Jelly Roll Morton's Scat Song	"
	Bert Williams (originally *The Pacific Rag* from the California years)	"
	Sweet Jazz Music	"
	Spanish Swat	"
	Discordant Jazz	"
	Melody with Break	"
	Fast Ragtime	"
	Melody with Riff	"
	A Slow Jazz Tune	"
1949	*Sammy Davis' Ragtime Style*	"

---

* Originals composed for *General's Tavern Tunes* series.
** All the above were transcribed from the Library of Congress recording sessions and copyrighted by Tempo-Music Publishing Co.

Buddy Bertrand's Blues   "

Albert Carroll's Blues   "

Boogie Woogie Blues (Crazy Chord   "
   Rag)

Game Kid Blues   "

Buddy Carter's Rag   "

Benny Frenchy's Defeat   "

Il Trovatore (A Transformation)   "

The Perfect Rag   "

Mama Nita (tango)   "

Muddy Water Blues   "

Soap Suds   "

Big Fat Ham   "

NOTE: The Melrose Bros. Music Company's and the Tempo-Music Publishing Company's copyrights are now controlled by Edwin H. Morris and Company, Inc., a division of MPL Communications, 39 W. 54th Street, New York, NY 10019 (ASCAP). The Southern Music Publishing Company's copyrights are controlled by Peer/Southern Music Publishing, 810 Seventh Avenue, New York, NY 10019 (ASCAP).

Appendix Two

The Records

For much of its life jazz was an aurally transmitted music. For more than half a century players and orchestras have learned from each other by ear and then made their own transformation of the rhythmic and harmonic material. Only recently have written arrangements intervened and then almost always the music has suffered. The shining exception was Morton's music. His scores were superb transcriptions of the free polyphonic style of New Orleans. Even so, without phonograph records, some of his music would have been lost to us, because much of it was worked out in the studio in collaboration with the virtuosos of his orchestras. Luckily, Morton was as fine an organizer and band leader as he was composer and so a fairly complete notion of his music exists on records. The high level of these records is indicated in the appreciations of the critics:

S. F. DUNCE, *Jazz Music:*
    "Just as I would recommend one specific record
by Jelly Roll Morton as being representative of jazz,
to the newcomer, so I would recommend Jelly Roll's
work in its entirety to those who have already been

captivated by jazz. There is no more enlightening collection of records to be found under the name of one man. Not all of the records are good, but they are of great variety and they illustrate jazz development and tendencies. Through all of them, like a golden thread, runs the insistent beat of Jelly Roll's uncompromising, incomparable piano."

HUGUES PANASSIÉ, *Jazz Information:*

"Jelly Roll Morton is one of the great figures of jazz music. . . . He is also one of the best pianists I have ever heard. . . . The music on every side is almost uniformly magnificent. . . . I must also mention the trio records. . . . It is through them that he gave us a very large part of his touching music . . . long before Benny Goodman's trio, which was presented to the public as an innovation and which always remained far below the Morton Trio's performances. . . ."

RUDI BLESH, *Shining Trumpets:*

"[The record] *Doctor Jazz* reveals most of the qualities of classic jazz in their fullest development. It is difficult to exhaust its variety: wide contrast of timbres; African polyrhythms; breaks; chain-breaks and solos; 'head' arrangement; free polyphony and Afro-American variation shown by the constant mutations of rhythmic pattern, tone, instrumentation, and melody."

BUD SCOTT:

"If you never heard Jelly Roll at his best, you ain't never heard jazz piano. . . ."

What jazzmen had known for forty years the young fans began to learn in the 1930's. Like Poe, jazz was first "discovered" by European critics; and at first there were more serious listeners for this music in Paris and London than in New York or Chicago. One of the English record collectors who had admired Jelly from afar met him at last in The Jungle Inn in Washington. His very British account provides a very amusing side-look at Mister Jelly Lord, who finally had encountered someone who knew more about his music than he did himself:

Morton had never heard of a record collector. I was the first one he had ever met. When I asked him if he had any of his old records, he laughed and said, "No, what would you want with any of those old things?" The idea that there might be people who collected and treasured his records had never occurred to him.

I didn't have all my Morton records in Washington, but the ones I did have I played over and over, asking Morton about personnels. Morton had forgotten what records he had made. He didn't like probing into the personnel of the records very much. Some of them he wasn't very proud of. He considered them dead stuff. He had been paid for them, had spent the money, and the public had forgotten them. He seemed to feel that they dated

him as a passé Chicago stomp man, when everything was swing and jive. He was willing to forget
them, too. When I would try to pin him down on
factual information, names, dates, and places, he
could stand it a long time, trying his best to remember, but after a couple of hours, he would edge
over by the window and look down in the street
longingly. When he got this jump-out-the-window
look in his eye, I knew he had had enough. He was
ready to go home. He was a musician and an entertainer. He had played the music and sung the
songs. Let someone else write the history.

It was almost immediately afterwards that Jelly Roll spun
out his saga for the Library of Congress microphone. What
a British discographer took for a dislike of history actually
seems to be something quite different. Jelly Roll's recording
career had been as much of a tangle as that of any other
prolific Negro musician. Years of work by absolutely tireless
jazz researchers had failed to clear up all the uncertainties.
There is nothing more boring, more self-deceiving, than the
attempt to write pop-music history in terms of recording
dates, personnels, and gossip about the mechanics of the recording industry. Jelly Roll was clearly filled with impa-
tience, as he was quizzed about recording sessions.
Nonetheless, he was also cocked and primed for our interviews at the Library of Congress; he had put his ducks in a
row, so to speak. He was ready to deploy his remarkable
gifts as a historian—almost total recall, especially for musical detail; his flare for storytelling; and above all, his sure

grasp of what had been meaningful in the life of his collaborators and the community that had fostered them.

A thorough list of Morton records has been compiled by Thomas Cusack, who normally teaches early Tudor drama in the Queens University, Belfast. His discography runs to twenty-two pages with a blinding number of footnotes and brackets. While it exhibits an uncanny knowledge of the smallest details of the Morton recording sessions, yet there are question marks about almost every recording date. The records give a sense of the frenetic period between 1923 and 1929 when Jelly was reaching for the big time. The titles with which he endowed his compositions, behaving here with a composer's scorn for program notes, give hints about his life and show, besides, the play of an ironic and fantastic imagination. Cusack's scholarship, complemented by comments from Mister Jelly Roll, reveals an artist of true creative passion at work in the unfamiliar and sometimes rather weird atmosphere of the record business. Jelly learned to work within the limits of the 10-inch 78 RPM record holding three minutes of music and he turned them out like hotcakes. . . . At the time this book was first published, *every known commercial record Jelly cut could be purchased*—if not on original labels, at least as unauthorized reissues. And I imagine this is still true . . .

There follows a chronology of Jelly Roll's recording activity. Although it has been superseded by more exhaustive accounts, it still gives one a sense of the period lacking in the more scholarly work.

"I made my first record," said Jelly Roll, "in 1918 for some company in California. Reb Spikes, Mutt Carey, Wade Waley, Kid Ory, and I recorded *The Wolverines* and *King Porter,* but we never heard from those records. I don't know why. Then on in Chicago, I cut piano rolls for the American, the Imperial, and the QRS Company. I don't know what happened to all those piano rolls." (So far three of these piano rolls have been discovered and reissued.)

CHRONOLOGICAL INDEX

DATE	PLACE	TITLE	GROUP	ORIGINAL COMPANY
1922 or earlier	Chicago?	*Dead Man Blues*	Piano Roll	QRS
		Grandpa's Spells	"	"

"About the time, in 1923," said Jelly Roll, "Fritz Pollard, the famous baseball player, introduced me to Ink Williams who was then a scout for the Paramount Recording Company. I got together a band (Nick Dominique—cornet, Roy Palmer—trombone, Townes—clarinet, Jasper Taylor—drums) and those records sold very big. I was to be paid by the side and I never have got all the money yet. We used a washboard in this record played by a crazy guy from New Orleans named Brown who stopped traffic in New York with that washboard of his."

June 1923	Chicago	*Big Fat Ham*	Orchestra	Paramount
		Muddy Water Blues	"	"

"Then I went with Gennet for a year and a half," said Jelly, "on a percentage basis. I helped the New Orleans Rhythm Kings out in making their big records, cut a flock of piano solos that were very, very big, and made plenty money for them. I never did keep track of how much I made. They wanted me to sign up for ten years, but I didn't want to work for a salary and I didn't want to be tied down. You see before that contract was up, I was recording for just about everybody else under different pseudonyms. Those days I used to call myself almost anything for a disguise and go on in and make the records. Naturally Gennet didn't like this too well. By the way if you want those pseudonyms, you can ask Lester Melrose in Chicago," Jelly grinned.

Aug. 1923	Richmond	*King Porter Stomp*	Piano solo	Gennet
"	Indiana	*New Orleans Joys*	"	"
"	Richmond	*Sobbin' Blues*	New Orleans Rhythm Kings (Mares, Brunies Rappolo and other white Creoles)	"
		Clarinet Marma-lade	"	"
		Mister Jelly Lord	"	"
Aug-Sept. 1923	Richmond	*London Blues*	"	"
		Milneburg Joys	"	"
		Grandpa's Spells	Piano solo	"
		Kansas City Stomps	"	"
		Wolverine Blues	"	"
		The Pearls	"	"

Dec. 1923	Chicago	*Someday Sweetheart*	Jazz Band (with Zue Robertson and Horace Eubanks)	Okeh
		London Blues	"	"
April 1924	Chicago	*Mister Jelly Lord*	Steamboat (with Kazoo, piano and banjo)	Paramount
		Steady Roll	Stomp Kings (Piano omitted)	"
April 1924	Chicago	*Mama Nita*	Solo	"
		35th Street Blues	"	"
June 1924	Chicago	*London Blues*	Solo	Rialto
?June 1924	Chicago	*Fish Tail Blues*	Kings of Jazz (Lee Collins, Roy Palmer and others)	Autograph
		High Society	"	"
		Weary Blues	"	"
		Tiger Rag	"	"
June-July 1924	Chicago	*King Porter Stomp*	Duet (Oliver)	"
		Weatherbird Rag (unissued)	"	"
		Tom Cat Blues	"	"
		My Gal	Trio (de Faut)	"
		Wolverine Blues	"	"
?Summer 1924	Richmond	*Mister Jelly Lord*	Incomparables	Champion
?July 1924	Richmond	*Copenhagen*	Acc. Kitty Irvin	Gennet

July 1924	Richmond	*Tia Juana*	Piano Solo	"
		Shreveport Stomp	"	"
		Mama Nita	"	"
		Jelly Roll Blues	"	"
		Big Fat Ham	"	"
		Bucktown Blues	"	"
		Tom Cat Blues	"	"
		Stratford Hunch	"	"
		Perfect Rag	"	"

"I began recording for Columbia and Victor about this time," said Jelly Roll, "but Jack Capp [later president of Decca] came to me and said that the Vocalion Company was about to go out of business and I must help him, so I went in and saved the business.

"From the time I started with Victor, using different personnels in the Red Hot Peppers Band, I was for years their number one hot orchestra, and that's the way they billed me."

Particularly to be recommended are *Black Bottom Stomp, The Chant, Grandpa's Spells, Doctor Jazz, Cannonball Blues, Shreveport Stomp, Turtle Twist,* and *Deep Creek.*

20 April, 1926	Chicago	*The Pearls*	Piano Solo	Vocalion
		?Frog-i-more Rag	"	"
		Sweetheart o' Mine	"	"
		Fat Meat and Greens	"	"
		King Porter Stomp	"	"
21 July, 1926	Chicago	*Dead Man Blues*	Acc. Edm. Henderson	"
		Georgia Grind	"	"

15 Sept., 1926	Chicago	*Black Bottom Stomp*	Red Hot Peppers (George Mitchell—cornet, Kid Ory —trombone, Omer Simeon —clarinet, Johnny St. Cyr —banjo, John Lindsey—bass, Andrew Hilaire—drums, JRM—piano)	Victor
		Smokehouse Blues	"	"
		The Chant	"	"
21 Sept., 1926	Chicago	*Sidewalk Blues*	Red Hot Peppers (add Barney Bigard and Darnell Howard—clarinets; with Lee Collins, possibly on the trumpet)	"
		Dead Man Blues	"	"
		Steamboat Stomp	"	"
16 Dec., 1926	Chicago	*Someday Sweetheart*	Red Hot Peppers (two extra violins on *Someday Sweetheart*, otherwise band same as for *The Chant*)	"

		Grandpa's Spells	"	"
		Original Jelly Roll Blues	"	"
		Doctor Jazz	"	"
		Cannonball Blues	"	"
4 June, 1927	Chicago	Hyena Stomp	Red Hot Peppers (Mitchell— trumpet, George Bry- ant—trom- bone, Johnny Dodds—clar- inet. Stomp Evans—alto sax, Bud Scott—guitar and banjo, Quinn Wil- son—tuba, Baby Dodds— drums, Lew Lamarr—vocal effects, JRM— piano)	"
		Billy-goat Stomp	"	"
		Wild Man Blues	"	"
		Jungle Blues	"	"
10 June, 1927	Chicago	Beale Street Blues	"	"
		The Pearls	"	"

		Wolverine Blues	Trio (Johnny Dodds—clarinet, Baby Dodds—drums)	"
		Mister Jelly Lord	"	"
21 Jan., 1923	Chicago	*Midnight Mama*	Levee Serenaders (Personnel unknown, except for Walter Thomas—tenor sax)	Vocalion
Same	Chicago	*Mister Jelly Lord*	"	"
		It Won't Be Long	Acc. F. Hereford	"
		Red Pepper Rag	Solo	?Gennet
?Early 1928	Richmond	*?King Porter Stomp*	Red Hot Peppers	Gennet
		?Someday Sweetheart	"	"
		?I've Seen My Baby	"	"
13 March, 1928	New York	*Sergeant Dunn's Bugle Call*	Dunn Band (Dunn—trumpet, H. Fleming—trombone, G. Bushell—soprano sax, J. Mitchell—banjo, Harry Hall—tuba)	Columbia
		Ham and Eggs	"	"
		Buffalo Blues	"	"
		You Need Lovin'	"	"

It must have been about this time that Jelly Roll began to have trouble with his bands. At any rate, from now on he changed his orchestras with almost every session. He demanded that his players follow "those little black dots," and so eager was he to prove that his "little black dots" contained the essence of jazz that he brought in Nathaniel Shilkret's sweet-clarinet player for one recording date. This man could read anything at sight and, working from Jelly's arrangements, he played so much hot clarinet that, ever since, the fans have been arguing about who this mystery man was. . . . The editor wishes that he could absolutely verify this tale.

11 June, 1928	New York	Georgia Swing	Red Hot Peppers (Ward Pinkett— trumpet, Geechy Fields—trom- bone, Omer Simeon—clar- inet, Lee Blair—banjo, Bill Benford— tuba, Tom Benford— drums, JRM— piano)	Victor
		Kansas City Stomps	"	"
		Shoe Shiners' Drag	"	"
		Boogaboo	"	"
		Shreveport Stomp	Trio (Omer Sim- eon—clarinet,	"

			Tom Benford—drums, JRM—piano)	
		Mournful Serenade	Quartet (add Geechy Fields—trombone)	"
11 June, 1928	New York	*Sidewalk Blues*	Trio (Ward Pinkett—trumpet, Tom Benford—drums, JRM—piano)	"
		Honey Babe	"	"
6 Dec., 1928	New York	*Everybody Loves Baby*	Red Hot Peppers (Edwin Swayzee, Ed Anderson—trumpets; Bill Cato—trombone; Russell Procope, Joe Garland, Paul Barnes—reeds; JRM—piano; Lee Blair—guitar; Bass Moore—bass; Manzie Johnson—drums)	"
		Red Hot Peppers	"	"
		Deep Creek	"	"

		You Oughta See My Gal	"	"
8 July, 1929	Camden, N.J.	Pep	Piano Solo	"
		Seattle Hunch	"	"
		Fat Frances	"	"
		Freakish	"	"
9 July, 1929	Camden, N.J.	Burnin' the Iceberg	Red Hot Peppers (Red Rossiter, Briscoe Draper—trumpets; Charlie Irvis—trombone; George Baquet—clarinet; Paul Barnes—soprano sax; Joe Thomas—alto sax; Walter Thomas—tenor sax?; JRM or Rod Rodriguez—piano; Barney ?—banjo; Harry Prather—tuba; Wm. Laws—drums)	"
		Courthouse Bump	"	"
		Pretty Lil	"	"
10 July, 1929	Camden, N.J.	Sweet Anita Mine	"	"

		New Orleans Bump	"	"
12 July, 1929	Camden, N.J.	Down My Way	"	"
		Try Me Out	"	"
		Tanktown Bump	"	"
13 Nov., 1929	New York	Sweet Peter	Red Hot Peppers (Henry Allen— trumpet, JC Higgin- botham— trombone, Albert Nicho- las—clarinet, JRM, Bud Johnson— guitar, Pop Foster—bass, Paul Bar- barin—drums)	"
		Jersey Joe	"	"
		Mississippi Mildred	"	"
		Mint Julep	"	"
Mid-Nov. 1929	New York	You Oughta See My Gal	R. Crawley (Freddie Jen- kins, Arthur Watsel—trum- pets; Joe Nan- ton— trombone; W. Crawley— clarinet; Johnny	"

			Hodges?—alto sax; JRM, Luis Russell—piano; W. Braud—bass; Barbarin—drums)	
		Futuristic Blues	"	"
		Keep Your Business	"	"
		She's Got What I Need	"	"
June 1930	New York	*Big Time Woman*	(Henry Allen—cornet, Wilton Crawley—clarinet, Charlie Holmes—alto sax, JRM—piano, Toddy Bunn—guitar)	"
		I'm Her Papa, She's My Mama	"	"
		New Crawley Blues	"	"
		She Saves Her Smiles for Me	"	"
11 Dec., 1929	New York	*I Hate a Man Like You*	Acc. L. Miles	"
		Don't Tell Me Nothin	"	"
17 Dec., 1929	New York	*Smilin' the Blues Away*	Trio (Barney Bigard—clarinet,	"

				Zutty Single-ton—drums)	
		Turtle Twist	"	"
		My Little Dixie Home	"	"
		That's Like It Oughta Be	"	"
5 March, 1930	New York	*Each Day*	Red Hot Peppers (W. Pinkett—trumpet, Wilber de Paris—trombone, Victor Houseman ?—clarinet, B. Addison—banjo, JRM—piano, Billy Taylor—bass, Cozy Cole—drums)	"
		If Someone	"	"
		That'll Never Do	"	"
		Looking for Bluebird	"	"
19 March, 1930	New York	*Little Lawrence*	Red Hot Peppers (W. Pinkett, Bubber Miley—trumpets; W. de Paris—trombone; Victor Houseman—clarinet;	"

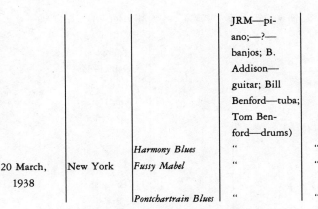

			JRM—piano;—?—banjos; B. Addison—guitar; Bill Benford—tuba; Tom Benford—drums)	
		Harmony Blues	"	"
20 March, 1938	New York	*Fussy Mabel*	"	"
		Pontchartrain Blues	"	"

The tides were running against Jelly Roll. He had hoped, he said later, to get Barney Bigard, Albert Nicholas, and other leading sidemen for the band he was asked to bring to Hollywood, but "Those gangsters and their gunmen said they'd kill me if I tried to get those boys away from the Savoy in Harlem." One day Billie Young, who helped in the office when she had no club date, broke out with that hoodoo rash. . . . The Victor contract was not being renewed. Jelly Roll tried to compete with the swing bands. He certainly played all the gig dates he could get in the next few years, ducking in and out of other bands. Only two recording dates are remembered, although others doubtless will be. With the Mannone orchestra he is said to have played with Bud Freeman, Artie Shaw, John Kirby, and others. . . .

4 April, 1930	New York	*When They Get Lovin' You Done Played Out*	Acc. B. Young	Victor
			"	"

2 June, 1930	New York	*Oil Well*	Red Hot Peppers (W. Pinkett,? —trumpets; Geechy Fields —trombone; Victor House-man?—clari-net; J. & W. Thomas —alto and tenor saxes; JRM—piano; Lee Blair—guitar; Billy Taylor—bass; Cozy Cole—drums)	"
		Load of Coal	"	"
		Crazy Chords	"	"
		Primrose Stomp	"	"
14 July, 1930	New York	*Low Gravy*	Red Hot Peppers (W. Pinkett—trumpet, Geechy Fields —trombone, Albert Nicholas —clarinet, JRM —piano, H. Hill—guitar Pete Briggs— tuba, Tom Ben-ford—drums)	"
		Strokin' Away	"	"
		Blue Blood Blues	"	"

		Mushmouth Shuffle	"	"
9 Oct., 1930	New York	*Gambling Jack*	Red Hot Peppers (Ward Pinkett —trumpet, Sandy Williams — trombone, — ?—clarinet, JRM —piano, Bernard Addison—guitar, Billy Taylor— bass, B. Beason—drums)	"
		Fickle Fay Creep	"	"
15 Aug., 1934	New York	*Never Had No Lovin'*	w. Mannone	Columbia
		I'm Alone Without You	"	"
? 1930 +	?New York	*?Kidney Feet*	w. Dave Nelson orchestra	QRS
		?Tomboy Sue	"	"
Reissued by Victor from recordings listed above		*JELLY ROLL MORTON* (Hot Jazz Series, Vol. 5) *Sidewalk Blues* *Dead Man Blues* *Burnin' the Iceberg* *Deep Creek* *Red Hot Pepper* *Pretty Lil* *Little Lawrence* *Pontchartrain*		

No further recordings are definite until Jelly Roll came to the Library of Congress in May 1939 and filled 12-inch acetate masters LC 1638 to 1688 and 2487 through 2489. These discs were the source of the series of twelve 12-inch albums compiled by Rudi Blesh and Harriet Janis and listed below. Since this extremely successful series went out of print, it has been reissued in whole and in part, and often pirated, by other companies. In 1980, these albums were "elected to" the National Academy of Recording Arts and Sciences Hall of Fame, with Alan Lomax as producer.

May-June 1938	Washington	*Saga of Mister Jelly Lord*	Piano solos, singing, talking.	Circle

Album 1—JAZZ STARTED IN NEW ORLEANS

Tiger Rag, Panama, Mister Jelly Lord, Sweet Papa Jelly Roll, Original Jelly Roll Blues, Ancestry and Boyhood, Boy at the Piano, The Miserere, Boyhood Memories, Hyena Stomp

Album 2—WAY DOWN YONDER

The Animule Ball (Parts 1 & 2), *Scat Song, Shooting the Agate, No Doubt the Finest Food, See, See, Rider, New Orleans Funeral*

Album 3—JAZZ IS STRICTLY MUSIC

Discourse on Jazz, Kansas City Stomp, Randall's Rag, Maple Leaf Rag, King Porter Stomp, You Can Have It

Album 4—THE SPANISH TINGE

*Mama Nita, Spanish Swat, New Orleans Blues, La Paloma, Creepy
Feeling, The Crave, Fickle Fay Creep*

Album 5—BADMAN BALLADS

*Aaron Harris, Robert Charles, They Were Tough Babies, Georgia Skin
Game*

Album 6—THE JAZZ PIANO SOLOIST

The Pearls, Pep, Ain't Misbehavin', Bert Williams, Jungle Blues

Album 7—EVERYONE HAD HIS OWN STYLE

Sammy Davis, *Pretty Baby;* Tony Jackson, Alfred Wilson, Albert
Carroll and Kid Ross, Mamie Desdoumes, *Mamie's Blues;* Albert
Carroll and Buddy Bertrand, *The Crazy Chord Rag;* The Game Kid
and his blues, *Game Kid Wouldn't Work;* Buddy Carter, Bad Sam,
and Benny Frenchy, *All That I Ask Is Love*

Album 8—JELLY AND THE BLUES

*Wolverine Blues, Low Down Blues, Michigan Water Blues, The Murder
Ballad, Winin' Boy*

Album 9—ALABAMA BOUND

Jelly Roll and Jack the Bear, *The Salty Dog, St. Louis, The Miserere,
Alabama Bound*

Album 10—THE JAZZ PIANO SOLOIST

Sweet Peter, State and Madison, Freakish, My Gal Sal, King Porter Stomp, Original Jelly Roll Blues

Album 11—IN NEW ORLEANS

The Broadway Swells, Buddy Bolden Legend, The Marching Bands, The Ragtime Bands, The Creole Song—*L'aut' Can-can, If You Don't Shake,* Indian Songs at the Mardi Gras

Album 12—I'M THE WINING BOY

It Was a Free and Easy Place, *Levee Man Blues,* Storyville—Hilma Burt and Tom Anderson, Sporting Life in New Orleans, Tony Jackson's *Naked Dance, I Hate a Man Like You, Honky-tonk Blues, Hesitation Blues, Winin' Boy* (2)

Jelly Roll tried frantically to arrange a comeback session in Washington with the help of his hot jazz friends. He brought a band of young unknowns together to make some "swing records," but they couldn't or wouldn't play the notes, and the only records that resulted were fine piano solos in the old style.

Late 1938	Washington	*Fingerbuster*	Solo	Jazzman
		Creepy Feeling	"	"
		Winin' Boy Blues	"	"
		Honky-tonk Music	"	"
?1938	Baltimore	*Winin' Boy Blues,* 12-inch	"	Private
		The Pearls, 12-inch	"	?Private

Coming back into New York in 1939, carrying the Washington knife wound and feeling his age at last, Jelly Roll nevertheless proved he was still master in his final Victor recording session, part of a series of hot jazz revival recordings which Panassié, the French critic, had arranged. Present in the Victor studio was writer Fred Ramsey, watching Jelly Roll in action for the first time. His vivid notes provide a fine portrait of band leader Morton:

Victor Recording Session of Jelly Roll Morton and his New Orleans Jazzmen, 1:30 P.M., Thursday, September 14, 1939. . . . An oblong room, draped completely with monk's cloth and with strips of the same hanging from the ceiling. Three quarters of the distance into the room a ribbon mike hangs from above—shining, bullet-shaped, small, yet dominating the room. Below it, platforms of various sizes and heights for the musicians. The men on the platforms looked very queer sitting way up there above the others. Claude Jones (trombone) and Sidney de Paris (trumpet) were in back on platforms with Zutty Singleton, his drums muffled with big hunks of mattress, close to the piano. Lawrence Lucie with his guitar stood in the crook of the piano. Next to him on a three-foot platform directly under the mike was Wellman Braud, Jelly's old bass man. Directly beside and in front of him, under the mike were Happy Cauldwell (sax), Albert Nicholas (clarinet), and Sidney Bechet (soprano sax).

As you know, Jelly Roll believes in rehearsals before recording dates to be assured the musicians aren't all over each other's notes in the middle of a

master. Sidney could not make the rehearsal, because of his job two hundred miles out of town, but
they left plenty of room for his solos. When he did
arrive Jelly seemed to know him pretty well and to
realize just the proper amount of discipline necessary to get the best work out of him as well as the
other members of the band.

Sidney didn't go right over and sit down beside
Nicholas. Jelly whispered to us, "I know the two
should be together, but they won't like it if I tell
them." Sure enough, after the boys had rehearsed a
bit, one of the engineers came out and suggested
that Bechet and Nicholas stand together on a platform directly under the mike. So it was arranged.

It's a tough job to keep a bunch of musicians in
line during a recording session and they need pulling together by a man they respect and one who
knows and loves New Orleans music as Jelly Roll
does. Jelly had made whatever loose arrangements
were necessary and I would say that the proportion
of arrangement to improvising was just about as it
should be—harmony parts with an indication of
whose solo should come at what time—a good feeling for placing the solos and for their content and
their sequence. In other words, Jelly Roll provided
a sketch of what the boys were to do and the rest
was up to them.

Nobody ever drinks at Jelly Roll's dates. Although this may spoil a lot of smooth-paper,
feature-article theories about hot music coming
from men who are liquored up, Jelly's discipline

certainly helped to keep the "jive in this session from becoming over-ripe."

After the practice number, the men were warmed up, confident and ready to begin. Sidney had the feel of the date, of the other men, and of the strong, guiding force of Jelly Roll. Thereupon he began to play some real solos. He was what the men called a "playing fool" on this date. And it was very amusing to watch him stare quizzically at the written notes, pretending to study them, look away, stalling for a moment just as Keppard is said to have done with the Creole band, and then play something that had them all looking at him.

They made a test to begin with. The signals: *buzz,* then a wait, followed by *buzz-buzz,* then count two and begin. Jelly Roll seemed to be amused that anyone would have to explain the signals to him, he'd been in the business so long. The tension between buzzes was tremendous, while everyone in the studio, including myself, counted two. I was waiting to catch the strains of the tune we had all heard so much about and never heard really played before —*I Thought I Heard Buddy Bolden Say.* When it came along it was a wonderful surprise. The melody is slow and very catchy. We were all surprised when Jelly started to sing the words and a little worried because we didn't want a session spoiled because of censorship of words. He explained at the end of the test, "I'm identifying the number in a conspicuous way."

For each master he sang a different set of words,

each one neatly taking care of the censorship problem—"I thought I heard somebody shout, 'We
gonna open up the window and let that bad air
come out,' " etc., . . . at any rate, the Longshore-
man's Hall atmosphere is thick on the record.

The test had to be cut for time—from five minutes down to three minutes, ten seconds. The en-
gineer began to look annoyed because he was using
one wax after another. . . .

"Come on," Zutty said, "make a master this
time. We using up all the guy's wax." Cauldwell
was getting impatient: "Let's go while spirit is on
us."

Jelly's pickup note was a discord and it didn't
come over the mike too well. The Victor man
protested about it, but Jelly defended himself,
"It's a discord, but it's supposed to be." Then, as
if this would make it all right, "It's an E Flat
diminished seventh"—and that held all of them
for a while.

"Watch for the pickup," Jelly gave them the cue
and they were off with Jelly singing, backed by
Bechet, Nicholas, Jones, the rhythm and muted
growls by Sidney de Paris. Jelly liked those growls,
said, "He's coughin'." Cauldwell played a fine half
chorus with a big tone for a tenor. Sidney got in
some very dirty choruses. . . . While they had been
rehearsing Sidney looked blankly at the music and
Jelly leaned from the piano and said, "You remember that, Sidney, don't you?" Sidney looked surprised and said, "Unh-uh." Yet he did remember it

and his choruses sounded as if they came straight out of tintype hall.

The *Winin' Boy* is very fine, a slow simple blues, not so easy to play as the faster stuff. Jelly sang the long refrain, with fine backing by Sidney de Paris using his mute close to the mike. And there was a duet between Bechet and Jones which, as Jelly put it, was a "pretty refrain."

During a pause Braud came over to us and said, "It wasn't a dance in New Orleans till they played *High Society,*" for that was the next number. Jelly said he'd fixed it up the way the bands really played it and they started out like the "best god-damned brass band you ever heard." The record turned out to be a duel between the two reeds, for, after a full brass opening, Sidney played his chorus and Nicholas answered him. It was wonderful hearing those two great reed men from New Orleans trying to cut each other on the greatest of all clarinet choruses. The rest of the band rode right on through to the finish, with plenty of trombone and a piano backing from Jelly that forced them along at a terrific marching pace. As he said, "Anybody can make a bad record—but anybody can't make a good one."

Didn't He Ramble described a New Orleans funeral. . . . The band led off with a few mournful strains of a funeral march, then Claude Jones walked to the mike and intoned in a sepulchral voice,

> *Ashes to ashes and dust to dust,*
> *If the women don't get you, the whiskey must!*

Then he turned away from the mike and let out a yowl of anguish that would have seemed weird if all the others hadn't joined in, moaning and carrying on in the best funeral manner, and Jelly, in the most mournful voice of all, wailing, "such a good man!" (As he told us later, "We doing just like those hypocrites down home who used to say nice things at a man's funeral and done all kinds of slandering when he was alive.")

The mourning died down. Zutty rolled his drums, Sidney de Paris let out a short staccato toot on his horn, while the tempo quickened and the men smacked their chops for the march back home. Then they were right in it, with Bechet playing around and away from the beat and de Paris going fast with a whacky horn. Before we knew it, they were finished, the music had stopped and Zutty was beating a slow, fading beat as the funeral band disappeared down the street. Claude Jones came to the mike and said, "He rambled till the butchers cut him down."

"That Claude Jones," Jelly yelled, "he's a natural preacher from Springfield, Illinois. He has such a soulful voice."

"1895," said Braud, without thinking what he was saying . . .

| 14 Sept., 1939 | New York | *Didn't He Ramble* | New Orleans Jazzmen (Sidney de Paris— trumpet, | Victor |

			Claude Jones—trombone, Happy Cauldwell—tenor sax, Albert Nicholas—clarinet, Sidney Bechet—soprano sax, JRM—piano, Lawrence Lucie—guitar, Wellman Braud—bass, Zutty Singleton—drums)	
		High Society	"	"
		Buddy Bolden's Blues	"	"
		Winin' Boy Blues	"	"
28 Sept., 1939	New York	*Climax Rag*	New Orleans Jazzmen (Sidney de Paris—trumpet, Fred Robinson—trombone, A. Nicholas—clarinet, H. Cauldwell—tenor sax, JRM—piano, L. Lucie—guitar, W.	"

			Braud—bass, Zutty Single-ton—drums)	
		Don't You Leave Me Here	"	"
		West End Blues	"	"
		Ballin' the Jack	"	"

"I have a subject of mutual benefit to discuss with you," wrote Jelly to Charles Smith. General Records had asked Jelly for an album of the old New Orleans favorites. "Jelly was extremely ill," wrote Mr. Smith, "and we used as many as four waxes on certain sides." The stand-out side, of course, was *Mamie's Blues,* which, everyone agreed, was "not commercial." Nevertheless it has kept the album in print ever since, and has been called the most beautiful of all jazz piano records. When General went on to make some "commercials" with a swing band composed of Henry Allen—trumpet, Joe Britten—trombone, Albert Nicholas—clarinet, Eddie Williams—alto sax, Wellman Braud—bass, Zutty Singleton—drums, and Jelly Roll—piano, the records died fast.

14 Dec., 1939	New York	Sportin'-House Rag	Piano solo	General
		Original Rags	"	"
		The Crave	"	"
		The Naked Dance	"	"
		Mister Joe	"	"
		King Porter Stomp	"	"
		Winin' Boy Blues	"	"
		Animule Ball	"	"

16 Dec., 1939	New York	*Buddy Bolden's Blues*	Solo	General
		The Naked Dance	"	"
		Don't You Leave Me Here	"	"
		Mamie's Blues	"	"
18 Dec., 1939	New York	*Michigan Water Blues*	"	"
4 Jan., 1940	New York	*Sweet Substitute*	Seven	"
		Panama	"	"
		Good Old New York	"	"
		Big Lip Blues	"	"
23 Jan., 1940	New York	*Why?*	Sextet	"
		Get the Bucket	"	"
		If You Knew	"	"
		Shake It	"	"
30 Jan., 1940	New York	*Dirty, Dirty, Dirty*	Seven	"
		Swinging the Elks	"	"
		Mama's Got a Baby	"	"
		My Home Is in a Southern Town	"	"

Spring, 1941, Los Angeles.—When death came along and closed and locked the keyboard, Mister Jelly Roll was in the middle of planning his next recording session of New Orleans music.

Appendix Three

Discography and Bibliography
Compiled by Gideon D'Arcangelo

In the years following the publication of *Mister Jelly Roll*, Morton's recordings have been reissued many times over. The following is a list of those still in distribution, along with some classic collections that should not be forgotten.

AVAILABLE RECORDINGS

All titles are available in compact disc and cassette formats, unless otherwise indicated.

The Complete Commodore Recordings, Vol. 1. Mosaic MR-123 [1988] (LP only).

The Pianist and the Composer, Vol. 1. Smithsonian Collection Recordings 043 (CD only).

Chicago: The Red Hot Peppers, Vol. 2. Smithsonian Collection Recordings 044 (CD only).

New York, Washington, and the Rediscovery, Vol. 3. Smithsonian Collection Recordings 045 (CD only).

Jelly Roll Morton: Complete Victor Recordings, Vols. 1–5. JSP

Records 321–325 [1991] (distributed by Rounder Records, CD only).

*Centennial: His Complete Victor Recordings.** RCA Bluebird 2361 [1991].

Jelly Roll Morton: Library of Congress Recordings, Vols. 1–3. Charly Records (Import) CD-AFS-1010-3.

Library of Congress Recordings, Vol. 1.** Solo Art 11 [1991] (CD only).

Piano Classics, 1923–24. Smithsonian/Folkways RF-47 (cassette only).

Folkways—Jazz Piano, Vol. 9. Smithsonian/Folkways FJ 2809 (cassette only).

Jelly Roll Morton, 1924–1926: Blues and Stomps from Rare Piano Rolls. Biograph 111 (CD only).

Jelly Roll Morton, 1923–24. Milestone Records 47018 (distributed by Rounder Records, CD only).

Jelly Roll Morton, 1926–1934. ABC Records (Import) 836199.

The Indispensable Jelly Roll Morton. Accord Records 982102.

The Complete Piano Solos, 1923–1939. Musical Memories 34000.

Doctor Jazz, Vol. 1, and *Didn't He Ramble,* Vol. 2. Black and Blue (Import) 59227-8.

---

* Gary Giddins, jazz critic of the *Village Voice,* strongly recommends the JSP set of Jelly's Victor recordings over the RCA/Bluebird set, citing the remarkably poor sound quality of the latter.

** Rounder Records is planning to reissue the complete Library of Congress recordings in 1993.

OUT-OF-PRINT LP RECORDS

Bob Greene's The World of Jelly Roll Morton. RCA Red Seal ARL1 0504 [1974].

Jelly Roll Morton and His Orchestra, Red Hot Peppers . . . 1929. RCA-French 741-070 (Black and White Series, Vol. 6).

Jelly Roll Morton, His Trio and His Red Hot Peppers . . . 1929–30. RCA-French 741-081 (Black and White Series, Vol. 7).

Jelly Roll Morton and His Red Hot Peppers . . . 1938–40. RCA-French 741-087 (Black and White Series, Vol. 8).

Giants of Jazz: Jelly Roll Morton. Time Life Records STL-J07.

Jelly Roll Morton Rarities. Rhapsody RHA 6021.

Jelly Roll Morton Baltimore 1938. Swaggie JCS 116.

DISCOGRAPHIES

For further discographical listings, the interested reader can look to the following publications:

Thomas Cusack. *Jelly Roll Morton: An Essay in Discography*. London: Cassell, 1952.

Laurie Wright, with special contributions by John H. Cowley et al. *Mister Jelly Lord*. Chigwell: Storyville, 1980.

Michael Hill and E. Bryce. *Jelly Roll Morton: A Microgroove Discography and Musical Analysis*. Australia: Salisbury East, 1977.

Rodney Simone. "Jelly Roll Morton Rollography." *Matrix*, no. 51 (February 1964): 14–17.

A BRIEF BIBLIOGRAPHY

Roy Carew. "Of This and That and Jelly Roll." *Jazz Journal* 10, no. 12 (1957): 10–12.

Samuel Charters. *Jelly Roll Morton's Last Night at the Jungle Inn*. London: M. Boyars, 1990.

Lawrence Gushee. "A Preliminary Chronology of the Early Career of Ferd 'Jelly Roll' Morton." *American Music* 3 (1985): 389–412.

Jelly Roll Morton. *Ferdinand "Jelly Roll" Morton: The Collected Piano Music*. Edited by J. Dapogny. Washington, D.C.: Smithsonian Institution Press, 1982.

William Russell. *A Jelly Roll Morton Scrapbook*. Copenhagen: Storyville, 1992.

————. "Morton and Frog-i-more Rag." In *The Art of Jazz: Essays on the Nature and Development of Jazz*, edited by Martin Williams. New York: Oak, 1959.

Gunther Schuller. *Early Jazz: Its Roots and Musical Development*. New York: Oxford University Press, 1968.

Martin Williams. *Jelly Roll Morton*. London: Cassell, 1962. Reprinted in Kings of Jazz Series. New York: Barnes, 1963.

About the Author

Alan Lomax, with his father, John A. Lomax, created the Archive of American Folk Song at the Library of Congress and published many anthologies, including *American Ballads and Folk Songs* and *The Folk Songs of North America*. Lomax produced the first albums of American folk song in 1939 and has edited more than a hundred recordings from all parts of the world. He is the director of the prize-winning *American Patchwork* PBS series. A Guggenheim and AAAS Fellow, he received the National Medal of Arts in 1986.